A City within a City

A CITY
WITHIN A CITY

The Black Freedom Struggle in
Grand Rapids, Michigan

TODD E. ROBINSON

TEMPLE UNIVERSITY PRESS
Philadelphia

TODD E. ROBINSON is Assistant Professor of History at the University of Nevada, Las Vegas.

TEMPLE UNIVERSITY PRESS
Philadelphia, Pennsylvania 19122
www.temple.edu/tempress

Library of Congress Cataloging-in-Publication Data

Robinson, Todd E. (Todd Ephraim), 1973–
    A city within a city : the Black freedom struggle in Grand Rapids, Michigan /
Todd E. Robinson.
        p.   cm.
    Includes bibliographical references and index.
    ISBN 978-1-4399-0921-8 (cloth : alk. paper)
    ISBN 978-1-4399-0922-5 (pbk. : alk. paper)
    ISBN 978-1-4399-0923-2 (e-book)
    1. African Americans—Civil rights—Michigan—Grand Rapids—History.
2. Grand Rapids (Mich.)—Race relations.   3. Grand Rapids (Mich.)—Social
conditions.   I. Title.

    F574.G7R63   2013
    323.1196'073077456—dc23   2012014737

Printed in the United States of America

030813P

CONTENTS

	Preface	*vii*
	Acknowledgments	*xvii*
	Abbreviations	*xxi*
1	"Rowing, Not Drifting": Black Organizational Reform before World War II	*1*
2	Citizens' Action: Managerial Racism and Reform Politics	*24*
3	The Suburban Oasis: The Origins of Segregated Space	*51*
4	The Mustache Saga: The Rise of Black Youth Protest	*91*
5	A Black Child's Burden: Busing to Achieve Racial Balance	*114*
6	Where Do We Go from Here? Setting the Course for Racial Reconciliation	*145*
	Conclusion: Secondary Cities and the Black Experience	*178*
	Notes	*187*
	Index	*217*

Illustrations follow page 84

PREFACE

In 1966, Karen L. Parker migrated from North Carolina to the city of Grand Rapids, located on Michigan's west coast. Like most black migrants who had arrived before her at the Michigan Central railroad station of the state's second-largest metropolis, Parker had an odd feeling that she had reached a place sequestered from the rest of state. In her diary, she recorded her initial observations of the city's built environment: "The architecture near town is old, stark, ominous. It feels so unfriendly! It's drab, dark and depressing. Stores close down on weekends, and downtown is practically empty."[1] Her premonitory thoughts about the city's unwelcoming structural design foreboded the bitter racial conflict that divided the city. Parker would soon realize that despite its remote location, Grand Rapids was not far removed from the racial enmity that fueled the upheaval so prevalent in many cities during the summer of 1967.

Although situated in the Rust Belt region, Grand Rapids as a city held no resemblance to the smoke-filled spatial contours that defined the industrial cities of the Great Lakes basin. Nestled away serenely in the southwestern corner of the state, it appeared instead that the Furniture City, as Grand Rapids became known, differed from the bustling industrial cities in Illinois, Indiana, Michigan, Ohio, and Pennsylvania. It was a community defined by a high rate of home ownership. Prior to World War I, roughly half the homes in Grand Rapids were owner occupied. In the post–World War II era, nearly 62 percent of the residents owned their own homes, and boosters "pointed with pride to the fact that the Furniture City claimed the nation's highest rate of home ownership among medium-sized cities."[2] Many residents believed that home ownership represented a powerful symbol of the "American Dream." Ostensibly, then, home ownership made Grand Rapids a better place in which to live, work, and do business.

Initially, the lure of social equality and economic opportunity brought black migrants to smaller northern communities, such as Grand Rapids, where they hoped to avoid the omnipresent discrimination existing in larger and more complex cities, such as Detroit and Chicago. Few actually did. As Parker determined, "The fair town of Grand Rapids is much like the town of Winston-Salem, maybe a half a degree better."[3] Parker, who had grown up in Winston-Salem, was the first black woman to enroll at the University of North Carolina at Chapel Hill. Initially unaware that she was a trailblazer, Parker later recalled, "I kind of discovered this when they put me in a dorm on the fourth floor, very top, in a room by myself and there was this empty bed, and I kept waiting for someone else to show up and nobody did."[4] Migration north did not alleviate Parker's sense of racial isolation and repudiation, as she soon experienced similar episodes of manufactured discrimination in her new hometown of Grand Rapids.

When she graduated from the University of North Carolina, Parker accepted a job as a copy editor for the *Grand Rapids Press*. After moving north, she observed, "I find people staring at me on the streets like I'm a freak or something." Puzzled by the dynamics of her new environment, Parker periodically recorded how the racial milieu of Grand Rapids resembled her experiences in the South. Discouraged by this reality, she told herself, "Be realistic—face up to it. You *know* not to expect more. Be calm. Be cool. Be rational. Be adult. Put up a good front. Don't let those white bastards know you're hurting like hell inside." She went on to note, "You wish they could see, without your having to tell them, that you're no different from them except for being black, and that you want and need the same things they do. . . . [E]ven here in the good NORTH [they] won't let me forget it."[5]

Parker tried to fit in. At her job, she noted, "I have to restrain myself in discussions if I want to keep any friends."[6] Although she managed to maneuver successfully behind the veil at work, Parker could not avoid the city's discriminatory housing market, which had hindered the black community for decades. She teamed up with her coworker Jessie, the only other black employee at the *Grand Rapids Press,* to find a home. They discovered that the places commonly recognized as black housing "were pretty crummy." And "the ones we liked," she explained, "canceled us out for one reason or another: no single girls, no girls, too young, etc. But we felt the primary reason was race. We shocked a few people. Several handed us the 'we just rented it' story." Informing the owners and landlords that they worked for the *Press* was no help. Parker recalled, "We visited one place where the landlady was a girl of about 25. She said right off . . . , 'There's only one problem, my tenants are all white. I don't mind myself, but they may move if I rent to you and I'll go in debt.'" Karen and Jessie found that, despite their professional credentials, white racism was preventing them, as it prevented other black residents of Grand Rapids, from securing decent housing.[7]

In a lengthy journal entry on June 20, 1966, Parker recalled a three-bedroom, two-story home with a full basement that she and Jessie had looked at: "The owner[s], a married pair of teachers, were a little surprised when they first saw us but took it all in stride and were amazingly courteous—the most courteous and cooperative people we had encountered." Thoroughly impressed by the home and the couple, Karen and Jessie decided to take the house. Accepting a check for half the rent, the owners said that the women could move in any time. Parker wrote, "We called parents, wrote friends, got changes of address at stores, called the movers and the telephone company. . . . [T]hen Jessie went out with a carload of belongings and the remainder of the rent."[8]

But the promise of decent housing quickly evaporated. "The landlord said he was sorry he couldn't rent to us," Parker reported. "He said his realtor had checked for our credit rating and couldn't find one for us. He also said he didn't think we could afford the rent." Although Jessie assured the landlord that their credit was in "good shape" and that she could provide the necessary documentation, the landlord held firm. "I found out later that night and blew my stack," Parker remembered. "I called Mr. Fehsenfeld [the landlord] and asked him to repeat the story for me. He said the credit rating business was the whole reason and that he was 'just sorry.'"[9]

The next day, representatives from the *Grand Rapids Press* discovered that neither Fehsenfeld nor his realtor had called the credit bureau; in fact, said Parker, "our ratings were fine." The two women filed a complaint with the local Human Relations Committee and the State Civil Rights Commission. Parker commented at the time, however, "It looks like it will be a long drawn out case," and "we still haven't found a place." Thus, she concluded, "There is hardly any advantage in being a Negro. It is a primary disadvantage. . . . [W]ell, here's to dear old Grand Rapids—my new 'home'"![10]

In only a few weeks, Parker had begun to learn how northern racism worked, and she continued to encounter discrimination in her search for decent housing. In one instance, she recalled, when she went to view an apartment complex with three vacancies, the landlady "said there weren't any. We told her we were told there were. She said, 'mine's not for rent' and slammed the door. We heard somebody inside ask, 'who was that?' [and] she answered, 'two Niggers. If they move in, I'll move out.'" Parker lamented, "It hurts to think about it. . . . [I]t seems like you're beating your head against a brick wall."[11]

Yet, like so many blacks in the city, Parker decided, "I wasn't going to give up. . . . [T]hey can take everything from you. But don't let them get your spirit. That's when you're gone." For generations, as she would learn, blacks in Grand Rapids had participated in their own fight for better homes, schools, jobs, and social equality, but despite decades of black resistance, a solidified racial system remained in place. As blacks challenged the city's inequities, whites continued to modify the system of racial oppression. As a newcomer to Grand Rapids,

Parker was learning about the complex system of "managerial racism" that dominated city life.[12]

At the heart of managerial racism was the notion that business leadership should govern American cities. During the 1940s, in particular, a coterie of self-described "progressive" Republicans challenged and defeated the city's established Republican Party machine controlled by Frank D. McKay and George Welsh. Eager to discard the political-party functionaries, progressive Republican reformers in Grand Rapids set out to establish a new civic engagement rooted in business expertise and efficiency. After World War II, the progressive coalition, primarily consisting of Chamber of Commerce business leaders, sought to transform the metropolitan landscape through housing, education, and economic policy. On the basis of the assumption that the "general welfare of the community could be best served by satisfying the concrete needs of business," the Chamber of Commerce set out to "build and develop . . . [the] Grand Rapids area into a community wherein . . . business [could] grow and prosper under [a] free and competitive enterprise system."[13] Exercising influence over city affairs, local business owners controlled municipal government and invariably directed the legislative process toward resolutions that they deemed desirable.

Although neighboring cities, such as Detroit and Chicago, were controlled by industrial unionism and Democratic-machine politics, Grand Rapids was a Republican-majority community that more closely resembled a business-run southern city. Even in comparison to other industrial secondary cities, such as Gary, Indiana, and Flint, Michigan, the political history of Grand Rapids reveals features distinct from those of other regions within the Rust Belt. Republican-machine politics dominated a number of small northern cities until the ascendancy of the New Deal coalition in the 1930s. Whereas politics in Gary and Flint mirrored the historical process, which saw the arrangement of industrial laborers into mass unions and the beginning of a number of important social reforms at the national level, Grand Rapids experienced a bitter divide within the Republican Party that resulted in two separate Republican coalitions. Tracing the political significance of conservatism in Grand Rapids, this book highlights the critical but often unnoticed impulse of conservative oppositional politics in the history of the urban North during the era of the civil rights movement.

Just as it did throughout much of the urban North, the Depression altered the political history of Gary and Flint. The shift from a long-standing Republican tradition to a Democratic stronghold marked the end of an era and the beginning of a major fundamental rearrangement in the political behavior of numerous other Rust Belt communities. Although historians debate the ideological substance and ultimate fate of postwar liberalism and civil rights, racial conservatism remains relatively untouched. Focusing on such cities as Chicago, Detroit, New York, and Oakland, historians Arnold R. Hirsch, Thomas J. Sugrue, Martha Biondi, and Robert O. Self have probed the racial tensions within the New Deal coalition. Collectively, their works explore the potential left-liberal alliance that unraveled "from within the New Deal bloc itself" during the 1940s and 1950s. As these recent studies illustrate, racial conflict over neighborhood and workplace integration indicates that the "'silent majority' did not emerge de novo from the alleged failures of liberalism in the 1960s; it was not the unique product of white rejection of the Great Society." Instead, backlash resulted from a "simmering white discontent" manufactured decades prior. Although this perspective repudiates the centrality of the 1960s to the decline of liberalism, it ignores the crucial history of a strong conservative coalition that shaped municipal- and state-level politics in many northern communities for much of the postwar period.[14]

Attempts to explain how the limits of liberalism hindered black demands often omit serious discussions of how racial conservatism further complicated the situation in the postwar era. As Anthony Chen has written, "The initial limits on 'freedom from discrimination' may have been set by southern Democrats and their constituencies, but the outermost limits of political possibility were set by conservatives, who enjoyed remarkable success in exploiting political institutions and the party system to their lasting advantage."[15] The scholarship on postwar urban and civil rights history has made tremendous strides in recent years, but it has not closely considered how conservative Republicans and business leaders initiated policies that transformed northern urban communities and stemmed the tide of civil rights as early as the 1940s. Racial conservatism formed a powerful obstructionist dimension during the postwar campaign for civil rights in the urban North. Such cities as Grand Rapids provided a controlled environment for the augmentation of statewide conservatism and served as relief valves for racial reform. The bulk of scholarly attention on the long civil rights era has been devoted to the rise and fall of liberal reform and reformers, but the urban North includes more than one community narrative. To be sure, Grand Rapids tells a critically important story of how the political and cultural impact of the American Right impeded protest politics at the local level in numerous northern communities during the civil rights movement.

Grand Rapids remained untouched by the Democratic prospects who influenced the heartland of industrial America. Instead, Republican politicians, such as Gerald R. Ford, who served for nearly twenty-five years as the representative from Michigan's Fifth District, and the powerful Chamber of Commerce controlled city life throughout the modern civil rights struggle. During this period, business leaders adopted the unofficial motto "What's good for business is good for the community" as their approach to the city's racial problems. Determined to build a city image of middle-class respectability, conservative city officials and business leaders routinely sacrificed black needs and interests for the "good" of the larger community. The story of American conservatism is an important and largely neglected piece of the story of the civil rights movement.

The belief that "municipal government is a business, not politics" implied that there was no room for the give-and-take of democracy. Business owners viewed societal disruption as akin to workplace conflict; both were detrimental to production. Therefore businesspeople and city officials avoided conflict and used the subtle and, indeed, effective approach of managerial racism to resist social change. This strict system of gradualism based on benevolent paternalism served as the primary method for handling race relations in Grand Rapids. Much like white progressives in Greensboro, North Carolina, Republican progressive reformers in Grand Rapids believed that conflict was fundamentally bad, disagreement denoted personal aversion, and consensus offered the only way to sustain a respectable and civilized community. To navigate this system of social control, blacks in Grand Rapids, such as Parker, used multiple strategies of resistance and accommodation to dismantle racial inequality.[16]

Initially, the quest for middle-class status and respectability shaped the terms and tactics of struggle for African Americans in Grand Rapids. As historian Randal Jelks correctly observes in *African Americans in the Furniture City: The Struggle for Civil Rights in Grand Rapids,* respectability was "the instrument used to reject racial oppression and assert a constructive communal identity." Although, as Jelks notes, respectability was "a defining and mediating role in community-building,"[17] understanding the paradoxes and limitations of the ideology of racial uplift was crucial. Respectability failed to overturn the patron/client relationship of blacks and whites in Grand Rapids. Instead, the racial uplift ideology ultimately worked to confirm the racist logic inherent in managerial racism by allowing whites to believe that "good race relations" existed in their community. Prior to the 1960s, black residents of Grand Rapids labored tirelessly to prove themselves worthy of full citizenship through racial uplift, yet these efforts seemingly reaffirmed notions of black pathology and strengthened both managerial racism and the conservative stronghold.

In addition, according to Kevin Gaines, "although uplift ideology was by no means incompatible with social protest against racism, its orientation toward self-help implicitly faulted African Americans for their lowly status, echoing judgmental dominant characterizations of 'the Negro problem.'"[18] Indeed, this was true in Grand Rapids, as blacks embraced respectability as a form of cultural politics in an effort to build a positive community identity and gain full citizenship status. However, heavy emphasis on behavioral norms narrowly defined the argument for black humanity and the measures deemed acceptable to achieve citizenship rights. It set the stage for gradual reform initiatives based on white Republican progressivism throughout the 1940s and 1950s. Whites interpreted the deferential poses that blacks employed to navigate managerial racism as evidence of authentic race relations. With racial equality still on the margins by the 1960s, however, dissatisfaction was growing in the black community and shifting the tide toward assertion.

When Parker arrived in Grand Rapids, the system of managerial racism was firmly in place. From a white perspective, it was unthinkable that the racial tensions prevailing in Detroit on July 23, 1967, would rock the quiet, conservative city of Grand Rapids just days later. But as the *Grand Rapids Press* reported, "The issues that fueled the upheaval were no less real in Grand Rapids than they were in Detroit: poverty, lack of opportunity, second-class citizenship and little hope for a better future."[19] These social conditions and a rise in student activism fueled urban unrest from 1965 to 1968. In the epilogue to his book, Jelks aptly notes, "'Blackness' became the new cultural symbol of urban respectability. The new rhetoric of blackness in the mid-1960s expressed a positive self-awareness within black urban communities as well as a growing resentment for white middle-class norms of behavior."[20] Although warning signs were apparent, business leaders felt no obligation to implement substantial change by altering the managerial format. Commercial success masked the deep-rooted racial animosities that led to the worst riot in the city's history.

Although a host of monographs have parsed the black experience in large northern cities, scholars have largely ignored the black freedom struggle in secondary cities, such as Grand Rapids, during the postwar era, except as an addendum to the main events that occurred in Chicago, Detroit, New York, Philadelphia, Milwaukee, and Los Angeles.[21] In fact, the majority of black Americans lived in nearly 150 midsize cities during the postwar era, and they made African American history in these regions. To be sure, the struggle for black equality could not be contained. Although the basic historical narrative of the black freedom struggle centers on climactic moments and a chain of physical encounters, Grand Rapids was often devoid of the heroic lunch-counter and bus-station incidents of southern civil rights activism. Perhaps this speaks to the often mundane, bureaucratic nature of civil rights organizing in smaller northern cities or our conditioning to expect some variation of the hostile confrontations of the South. Yet the freedom fight in Grand Rapids was no less real or meaningful. In situating the black freedom movement in Grand Rapids, I employ historian Hasan Kwame Jeffries's concept of "freedom rights" to express the scope of black aspirations and goals, abandon the false dichotomy between civil rights and black power, and represent the fluidity and malleability in the way black people lived this history.[22]

Although recent scholarship has convincingly argued that the Montgomery-to-Memphis framework captures only one part of a larger battle that extended further back in time and transcended regional distinctions, it still narrowly conceives the black freedom struggle as having its most vibrant moments in larger cities. The new scholarship suggests that the black experience in these cities was mirrored throughout the urban North. This was not entirely the case, and the absence of focus on how the political culture and the social and economic conditions of these smaller urban communities (Grand Rapids, Michigan; Springfield,

Massachusetts; Gary, Indiana; and Sacramento, California, to name but a few)
transformed the black experience in the postwar era distorts our understanding
of the past. Further research is needed to explore the similarities and differences
between the freedom fight in smaller and larger urban cities and among smaller
communities as well.

A City within a City broadens our understanding by telling the story of how
blacks in Grand Rapids led lives of dignity and meaning despite experiencing
white racism in a smaller urban setting.[23] Because the process of city building in
the postwar era, a period marked by suburban investment and urban disinvestment, was a critical turning point in the northern black freedom movement,
this history demands attention.[24] In postwar Grand Rapids, decentralization,
neighborhood backlash, and downtown redevelopment established a spatial
geography of privilege. As in Richmond, Virginia, in the postwar era, race
loomed large in the political and planning history of Grand Rapids. Although
whites recognized the deplorable housing conditions that blacks faced in both
cities, no resolution that did not sustain the existing segregated landscape
proved viable. Moreover, in both communities, business leaders maintained
power through an at-large city commission election and the appointment of
a city manager. As white out-migration increased, the business community
looked to annexation as a way to hold sway over the expanded suburbs, yet, in
both cities, business leaders faced strong resistance from the suburbs. As a
result, in the 1960s, Grand Rapids and Richmond instituted significant urban
revitalization programs in an effort to compete with their suburbs for jobs and
for residences.

Unfortunately, histories of the great freedom struggle and the postwar spatial transformation are told separately. Examining the interconnections between
the histories of postwar city building and the black freedom fight illuminates
how race shaped the contours of urban life. It also highlights the role of black
agency in the postwar campaign for quality-of-life issues.[25] Whereas works by
Hirsch and Sugrue clearly articulate how white neighborhood resistance surfaced and limited black housing opportunities in the postwar era, they focus
almost exclusively on ethnic white backlash. This book uses Grand Rapids to tell
the contested story of urban stratification with blacks centered as primary agents
in the complex history of city building. Understanding the intricate nature of
urban life in secondary cities is crucial to understanding why blacks did not,
ultimately, achieve equal housing or schooling in the post–World War II era and
to discerning how blacks shaped, resisted, and coped with these metropolitan
changes.

Inextricably linked, housing and schools greatly influenced the politics of
race and metropolitan development in postwar society. Given the complex
nature of structural racism, it is imperative to consider these arrangements rela-
tionally and to value these spaces as important arenas for race, class, and power

battles that affected entire communities.[26] Accordingly, *A City within a City* examines the interconnected forces of race, housing, and schools in a way that alters the conventional view of the urban crisis from mere economic restructuring to a perspective that illuminates the emerging coherency of spatial racism in the postwar era. Thus, it provides a new framework for understanding the postwar struggles to shape and control metropolitan space.

This framework also shifts the narrative away from blacks as mere objects of economic forces and racism.[27] Considering the agency of multiple black constituencies and their interior struggles, this book argues that blacks were central historical actors and explains the motivations for and the significance of black activism in the postwar era. This approach means moving beyond an examination of external forces alone to an investigation of the black urban experience on the ground level to capture the sense of life that reveals the varying choices, negotiations, and decisions that blacks faced and that occasionally pulled them in different directions. This distinct vantage point provides an intimate understanding of urban space and race. Although race united blacks, racism was not the only determining framework of the black urban experience. Despite shared aspirations, varying strategies often divided black coalitions, and not all strategies proved equal.

The story of schools and housing is also part of the long civil rights movement.[28] Recently, historians have recognized that the temporal and ideological sweep of the twentieth-century freedom struggle stretched beyond the older Montgomery-to-Memphis framework. *A City within a City* examines one battleground in the civil rights movement, but it adds several new dimensions to the story. First, it shifts the focus from how the promises and limits of the liberal–civil rights coalition shaped the future of racial politics in urban America to an understanding of how racial conservatism shaped the battle over property, housing, and schools and the trajectory of black urban struggle. Second, it focuses on teenagers as leading political actors in the struggle for racial justice in the North. No one played a more important role in shifting the politics of race than secondary students in Grand Rapids. Through their demands for black history courses, black teachers, better facilities, and support for black students, young people dramatically shaped the course of the black freedom struggle. Understanding black youths' emphasis on racial dignity, cultural heritage, and the power to determine their black identity free from the restrictions of white authority in Grand Rapids advances our understanding of the highly complex nature of urban race relations in the postwar era.[29]

The postwar reshaping of the American metropolis represented a moment of historical possibility to reduce racial anxiety and resolve the American dilemma. Instead, conservatives in Grand Rapids blended a discourse centering on individualism, property rights, a market-based meritocracy, and limited government intervention to direct and control the postwar city-building process.

Although this process in northern communities was often categorized as "de facto segregation," Grand Rapids illustrated that government officials, at the local level, significantly influenced the process of building American urban areas. Beneath the veneer of de facto segregation lay a tri-level system of "northern managerial racism," which funneled blacks into declining neighborhoods complete with poorly funded and underequipped schools, thus functioning to institutionalize race relations in Grand Rapids. This book demonstrates that space was a racially coded category that individuals actively constructed and reconstructed, and, despite multiple forms of black protest, this contested struggle ultimately produced a harsh landscape of northern inequality.

ACKNOWLEDGMENTS

Like all book projects, this one benefited immensely from the professional and personal support of a number of extraordinary people. I would be remiss if I did not take this opportunity to acknowledge their contributions publicly. In particular, I am indebted to Matthew Lassiter, a mentor and friend, who read and offered feedback on every draft of the manuscript. His insights were signposts that helped me find my way and strengthened the arguments of this book. I am also grateful to a number of scholars, especially Matthew Countryman, Matthew Daley, Randal Jelks, Peter Kuznick, Earl Lewis, Jeffrey Mirel, Randy Monhollon, Abigail Stewart, and David Winter, to mention but a few, who read and reviewed all or parts of the manuscript. Their key suggestions helped shape this book.

I thank all my colleagues in the History Department at the University of Nevada, Las Vegas (UNLV), for their support and camaraderie. In particular, I am indebted to John Curry, Joseph Andy Fry, David Holland, and Colin Loader for taking time out of their own busy schedules to read portions of the manuscript and provide instructive commentary at critical junctures. David Tanenhaus, my mentor since I arrived at UNLV, also deserves special mention for reading numerous drafts and providing a critical review of my work with kind support. Furthermore, I thank all my graduate students at UNLV for their engaging conversations, in particular Summer Burke and Colin FitzGerald.

In addition, I thank all the archivists and librarians at the numerous archives I consulted, including the Bentley Historical Library; the Gerald R. Ford Library; the Michigan Regional Archives; the Hekman Library and Heritage Hall at Calvin College; Special Collections at the Kalamazoo College Library; the Library of Congress; the National Archives; and the Grand Rapids City Archives and Records Center, especially William Cunningham. Specifically,

I thank everyone at the Grand Rapids Public Library who helped me collect and locate precious local documents. In particular, I am grateful to former city historian Gordon Olson for his guidance and research assistance and M. Christine Byron, Karolee Gillman, and Ruth Van Stee for assisting me at every turn. I also thank Ben Boss, Heather Edwards, Melissa Fox, Tim Gleisner, Will Miner, and Julie Tabberer for all their archival expertise. I am also grateful to all the people of Grand Rapids who took time to meet and speak with me, including but not limited to Vernis Schad, Roger Wilkins, and Helen Jackson Claytor, whom I had the pleasure of interviewing before her passing in 2005.

I was also extremely fortunate to have a team of experts shepherd my book through production. My editor, Micah B. Kleit, enthusiastically embraced my ideas and extended me the opportunity to join the Temple University Press family. Micah surrounded me with a group of skilled professionals, including Joan S. Vidal, Lynne Frost, Gary Kramer, Irene Imperio Kull, and Linda Hallinger, who all graciously provided assistance in developing this book. In particular, I thank Joan S. Vidal and Lynne Frost for not only their technical expertise but also their patience, thoughtfulness, and kind words during a difficult period in my life.

Additionally, I thank my friends and family. My friends encouraged me throughout the book project. Most especially, I convey my deep appreciation to Cameron Allen, Jemel Buck, Marko Krivokapic, Audu Mark, and Yannis Pappas, who kept me sane, made me laugh, and helped put everything in proper perspective. Also, a number of wonderful people have helped my family adjust to life in Nevada, including the Celano, Horinger, Jimenez, Magrisi, and both Martinez families. I thank them all for embracing my family and providing much-needed relief during this arduous process. I also extend thanks to my own family. I am extremely grateful for my many cousins, uncles, aunts, and extended church family members—too many to name here—who all contributed significantly to this book by setting high expectations for me and believing that I could approach them. I offer my gratitude to my wife's family in Michigan for opening their homes to my family while I researched and wrote. (Thanks, Mom Cindy.)

Finally, I extend special thanks to my sister, Renee, for her encouragement throughout the years and to my brother, Trey, for providing me with helpful guidance and support my entire life. I am grateful to Trey for reading every draft of the manuscript and providing useful feedback during our golf sessions. I also thank my beloved son, Kaleb, for bringing me tremendous joy on a daily basis and for reminding me of life's simplicity. (Son, I am proud of all you have accomplished at such a young age; you truly are remarkable.) And to my two daughters, Isabella and Ava, I offer thanks for the tea parties, fashion shows, and children's literature. My kids have provided me with laughter, hugs and kisses, and timely distractions that remind me of life's most precious moments.

That said, my deepest gratitude goes to my wife, Melissa, for being my pre-eminent source of inspiration and for being there for me during every phase of the publishing process. She refused to let me become discouraged. I thank her for her enduring love and for the abundant emotional and spiritual support she has provided during every step of this journey. (Melissa, I love you.) Last, but not least, I offer a warmhearted thank-you to my parents, Margaree C. Robinson and Dr. Bryant Robinson Jr., who have been my greatest source of inspiration. This book would not have been possible without them. They have taught me patience and persistence, given me love and guidance, and made immeasurable sacrifices for my family and me. I dedicate this book to my parents as a small keepsake to remind them that their struggle is not altogether lost on their son, who loves them immensely. (Mom and Dad, please, keep pressing on; I thank you with all my heart.)

Abbreviations

BUC	Black Unity Council
CAP	Community Action Program
CSC	Campau School Committee
FEPC	Fair Employment Practices Commission
FHA	Federal Housing Administration
GRNAACP	Grand Rapids National Association for the Advancement of Colored People
GRPD	Grand Rapids Planning Division
GRREB	Grand Rapids Real Estate Board
GRSB	Grand Rapids School Board
GRSC	Grand Rapids Study Club
GRUL	Grand Rapids Urban League
HOLC	Home Owners' Loan Corporation
HRC	Human Relations Commission
KKK	Ku Klux Klan
MCRC	Michigan Civil Rights Commission
MSACW	Michigan State Association of Colored Women
NAACP	National Association for the Advancement of Colored People
NAREB	National Association of Real Estate Brokers
NUL	National Urban League
OEO	Office of Equal Opportunity
OJT	On-Job Training
PVL	Progressive Voters League
SNCC	Student Nonviolent Coordinating Committee
UHPA	Union High Parents Association
VA	Veterans Association

1

"ROWING, NOT DRIFTING"

Black Organizational Reform before World War II

Black Settlement in Grand Rapids

During the First Great Migration, nearly 1.6 million black southerners headed north between 1910 and 1940. Initially, almost 40 percent of them settled in eight large cities, five of which were in the Midwest, but many ended up in smaller "off-line" locations, such as Grand Rapids.[1] Many blacks "were only temporary guests" in the larger cities before moving on. The influx of black migrants in Grand Rapids before World War II underscored the extended migratory streams that flowed beyond big cities and gave rise to new vibrant black communities in such second-tier cities.[2] Patterns of black life in these cities often diverged from rather than replicated those of the larger metropolises.

In the primary cities, dramatic urban change compressed blacks into ever-more-constricted neighborhoods and ultimately produced physical ghettoes. Some secondary cities, such as Gary, Indiana, which adjoins Chicago, did indeed have patterns of segregation similar to those of their larger counterparts. However, such cities as Grand Rapids and Lansing exhibited characteristics different from those of the archetypical model. White restrictions and prohibitions there were principally aimed at establishing a rigid occupational structure and de facto segregation rather than a fully segregated residential structure. Blacks in such places as Grand Rapids and Lansing were not "knit together . . . by black institutions that nurtured them" in districts that "assumed the pattern of a self-contained city" as they were in New York, Chicago, and Detroit.[3] Although African Americans were lured by the same desire for educational opportunities, better living standards, and employment opportunities as their neighboring counterparts, their settlement experience contrasted sharply.

Located 150 miles northwest of Detroit and 170 miles northeast of Chicago, the Furniture City fed off both locations. The black community there grew from

665 in 1910 to 2,795 in 1930,[4] a pattern shared by other secondary cities. In Lansing, the black population increased from 354 in 1910 to 1,638 by 1940. Although larger metropolitan areas experienced a greater numerical increase of black migrants, the population growth in numerous midsize cities was substantially higher in proportion to their previous black populations. The dispersion of black migrants into secondary cities had significant consequences.

The manner in which blacks reached Grand Rapids varied. According to a 1940 National Urban League (NUL) study of 319 black migrant families in Grand Rapids, more than half relocated from midwestern or Rust Belt states, with most of the remainder arriving directly from the South.[5] In the absence of "migration clubs" and other critical migratory networks vital to the process of "chain migration," they relied on local black organizations, such as the Grand Rapids Study Club (GRSC), the Grand Rapids National Association for the Advancement of Colored People (GRNAACP), and the Grand Rapids Urban League (GRUL), to forge a dynamic black community. These three institutions represented different strategies in the grassroots insurgency that challenged the northern version of Jim Crow. Their roles are best told in the individual life histories of their members in the two decades before World War II.

In 1927, Lucille Skinner moved from Kansas City to Grand Rapids, where she met and married her husband, Floyd, who had graduated from the University of Michigan School of Law and returned to Grand Rapids to practice. Oliver M. Green, a World War I veteran, also earned a Michigan law degree and became an attorney.[6] Among his many accomplishments, Green received the distinguished honor of being the first black elected to the Grand Rapids Bar Association in 1925. Emmett Bolden was born and reared in Grand Rapids. After graduating from Howard University, he returned to open a dental practice. Milo Brown came to Grand Rapids from Cassapolis, Michigan, attended Worsham College of Embalming in Chicago, and returned to become Michigan's first black mortician outside Detroit. Sarah Carter moved with her family to Grand Rapids from Alabama in 1922. She married Henry Glover, a chauffeur, shortly thereafter and in 1927 was hired as a maid at a local hospital. Lucille Skinner became the president of the GRSC, and Sarah Glover an active member. Floyd Skinner, Oliver Green, Emmett Bolden, and Milo Brown became active members of the GRNAACP. The activities of these individuals joined those of others to develop a sense of community in the face of conspicuous and often hostile white discrimination before World War II, after which "Michigan's Jim Crow customs were often disguised in arguments about free enterprise and the freedom of association."[7]

Northern Jim Crow

In early November 1924, nearly six thousand Ku Klux Klansmen representing more than fifty counties descended on Grand Rapids for a three-day Western

State Klonvokation. The Michigan Klan, with membership projected at nearly twenty thousand, joined with locals in preparation for their first public rally in the city. Local Klansman Wilbur Ryman presented the request for the parade permit, assuring city officials that his "organization [was] not in the business of violating the law."[8] He guaranteed city commissioners that the parade would not be disruptive, noting as evidence the Klan's "orderly handling" of much larger gatherings ranging from 150,000 to 200,000 people and recent parades in Lansing, Saginaw, Adrian, Tecumseh, Jackson, and Kalamazoo.

Inspired by a common message that condemned "foreigners," in particular Jews and blacks, the Ku Klux Klan (KKK) adapted its message to suit specific resentments of a particular community.[9] Northern Klan members traveled throughout the state of Michigan and made their presence known "in many communities with parades, picnics and campaigns to elect friendly officials."[10] With remarkable success, the Klan mobilized large numbers in the Midwest, particularly in Michigan, Illinois, Ohio, and Indiana. By the early 1920s, the KKK even established a "club" at Gerald R. Ford's high school, South High, which was considered one of the most prestigious secondary schools in Grand Rapids.[11]

Local law enforcement permitted public displays of white supremacy, and state laws and city ordinances placed minimal restrictions on KKK parade demonstrations. Even though an area Klansman had set off three bombs just months prior in Traverse City, Michigan, city officials in Grand Rapids maintained they lacked authority to stop the impending rally. Ganson Taggart, the city attorney for Grand Rapids, proclaimed that the City Commission had "the right to refuse or grant a permit for a parade" only if participants decided to wear masks forbidden by law.[12]

The 1924 parade was canceled due to inclement weather, but the Klan finally held its procession on Independence Day, July 4, 1925, complete with a band and multicolored floats promoting its principles. The event gave spectators a firsthand look at the KKK in all its ceremonial glory as the junior order or youth division, women of the Klan, and Klansmen marched unmasked throughout the streets of downtown Grand Rapids.[13]

The Klan parade was only the most dramatic episode of a range of proscriptions of race mixing in public institutions, social activities, and employment in and around Grand Rapids. Discriminatory signs located in the windows of restaurants and businesses up and down Division Street declared, "Prices subject to change without notice." Even a basic commodity, such as coffee, routinely cost black customers five times as much: They paid fifty cents, while whites paid only ten cents. Although no overt campaign existed to drive out blacks living in Grand Rapids, as there had been in Gary, Indiana, blacks realized that Jim Crow pervaded every aspect of public life.[14] Few social, cultural, and economic options were available for blacks in the city. The city's social clubs, theaters, restaurants, and hospitals banned or restricted blacks.

Lucille Skinner recalled, "In the 1920s, Blacks were not even allowed to enter the building of White literary clubs."[15] William Gaines, a black plumber, recalled in 1904, "If a colored man goes into some of the restaurants here and asks to be served, the proprietors tell him to go way back in some dark corner. In some places they come out plainly and tell him that [they] do not wish for his patronage and they will not entertain him."[16] Similarly, in 1913, Reverend Henri Browne faced the harsh reality of discrimination in Grand Rapids when a storeowner refused to sell him a pair of shoes simply because he was black.[17] Blodgett Memorial, Butterworth, and St. Mary's, the city's three major hospitals, assigned patients to segregated wards.[18] In addition, "Negro and white insurance clients are segregated in the records. . . . Negro clients are on pink sheets, while those of white are kept on white sheets."[19] These are only a few examples of the countless stories of discrimination that represented a codified system of prejudicial treatment in Grand Rapids.

Sarah Glover's experience was typical of many black women in Grand Rapids before World War II. Like several female migrants who entered the city with high school diplomas in hand and training experience at their disposal, they found themselves relegated to positions in domestic service. The prejudicial treatment Glover encountered upon arriving in the city surprised her. She later reflected, "I came from the South where all we knew was discrimination. When I came here, I thought it wouldn't be as bad, but I soon found out it was undercover. In the South you knew where you couldn't go. Here you had to guess." Although she had been employed as a teacher in the South, in Grand Rapids Glover came up against the school board's policy not to hire black teachers in the 1920s, leaving her with few options in her new Midwest community.[20] She "wanted to stay busy, so when a lady leaving the hospital needed a companion," she took the job. She received greater compensation for her services as a companion in the North than she did as a teacher in the South, but she still dreamed of a teaching job.

In 1927, Glover accepted a job as a maid on the semi-private and private floors at Blodgett Hospital. For seventeen years, she scrubbed floors and performed a number of housekeeping duties throughout the hospital. After completing her daily tasks, she assisted the nurses. "The nurses used to call me 'Miss Sunshine' because I would cheer up the patients," Glover recalled. "I'd come over and say you look good today and crack a joke. That used to get most of them smiling again." But life did not always smile back at Glover. Although she acquired years of practical experience feeding and caring for patients, she "was rejected as a nurse's aide because of her skin color." Although not formally recognized as a valuable asset, Glover's ability to perform nursing duties allowed the white nurses time to handle additional tasks. Yet hospital officials determined that promoting Glover "was against the rules," and they continued to pay her only for maid service, despite the fact that her routine and responsibilities closely resembled those of a nurse's aide.[21]

Discriminatory practices were not limited to public accommodations and private institutions. Blacks faced a rigid color line in employment that dated back to the turn of the century. The restrictions placed on blacks applied to public and private employment opportunities. Examples are numerous. According to NUL records for 1940, of the 1,330 workers employed in various municipal offices, only 10 were black, 9 of them in menial jobs. The Board of Education, with 1,186 employees, had only 1 black worker, who worked in the maintenance department. The Bureau of Public Health Nursing, Michigan Social Security Area Office, Michigan State Employment Service (Grand Rapids Office), local office of the Federal Works Agency (WPA), and the Kent County Board of Social Welfare had no black workers among their nearly three hundred employees collectively.[22]

Blacks found employment prospects limited even in quasi-public institutions. The eight public utilities, for instance, with more than a thousand workers, employed only three black workers as janitors. Similarly, exclusionary trends were evident in four insurance companies. These companies together employed more than a hundred workers in their Grand Rapids offices, but not a single black person. This pattern of discrimination was replicated in local banks. Despite the fact that blacks provided revenue from property mortgages and rental units, only one black person secured a job—as a maintenance worker—in seven banks that employed more than three hundred people.

These discriminatory practices became the standard for private enterprise. In Grand Rapids, the emergence of the furniture industry proved essential to the growth of the city's economy. With more than fifty-four furniture makers in the city by 1910, the federal census reported, "by far the most important industry [was] the manufacture of furniture," and it recognized Grand Rapids as the "center of the furniture industry in the United States."[23] By 1910, "one in every three wage earners found work in the furniture factories."[24]

But manufacturing jobs in the Furniture City remained closed to black residents. For some time, owners of industry used labor unions to justify the maintenance of racial barriers. They argued that white laborers would protest the use of black workers in the plants. Although most unions discriminated against minority laborers, often the union views of exclusion simply reinforced employers' discriminatory hiring policies. The preferential hiring practices ensured employment opportunities for the growing supply of immigrant labor. Dutch and Polish newcomers, in particular, benefited from the available jobs, providing a sufficient labor pool for employers disposed against hiring black laborers.[25]

The Dutch and Polish communities were well established in Grand Rapids. By 1910, Dutch immigrants were easily the most sizable immigrant group in Grand Rapids, making up 42 percent of the city's population. Germans were second, constituting nearly 17 percent.[26] In her study of ethnic groups in the city, Mary Patrice Erdmans notes, "The foreman and shop floor managers were likely to be native-born German Americans and Swedish Americans, while the skilled and unskilled workers were Dutch (60 percent) and Polish (25 percent), primarily immigrants."[27] The Immigration Commission records of 1911 indicated that on average, the Dutch earned nearly 8 percent more than Poles in the furniture industry.[28] Thus, Polish immigrants "made lower wages, they were in more unskilled positions, and they were more likely to be paid by piecemeal," placing them "on the bottom stratum in factories."[29]

Although Polish laborers occupied the lowest rung in the furniture industry, blacks remained on the outside looking in. This "lockout" continued well into the 1930s, as the two leading industries in the city, furniture and automobile manufacturing, "refused to hire black workers."[30] In lieu of skilled jobs, blacks labored primarily in unskilled service occupations, such as busboys, bellboys, waiters, porters, and maids.

A few industries in the city had closed-shop agreements in Grand Rapids. A knitting-mill official noted, "Only whites can be employed [on] account [of] many female employees."[31] The Nash-Kelvinator Corporation, which employed nearly three thousand workers, also had an agreement with the United Automobile Workers of the Congress of Industrial Organizations (CIO). However, an administrator for the company reported that the plant had "no jobs suitable" for blacks. The small number of black industrial workers was not a result of union bias. A 1940 study conducted by researchers from the NUL noted that "Grand Rapids [was] not a union-controlled town." Instead, it explained, "the Negro does not, to any great extent, have the union as a barrier to his entrance into the majority of industrial establishments." Nevertheless, the study revealed a number of prejudices present in industrial hiring practices. Therefore, although union restrictions should not be disregarded, the "Negro's plight" went "beyond union restriction in this community."[32]

By the late 1930s, the furniture industry in Grand Rapids had lost ground to "newer centers of furniture manufacture in the South and West." By then the two "most important single industries and the largest individual employers [were] General Motors Corporation—Stamping Division plant, makers of body parts, and the Kelvinator Division of the Nash-Kelvinator Corporation, makers of mechanical iceboxes, etc." But the pattern of discrimination remained intact. Each of these industries employed roughly two thousand workers, but virtually no blacks.[33]

The NUL study disclosed a number of reasons why industries in Grand Rapids refused to hire blacks. Comments from industry administrators, which ranged from "habit and custom dictates" to "employees would object if we hired Negroes to work beside them," revealed a managerial policy that explicitly banned black industrial workers. In 1928, the president of the American Seating Company, which had nearly 1,300 white workers and no black laborers, expressed concern over the absence of minority workers. He explained, as did a number of industry officials, that no policy suggesting racial restriction existed in his company. Instead, he said no "competent" blacks had applied.[34]

Blacks who applied were kept out by a citywide closed-door policy. Like Glover, who was excluded from the nursing profession, black women workers faced an impossible job market. Although white women worked largely in white-collar jobs, black women could labor only in domestic and personal service roles. According to the NUL occupational statistics for 1930, "Over 60 per cent of Negro males and 93 per cent of Negro females were employed in occupations classified in the laboring and the domestic service classes."[35]

In the face of rigid exclusionary customs in virtually every facet of urban life, blacks in Gary and Grand Rapids demonstrated a complex sense of political consciousness. Despite relatively small numbers from 1900 to 1940, the black community in Grand Rapids organized to resist northern Jim Crow. It is important to note that although the black population in both communities was increasing, Gary's black population far surpassed that of Grand Rapids. In 1930, the black population in Gary reached nearly 18 percent of the total population of 100,000, while blacks in Grand Rapids remained at less than 2 percent of the total population of 165,000. The black population in Grand Rapids displayed a collective defiance, which had roots in the growth of local black institutions. Although not always as combative as Gary's black population, blacks in Grand Rapids challenged racial injustice in a multitude of ways, making their opposition to oppression known.

To navigate the racial impediments that white citizens devised, blacks turned inward for solutions. Repression intensified segregation, and discrimination ultimately spawned an organized self-help movement among blacks in Grand Rapids that was designed to enhance their state of affairs. Blacks closed ranks, reaching out only sparingly and strategically, in response to the pervasive disaffection among whites, and they pledged a commitment to self-help and racial solidarity. It "was mainly a black do-it-yourself effort which struggled beneath the surface of other public affairs."[36]

This movement came at a point when the minority community was quadrupling, and black residents placed a premium on social welfare and respectability. The unprecedented push for change came from all angles, but this chapter focuses primarily on the efforts of the Grand Rapids Study Club (GRSC), the Grand Rapids National Association for the Advancement of Colored People (GRNAACP), and, to a lesser extent, the Grand Rapids Urban League (GRUL), which was not formalized until 1942 and formally incorporated in 1943.[37] Although such organizations as the GRSC placed a premium on self-improvement, such groups as the GRNAACP attempted to dismantle the public relevance of northern Jim Crow. At times these two divergent tactics generated tensions within the black community reminiscent of the civil rights protest ideology put forth by W. E. B. DuBois and Booker T. Washington's pragmatic self-help model. However, to categorize these groups narrowly fails to capture the internal disagreements that represented the complexity and fluidity of the individual members. The GRSC, the GRNAACP, and the GRUL utilized different approaches, but they sought to accomplish analogous goals. The strategic divisions merely reflected a small variation of how blacks confronted the injurious and offensive nature of discrimination in Grand Rapids. Self-improvement directly addressed the internal needs of the marginalized black community, while the outward battle against northern Jim Crow forced full recognition of black legal, social, and economic rights. Therefore, at times, it was necessary for the black community in Grand Rapids to embrace both strategies.

Such organizations as the GRSC, the GRNAACP, and the GRUL emerged as sites of refuge for blacks living within the Jim Crow parameters of Grand Rapids. Each association, as documented by the GRUL, worked "toward the elimination of discrimination, segregation and prejudice from the general American scene, and work[ed] toward first-class citizenship for all Americans."[38] The chronicles of black organizational reform efforts exist as an integral part of the history of black racial uplift in small urban communities during the twentieth century. Exploring this spectrum of organizations helps map the development of a dominant intraracial approach to racial advancement, and it illustrates how the attitudes and practices of reform organizations affected the lives of fellow black citizens within the inner city. The testimonials of these societies are also part and parcel of the larger narrative documenting the black urban experience in cities throughout the country, encapsulating the aspirations and experiences of black migrants new to the urban arena. Furthermore, these testimonials illustrate the types of programs and services that blacks established to meet the political, social, and cultural needs of their community despite racial adversity. Thus, the individual and collective action of blacks in Grand Rapids to dismantle the public arm of segregation represent a crucial moment in the city's black freedom struggle.

Sisters in the "By-and-By"

Every Thursday, Glover "would get off work early as a maid at Blodgett Hospital and ride a streetcar to the [GRSC] meetings." Through her membership in the GRSC, Glover found some relief and encouragement. The racial and gendered nexus among black women of the club provided a much-needed release from the constant reminders of degradation within the polarized city. Racially banned from such organizations in the white community and exiled from recognized leadership positions in male-dominated black institutions, black women found in the GRSC a place to congregate and share ideas. Moreover, clubs afforded black women "an opportunity to escape from the confines of their religious domains, freely express their views, fully engage the political issues of the day, and actively participate in an organization that gave full vent to their talents."[39] Glover proclaimed, "I joined because there was no place to go for black women to study. And they would charge a fee of 25 to 50 cents if you didn't study your topic. Course that was a lot of money back then."[40] Most of the members in the club, domestic servants like Glover, could not afford to forfeit their weekly earnings, but the thought of intellectual development and community made the risk worth it. Forced to work jobs below their qualifications and left with few avenues to pursue their love of learning, they turned to the meetings of the GRSC for intellectual stimulation, social relief, and political activity.

The GRSC, which had been in existence since 1901, was formally organized on November 10, 1904, by several black women at the home of Louisa Gaines. Its purpose was to "provide helpfulness in study, sewing, and general charity."[41] However, the GRSC's self-help mission, which emphasized continued learning, quickly evolved into a much more comprehensive ideological mission devoted to improving the lives of the black community. The Grand Rapids Ladies Literary Club and Women's City Club barred black women. Born of discrimination, therefore, the GRSC promoted educational, social, and moral uplift as well as economic improvement as the pathways to racial progress. The philosophy of self-improvement and racial solidarity among the GRSC members served as a counter to white disaffection toward black causes and needs. According to the club song entitled "Smiles":

> There are clubs that stand for progress
> There are clubs that stand for fame
> There are clubs that only strive for
>   Pleasure, and each day
> Make life a selfish game
> But our club is ever pressing onward
> We don't drift, but row against the
>   Stream
> We are large in word, in thought, in action
> We are proud of our Study Club.[42]

GRSC members extended this ideology to the black community, and many women received their first involvement in civic affairs through the GRSC. Some members simply sought the camaraderie of the all-black female association, while other black women found refuge in the club's message and goals.

An affiliate of the Michigan State Association of Colored Women (MSACW), the GRSC participated in a larger black women's club movement that united black women in the state and across the Midwest. Founded in 1898 at a Chicago meeting of the National Association of Colored Women's Clubs, one of the nation's most established women's organizations that had more than one hundred thousand members, the MSACW clubs proved critical in the creation and maintenance of networks for black migrants.[43]

Such organizations as the GRSC facilitated migrant adaptation to the city. Without established migratory networks, the GRSC proved critical in the development of the city's black communal infrastructure. GRSC members exemplified what historian Darlene Clark Hine describes as "the connection between migration and black social-class formation and between migration and the rise of protest ideologies which shaped the consciousness of the 'New Negro.'"[44] This group of remarkable black women came together to address their needs and the larger concerns of the black community. According to the *Grand Rapids Magazine*, "This revolution wasn't born in the front parlors over brandy and cigars, but in the kitchens over rising loaves of bread and in the laundry rooms over soapy washerboards."[45] In their effort to carve out a modicum of dignity, these women made a conscious decision to battle the iniquitous racial system that denied minority residents of Grand Rapids social autonomy, respectability, and intellectual dominion. Incorporating politics and pleasure, black working women in the city established the first organizational structure that turned segregation into "congregation." As historian Earl Lewis aptly writes, congregation "symbolized an act of free will, whereas segregation represent[ed] the imposition of another's will. . . . [Blacks] discovered, however, that congregation in a Jim Crow environment produced more space than power. They used this space to gather their cultural bearings, to mold the urban setting."[46]

During the Jim Crow era, black working people carved out social space and constructed what historian George Lipsitz calls a "culture of opposition" through which to express their own concerns as well as social and cultural practices outside the spotlight and gaze of white authority. The GRSC provided such a social space for black women in Grand Rapids. The all-black club presented its members with a refuge from the daily humiliation and indignity of racism and the day-to-day degradation of domestic labor. The social environment of the GRSC afforded black women the occasion for fellowship with likeminded thinkers in a collectivist setting free from outside influences, including black men. In this forum, black women registered their discontent, developed inspirational companionship, and derived a degree of political and social autonomy.[47]

Such a space proved especially valuable in the early 1900s, as a trickling of migrants moved to Grand Rapids from the South and Midwest. Blacks migrated to escape economic hardships, racial oppression, disfranchisement, and violence, but they found that a variation of each obstacle existed in Grand Rapids. The city's racial atmosphere did not bode well for crafting solutions to educational, social, and economic concerns in interracial cells. Therefore, black women created solutions from within to improve and protect their community. Because wealthy furniture makers and other employers recognized Thursday as the maids' day off, the GRSC made Thursday afternoon its weekly gathering date. Not all businesses provided maids with an entire day off on Thursday; many employers made their domestics work a half-day. However, this restriction did not deter many of the members from convening at the weekly meeting. These women hurried through their duties inside the homes of wealthy white businessmen and rushed off upon completion to catch a streetcar after work to make the 2:30 P.M. start time.[48]

Initially, many women joined the GRSC because no other outlets for continued education existed for black women. As vital as the local NAACP chapter and the NUL, which evolved later in Grand Rapids, the GRSC enriched the lives of blacks living in the city. These women created a space for themselves and their families to escape rigidly enforced inequality. Elizabeth Tolliver, a club member, remembered vividly during the Jim Crow era that black women in Grand Rapids "just wanted to feel free to go where we wanted to go." The GRSC allowed black women to forge important kinship bonds. "We felt that keenly," she stated. "They [the white community] encouraged us to meet on our own. I hope they didn't think we wanted to be in their club."[49] Tolliver's sense of black pride resulted from the autonomy of the GRSC. According to historian Robin D. G. Kelley, the form of congregation experienced by members in the GRSC permitted "black communities to construct and enact a sense of solidarity; to fight with each other; to maintain and struggle over a collective memory of oppression and pleasure, degradation and dignity; to debate what it means to be 'black,' 'Negro,' 'colored,' and so forth."[50]

Lucille Skinner, who had been a member of the black Study Club in Kansas City, understood that the GRSC embodied the virtues of reform needed for communal self-improvement in a segregated city. The GRSC's emphasis on educational achievement among black women immediately prompted Skinner to join the movement toward a meaningful social, political, and educational alternative to northern Jim Crow in Grand Rapids. A natural leader, Skinner was appointed the club's president in 1928, and she began to build lasting relationships with other black migrant women also committed to self-help.[51]

Few black families lived in Grand Rapids during the late 1930s when Tolliver migrated to the area and married the pastor of True Light Baptist Church. The GRSC provided the expanding black community with a place to socialize. "There was never a dull moment. We'd have parties, teas and guest programs," Tolliver explained. "Some of the guests brought in by the club had national reputations for the black cause," including such notables as black poet Langston Hughes, black author and television journalist Louis Lomax, the Fisk Jubilee Singers, and former Howard University Dean William Pickens.[52] In the 1930s, Pickens journeyed to Grand Rapids to address the GRSC twice, and on his second visit he "was appointed an honorary member" of the club, becoming the first inducted male member.[53]

Grand Rapids Magazine reported that black women employed as domestic servants began asking critical questions, such as "How were [blacks] faring in other parts of the country? How could [blacks] in Grand Rapids stay informed on the issues?"[54] The programs organized by the GRSC exposed the black population of Grand Rapids to the most current and innovative thinkers in black culture and race ideology. Moreover, racial uplift extended beyond rhetoric for the members of the GRSC. Every day club members set aside the harsh realities and demeaning nature of discrimination that occurred in the work sphere and the public sphere. The GRSC was a space absent of racial judgment and male influence. Moreover, the club further reified the personal self-improvement beliefs posited by each of the individual female members. The internalized belief of racial uplift shared among the members defined their social status within the community. Although they were domestic servants on the surface, underneath the sheath existed well-read, self-aware, complex women who prided themselves on achievement. The women of the GRSC embodied the spirit of self-reliance. In an effort not only to satisfy their own incessant desire for accomplishment but also to motivate and steer the burgeoning black community toward success, the club women put their motto "Rowing, Not Drifting" into daily practice.[55]

For instance, in the early 1920s, club member Hattie Pinkney established the Christmas Savings Club within the organization. Initially, club members designated the money for social venues and communal entertainment. Deliberation among the club members sparked an alternative use for the funds in 1928. At that time, GRSC records indicated, "people were buying lots, and building cottages in Idlewild, and it seemed a wise course for us, also, to put money in lots up there." The investment in property, it continued, represented a successful venture in which the women of the club pooled their resources, and in April 1928 the GRSC purchased several lots. Also known as "Black Eden," Idlewild was one of the few vacation resorts that permitted blacks to purchase property. Despite the attraction of a vacation home in rural northwestern Michigan, the members of the club voted not to build a clubhouse in Idlewild. Rather, according to the GRSC report, "An offer was made and the lots were resold, the money banked." The money acquired from the Idlewild investment ultimately served as a substantial contribution toward the purchase of the GRSC headquarters in 1935, located on 427 James Avenue in the central city. Previously, GRSC members had rotated hosting the meetings "until funds were saved to purchase a building."[56]

Exclusive affairs, such as the GRSC's annual anniversary dinner and the Membership Tea, also secured funds for developmental projects in the black community. Such events, whether the annual anniversary dinner or a simple potluck dinner, afforded black community members opportunities to satisfy their social cravings while simultaneously providing essential funds for community uplift projects. Some of the affairs were extremely elegant and afforded blacks an opportunity to shed their work uniforms and dress up in their best evening apparel. "Seeing oneself and others 'dressed up,'" Kelley writes, "was enormously important in terms of constructing a collective identity based on something other than wage work, presenting a public challenge to the dominant stereotype of the black body, and reinforcing a sense of dignity that was perpetually being assaulted."[57] GRSC member Skinner recalled that in "those days, everyone dressed up for functions such as these especially if they were at night."[58] GRSC members orchestrated a number of gatherings that provided blacks with a recreational space filled with entertainment for working-class families.

The personal time, money, and effort sacrificed by these women often went unacknowledged, yet GRSC members and their supporters labored hard with extreme pride for the betterment of the black community. As the GRSC tune "I Love a Parade" pronounced, the organization provided blacks with a place of congregation. According to the song:

> We want a Club House
> A Place we can meet and get off the street
> And have lots of fun.
> We want a Club House
> A place of our own that we can call home
> And bring in our friends.
> That you can't come here
> That you can't go there we'll nevermore hear.
> Our children can dance, our children can prance
> They'll run, skip and play and no one will say; nay; nay.
> We want a Club House
> A place we can meet and get off the street
> So, we want a Club House.

Thus the GRSC, through its extensive network of leisure activities, quickly evolved into "a popular site for various social functions within the black community because there were few other places to go."[59]

But the GRSC functioned to satisfy much more than a social dimension in the lives of its members; it also catered to their intellectual needs. In 1928, newly appointed GRSC president Skinner "saw to it that members kept up with their subjects, and made sure they turned them in on time."[60] Each meeting was designed to widen the scope of knowledge of every member. According to one report, "Consistent with their dedication to learning, each member also [was] expected to recite a quote and verse that ha[d] inspired them since they last met."[61] Also, the highlight of each meeting included a special guest speaker or presentation from a club member. GRSC members selected research topics of interest. If club members could not determine a topic, then "they were assigned a subject by the committee,"[62] and they were expected to present their topic to the group. Discussions focused on, but were not limited to, such issues as birth control and sickle cell anemia as well as race relations in the United States and abroad.

Most of the women used the lessons learned from their organizational experience in the GRSC to support other civic groups in the city. Glover and

Skinner, like many of the club members, maintained active memberships in other communal organizations, such as the GRNAACP, the GRUL, the Progressive Voters League (PVL), and the Grand Rapids Civic Club. Glover recalled how, as a member of the PVL, she "went from house to house to encourage people to register and vote." She continued, "We tried to show them the necessity of voting and we ran two or three people for the City Commission." Actively engaged in traditional politics, during the years of the Depression, Glover and other organizers of the PVL paid workers to take people to the polls, because most did not have money. Covering such expenses as gas facilitated political participation among blacks otherwise unable to get to the polls. According to Glover, there "was a lot of footwork in those days" as workers went "house to house" to spread general political awareness, because so many people did not have telephones.[63]

Such members as Glover epitomized the "row" and "not drift" mentality of the GRSC. Glover "never stopped trying," despite the many obstacles of inequality she was forced to endure. Eventually, Glover's determination produced tangible results, and she spread her rowing ideology within the Grand Rapids black community. Although she participated actively in other organizations, the security and autonomy afforded by the exclusively female organization made the GRSC a unique and special place where black women could congregate.

Their shared labor and discrimination experiences undoubtedly brought GRSC members closer together. They had not only a common passion for learning but a working knowledge of the difficult and often dirty work associated with domestic labor. The physically arduous domestic work also came with an equally strenuous mental strain. The humiliation of performing maid services intensified among the members, because they had acquired education and were engaged in establishing a vibrant black middle-class community. Although the domestic service work regularly chipped away at their self-esteem, the club reaffirmed their self-respect and validated their worth. "Blacks could not go where they wanted to go, or do what they wanted to do, they had to make their own activities," Skinner recalled.[64] The club afforded its members an opportunity to create their own identities as black women in Grand Rapids. That is not to say these women did not sustain their identities in the work or home sphere; rather it recognizes the multipositionality of their identities and acknowledges the obstacles of race and sex in both settings.

The Early Struggle for Integration

DuBois arrived in Grand Rapids in 1917 to cultivate the seeds of change. He delivered a talk to the Sunday Evening Club, sponsored by the Park Congregational Church. Although DuBois's talk, entitled "The World's War and the Darker Races,"[65] received a moderate response from the *Grand Rapids Press,* the address resonated among blacks in the community and inspired the formation of a local chapter of the NAACP.[66] Nearly fifty black residents gathered two years later, on January 3, 1919, with the Great Lakes district organizer of the NAACP, Rev. Robert W. Bagnall, to charter the Grand Rapids chapter. The attendees paid a single dollar and in return received a subscription to *Crisis* magazine and membership in the NAACP. It took only twenty-two days for the NAACP's national office to confirm the charter for the Grand Rapids branch.[67]

In the wake of the KKK rally in 1925, dentist and NAACP member Bolden decided to challenge the growing parameters of Jim Crow in the city. Bolden knew that despite the close residential proximity, in the early decades of the twentieth century, whites in Grand Rapids preferred to keep the races socially separated in all aspects of public city life. Blatant forms of discrimination in restaurants, theaters, and even health facilities revealed an unmistakable color line. However, reluctant to accept the increasing racial animosity, blacks organized the Grand Rapids branch of the NAACP to help eliminate the strictures of racial discrimination. The leadership of the GRNAACP represented a burgeoning population of black professionals. Their guidance shaped the organizational and ideological goals of the GRNAACP and most of the total black community reform efforts prior to World War II.

Bolden's action came at a time when the KKK's parade raised racial tensions in the community. But he embodied a spirit of determination and heightened expectations. Bolden promptly allied himself with an emerging cadre of local black activists with similar credentials and aspirations to challenge Jim Crow, including attorneys Green and Floyd Skinner; another dentist, Cortez English; and physician Eugene E. Alston. This new generation of college-educated professionals began their careers inspired by the "New Negro Movement" of the Roaring Twenties, which centered on an extraordinary proliferation of black writers, artists, musicians, and actors. Although known broadly as the Harlem Renaissance, the "New Negro Movement" did not take place exclusively in New York. The cultural flowering of black self-confidence in artistic works, public life, and politics arose in communities across the United States. Although blacks in Grand Rapids welcomed self-determination, the ideological fervor of the emerging leadership cadre around Bolden firmly believed it was necessary to lessen race discrimination. The enforcement of northern Jim Crow and the growing sense of assurance and confidence among the rising urban black middle class made the city a fertile environment for the efflorescence of black pride and organization.[68]

Although professionals were well represented in the new NAACP chapter, membership also included many with less prestigious occupations. A railroad porter, Thomas E. Benjamin, served as president; the vice president was a waiter, Basil Ray; a custodian, J. Ed Jones, and a printing superintendent, George M. Smith, filled the offices of treasurer and secretary, respectively. This union of professionals and ordinary black residents charted the course for the GRNAACP and began a strategic assault against inequality within the city limits.[69] Within a year, GRNAACP Secretary Smith founded the *Michigan State News,* which, according to historian Randal M. Jelks, "became a statewide promotional vehicle for the NAACP."[70] Perhaps the most important contribution came from members' willingness to challenge the implicit foundation of northern Jim Crow.

On the evening of December 14, 1925, Bolden attempted to purchase mainfloor seat tickets for a vaudeville show and film downtown at the old Keith Theater. Bolden no doubt could afford such seating, but the color of his money was not the issue; rather, the color of Bolden's skin presented the most immediate difficulty. According to a *Grand Rapids Press* article, "It took guts—or sublime ignorance—in those days for a black to ask for a seat anywhere but in the balcony." The balcony section, dubbed sarcastically by whites as "Nigger Heaven," was a concession to the blacks' wanting to experience the fine arts, but only under the restrictions of segregation. Bolden did not agree with the spurious idiom, and he sought to experience the white man's heaven situated on the first floor.[71]

The theater employees gave Bolden the customary runaround. And although that road had a certain familiarity, "it wasn't something he'd learned to live with." Bolden's determination on that night intersected with good fortune, as a white man standing in line behind him overheard part of the exchange at the right time. As a dental supplier, the white gentleman came into frequent contact with Bolden. He inquired about the conversation and asked whether Bolden intended to go to the show. Instead of creating a scene, the doctor simply said that "the main floor, where he wanted to sit, was said to be sold out." Incredulous, the white dental supplier responded, "I don't believe it," and he stepped up to the window and without delay purchased two tickets located on the main floor.[72] Clearly, the theater accepted money from both black and white patrons, but money from a black hand could buy only a seat in the lessglamorous "Nigger Heaven" section of the theater. Bolden found this situation offensive and unacceptable, as did his white acquaintance, and both were willing to stand for justice. Bolden took the next step and brought a civil rights suit against the theater.

It was not the first such case in Grand Rapids. Nearly five years earlier, a verdict by Judge M. L. Dunham awarded the sum of $250 to Rev. William Nelson DeBerry, pastor of St. John's Congregation Church in Springfield, Massachusetts; Rev. Alexander C. Garner, a pastor in Washington, D.C.; and Rev. Charles Wesley Burton, pastor of Lincoln Memorial Church in Chicago, Illinois. The three black pastors came to Grand Rapids to attend the National Congregation Council of America conference. On Sunday, October 26, 1919, they walked into the Livingston Hotel, intending to eat dinner at the hotel cafeteria. The manager of the cafeteria, Robert E. Jones, refused to serve the black ministers and declared that people of color could not dine within the hotel premises. That year the legislature had revised the Civil Rights Act of 1885, which guaranteed to all equal access to public accommodations regardless of race, creed, or color.[73]

Bolden's case also appeared to be a clear civil rights violation. "One of the several local theaters to draw a color line," city historian Gordon Olson writes, "the Keith restricted individuals of African descent to seats in the balcony."[74] The enforcement of Jim Crow troubled not only Bolden but also other members of the newly originated NAACP chapter. With the support of the GRNAACP, Bolden filed suit in Superior Court against the theater's holding company, the Grand Rapids Operating Company. Green served as counsel for Bolden, while Skinner, still a law student, assisted with legal research.

Under Michigan state law, discrimination in public accommodations was forbidden in any form.[75] Green contended that under Michigan law and the Civil Rights Act of 1885 (amended in 1919), the holding company clearly denied Bolden equal access. This was part of a strategy to combat the practices of businesses that ignored the law and required blacks to enter in separate entrances, pay higher prices for commodities, and assemble in segregated sections without consequence, despite the fact that the civil rights statute outlawed prejudicial bias based on race, creed, or color in all public spaces.

In 1925, Green filed three cases of discrimination against the Keith Theater, aiming to substantiate a regular pattern of prejudicial treatment in its daily operation. In each instance, Green based his suit on discriminatory seat assignments based on racial preferences. The court decided to combine the first two lawsuits, which were filed separately on April 10, 1925, into one in *Glenn v. Grand Rapids Operating Corporation*.[76] William Glenn and Roger Grant, the litigants in the initial suits, were both born and raised in Grand Rapids. Both had graduated from high school and received jobs as porters at the Pantlind Hotel, and the GRNAACP hoped their respectable status would assist them in their case. Although Green stated that he won the case, perhaps with a negotiated settlement, the GRNAACP wanted the discrimination issue settled entirely.[77]

Bolden, Green, and the GRNAACP remained determined to eradicate the application of Jim Crow within the Grand Rapids community. It did not hurt that Bolden, unlike Glenn and Grant, had a formal education after high school and managed to secure an elite occupation. A well-known athlete in the community and an accomplished professional, he ran as a candidate for the Grand Rapids School Board. Although he finished dead last, receiving only 1,165 votes, his candidacy provided much-needed publicity for his discrimination lawsuit, which had received minimal attention from the local press.[78] Moreover, the Keith Theater's defense attorney, Julius Amberg, filed numerous motions, which he hoped would exhaust the prosecution's financial resources. It nearly worked, but Green overcame financial hardships to keep the case open. Additionally, as noted by historian Jelks, "To add insult to injury, during this time a police officer beat Green for entering the front door of the police station."[79] Although Green filed suit against the officer, he subsequently dropped the charges.

The holding company held firmly to the position that as a private enterprise, the theater could exclude any individual regardless of the condition, and Judge Leonard Verdier agreed. Verdier had a reputation for making racist decisions. Just months before, he had sentenced a black man to life in prison for armed robbery and had declared at sentencing, "If you were in some other states, you would have been lynched."[80] Although the initial decision supported the holding company, Green appealed to the Michigan Supreme Court, which subsequently overturned the decision on June 6, 1927. Although the decision went almost unnoticed in the local press, the verdict captured the headline of the *Chicago Defender*: "Court Rules Against Jim Crow Tactics: Reverses Decision in Theater Case."[81] Bolden eventually received approximately $200 in compensation for damages, but the victory produced a more satisfying result for blacks by forcing the Keith Theater to dismantle its segregated seating policy. The trial represented a political milestone for blacks within the community. For such blacks as Brown, this landmark decision served as inspiration to attack additional injustices throughout the community.

As a charter member and officer of the GRNAACP and charter member and eventual president of the GRUL, Brown embraced a politics of struggle that wove together various approaches designed to achieve favorable circumstances for urban blacks. His self-determination often caused Brown to have minimal tolerance for blacks who did not share his devotion to breaking down racial walls. "I tell them that they have to get on the ball," he proclaimed. "They have to qualify themselves for better jobs of all kinds. What they need is more and greater motivation. I keep telling them not to give up."[82] Brown embodied the steady persistence of black activists in Grand Rapids. He also epitomized how ordinary black citizens fluidly crossed organizational lines labeled integrationist or separationist. Like so many blacks in Grand Rapids, Brown constructed a pragmatic politics of survival that contradicted absolute dichotomies between civil rights and black power.

Brown purchased a house at 603 Jefferson Avenue from which to operate his mortuary business. The Depression of the 1930s forced him to move into a residence that accommodated both his family and his business within a single unit. He continued to work and live there, after several remodeling endeavors, well into the 1960s. Although he had no problem developing his business, families often had difficulty paying for the services rendered. Over the years, Brown "developed a plan for his clients to prepay for the funerals the families might have."[83] He set the money aside in a special bank account, and the interest drawn on the money submitted by the family was returned to them. The agreement resolved the complications on both sides, as it allowed Brown to get paid on time and let families concentrate on emotional matters during a time of critical loss.

Brown's business acumen led to entrepreneurial success. The Brown funeral home expanded from a one-man shop to a business that employed an additional four full-time and four part-time workers. As Brown established himself within the community, black residents began to call on him for matters unrelated to work. "They started dropping in or calling me on the phone," Brown attested, "to ask for advice and help of one kind or another. I became a counselor without portfolio." It was clear that Brown's decades of service engendered trust among the black community.[84]

Brown did not work alone in his efforts to defuse racism in the community. Aware of the harm caused by Jim Crow, Skinner actively combated discriminatory forces. A lawyer with "exceptional power and skill," Skinner generally represented clients who were poor and black. His efforts for change, although extensive professionally, also came in the form of civic activity, as Skinner served as the president of the GRNAACP for five terms.

Throughout the Great Depression, Skinner and Brown used the GRNAACP platform to engage in local politics. Cofounded by Skinner and Brown in 1926, the PVL worked diligently to organize black voters to win political concessions in a corrupt system of city politics. As forerunners of the voting rights movement during the 1920s and 1930s, "we knew where every black in town lived . . . and we organized in every way we could think of to get all of them to vote," Brown recalled. "We used the telephone to remind them of upcoming elections and set up a transportation service to get those to the polls who didn't have cars or another way of getting there."[85]

The PVL ran black candidates for local municipal offices, including Smith for City Commission and Brown for mayor. Although unsuccessful in its attempts to win an elected position, the organization continued to make its presence known. In particular, Skinner headed the PVL fight against City Commission candidate Harry C. White, who advocated segregated neighborhoods throughout the city. The PVL successfully launched a campaign to organize black voters in opposition to White in the third ward and proved an "effective means of marshaling the black community's voting power."[86] "We were too militant to be scared," said Brown. "Walking house to house, block to block, members of the Progressive Voters League registered between 1,400 and 1,500 of the city's black population."[87] The ability to organize so effectively ultimately produced patronage from the local political machine in the form of employment opportunities for blacks at the Civic Auditorium and at the polling stations in city elections.[88]

In many ways, Skinner embodied the integrationist aspirations of Smith, founder of the *Michigan State News*. Both remained emphatically opposed to any hint of segregation, and their integrationist beliefs led to internal conflict in the black community surrounding the creation of the GRUL and, subsequently, the establishment of a separate recreational facility for blacks.

Contradictions of Activism

In June 1927, the city's Interracial Council, made up of black and white Protestant church affiliates, researched the recreational needs of the local black youth. With Ethel Burgess at the helm, and joined by committee members Thomas E. Jefferson, Vivian Gould, Daniel B. Lampkins, and C. C. Stillman, the Interracial Council decided to begin with a comprehensive study of the black community.[89] Burgess wrote to Eugene Kinckle Jones of the NUL to request assistance in conducting the citywide survey. Jones agreed and assigned Charles Johnson, the director of the Department of Research and Investigations, to complete the study for a $400 fee.[90]

At the request of the Grand Rapids Welfare Union, the agency responsible for the distribution of funds to social service organizations, Jones was invited to come to Grand Rapids on September 22, 1927, to discuss the importance of local black recreational centers. Jones also suggested, "Wherever the Negro population of 1,000 or more is recorded, there is a need for a special Negro social worker."[91] The notion of a professional black social worker resonated with the Interracial Council. Shortly thereafter, the group suggested that "a Grand Rapids branch of the National Urban League be organized for the promotion of social work among colored people, that a trained Negro social worker be employed and that the Grand Rapids Urban League, if and when organized, be made of a member of the Welfare union."[92]

Many NAACP activists opposed the creation of the GRUL. Black leaders, such as Smith, Bolden, and Skinner, according to historian Jelks, believed "self-segregation was just as bad as the policies of formal and informal Jim Crow."[93] Hoping to find clarity, the chair of the Interracial Council, Ida W. Wilson, wrote to DuBois on December 28, 1927. The Interracial Council, she stated, "work[ed] for the betterment of the Negro population of about 5,000 and other residents of the city." With segregated YMCA and YWCA facilities, she wondered "how best to address the needs" of the black community and at the same time confront "the problem of segregation" in the community.[94] She also requested that DuBois come to Grand Rapids and address these issues. DuBois accepted but noted, "I would not like to express my judgment concerning a racial policy in a city that I know practically nothing about." His response captured the complicated nature of race in such cities as Grand Rapids. He added, "I am opposed to racial segregation as a principle but I am compelled to recognize it continually as a fact. How, where, and when principle can be successfully defended must, of course, be a matter of judgment among those who know all the circumstances."[95]

In 1928, a study of Grand Rapids conducted by R. Maurice Moss for the NUL concluded, "Justifiably or not, this is the issue which has overshadowed every other matter before the Interracial Council; the issue on which the most intense feeling has been aroused; the issue toward whose solution the least progress has been made."[96] In his interviews with local black leaders, Moss discerned the contempt blacks reserved for the local YMCA and YWCA. Despite the use of public funds to build community swimming pools, each organization regularly banned black usage. Moreover, YMCA administrators openly admitted to their prejudicial selection of patrons but noted that if the organization permitted blacks entrance, it would result in "serious defection on the part of their present white membership."[97] Separate accommodations, according to YMCA officials, would easily remedy issues on both sides. Moss seemed inclined to concur: "Negroes entertain the conception of these Associations as on par with hotels, railroads, etc.—that is, public affairs which should be open to everyone on an equal basis and which, if necessary, may be forced by law to make available to Negroes their facilities"[98] However, he considered the two organizations similar to private agencies with the ability to select their clientele. This sentiment echoed the argument of the owners of the Keith Theater in Bolden's case. Therefore, such men as Moss, Skinner, and Smith skeptically assessed the NUL's agenda in Grand Rapids. On the surface, the NUL's position and Moss's reasoning appeared to contradict the integrationist strategy of the GRNAACP.

In the spring of 1930, when the Interracial Council endorsed the idea of establishing a separate Grand Rapids Negro Welfare Guild to address the recreational needs of the black community between the ages of sixteen and twenty-one, Skinner adamantly objected. Although it appeared the Negro Welfare Guild would offer services that such organizations as the YMCA and YWCA refused to offer to black residents, Skinner viewed the separate organization as a continuation of northern Jim Crow. Burgess argued that the GRNAACP missed the point. In a sixteen-point response, she noted that several members of the Welfare Guild also maintained dual membership in the GRNAACP. Moreover, she noted, the real issue—the needs of local black youth—remained neglected. "We wish supervised recreation for their idle time," she stated. "It is only in organizations of his own race," Burgess continued, "that the Negro youth is trained in leadership."[99] That northern Jim Crow made both approaches necessary was a reality both sides failed to fully recognize. However, the Great Depression muted most of these internal concerns, as the black population in the city actually declined and blacks became less reliant on social agencies and more dependent on state and federal aid.

Skinner's position contained a degree of irony. In the face of "racial barriers in places of public accommodation such as restaurants, bars, nightclubs," he established a regular opportunity for blacks to enjoy nightlife. Although white audiences enjoyed black performers, such as Cab Calloway, at the Ramona Gardens dance hall, blacks waited in the back alley with the hope that Calloway would come out during intermission.[100] Skinner and Brown sought to ease the social humiliation experienced by blacks banned from places of leisure, such as Ramona Gardens, so together they founded Club Indigo, which was located on

South Division near Wealthy Street. Club Indigo provided an atmosphere in which blacks could freely associate and indulge in leisurely activity among friendly faces. While socializing at Club Indigo, blacks could listen to "the best black jazz musicians . . . and the finest black entertainers, headliners from Chicago, Detroit and other Midwest cities."[101] Organized social amusement among blacks served as a critical form of escape from the constant degradation encountered on the job and in hostile public spaces.

Club Indigo served a crucial need for black residents restricted from white entertainment venues, yet it seemed to stand at odds with Skinner's integrationist stance. Moreover, Skinner's wife, Lucille, was the president of the GRSC, which advocated a self-help formula for the black community. These contradictions reveal the complexities in minorities' opposition to the world of Jim Crow. From the public legal efforts of the GRNAACP to the behind-the-scenes infrastructure established by such organizations as the GRSC, blacks agitated, built coalitions, and closed ranks to survive in the city. Although these groups operated from varying vantage points, their efforts remained complementary to the struggle for freedom. Blacks needed the vibrant communal stability provided by the GRSC, but at the same time, they had to confront northern Jim Crow head on to exercise their full rights. GRNAACP activists did exactly that.

These combined efforts constituted the collective "Row, Not Drift" mentality of the black community prior to World War II. The entire black community identified with the humiliation of race prejudice; however, the process of finding relief often varied, contingent on the issue of the day. Despite the fluidity of responses from within the black community, the constant target remained overt racial discrimination. This was soon to change, providing a host of problems for the black community. On reflection, Brown commented that racism post–Jim Crow was "more subtle and less easy to define or root out. We still have a way to go." Thus, as blacks successfully managed to peel back the layers of Jim Crow and step out of "Nigger Heaven," many found themselves fighting for nonexistent work positions, social mobility, and respectability in a white man's hell. Black organizations geared toward self-improvement set the agenda for what Jacquelyn Dowd Hall calls the "long civil rights movement." In Grand Rapids, however, it was less of a movement in the traditional sense and more of a long freedom struggle for black equality. Their efforts affected the city's political, social, cultural, and economic fabric. Paradoxically, for each success that black actors experienced in Grand Rapids, whites seemed to engineer a more potent responsive form of racism. Although blacks triumphantly challenged northern Jim Crow in public accommodations and even secured new employment positions, by the late 1940s, whites had constructed an inconspicuous form of managerial racism designed to limit black progress while maintaining the city's prestige and economic prosperity. It became clear that racism was not a static feature in Grand Rapids; rather the forces of racism continued to evolve in extremely complex ways.

Numerous daily acts reminded blacks in Grand Rapids that the ominous reality of racial violence and discriminatory conduct was part of northern life. Yet the long fight for freedom in secondary cities, such as Grand Rapids, has remained situated on the periphery of conventional civil rights narratives, which focus primarily on the South and larger northern cities. Even though recent studies have turned their attention to civil rights and black power in the North, these works have overlooked the intense struggle for freedom in such places as Grand Rapids and the people who made that history, such as Lucille Skinner, Sarah Glover, Elizabeth Tolliver, Louisa Gaines, Hattie Pinkney, Emmett Bolden, George Smith, Oliver Green, Milo Brown, and Floyd Skinner.[102]

2

CITIZENS' ACTION

Managerial Racism and Reform Politics

City of Hope

Despite a decade of depression, which heightened the level of inequality between blacks and whites in the city, the black population in Grand Rapids had several reasons for believing their grievances would receive greater consideration in the post–World War II era. First, the unheralded acts of black resistance began to dismantle the overt signs of Jim Crow in the city. A stable coalition of civil rights organizations successfully challenged the racial barriers that openly excluded blacks from stores, hotels, restaurants, and numerous public accommodations. It appeared that blacks would face less hostility and benefit from greater access to commercial establishments throughout the city. Second, a reform movement surfaced in the late 1940s to address corruption in city government. Its emphasis on democratization of city politics offered a glimmer of hope that increased municipal social and economic awareness would result in changes in the conditions affecting urban black life. It remained to be seen, however, whether political and economic reform would translate into racial justice for a severely deprived black community.[1]

Concerned with political corruption and manipulation of the democratic process, self-proclaimed "progressives," mainly within the Republican Party, launched a vigorous assault against the Republican political machine led by Frank D. McKay and George W. Welsh. Blacks believed the promise of good government would lead to a more just allocation of city resources. Better government officials, encouraged by the Chamber of Commerce, promised to improve living standards and address the educational needs of children as well as ameliorate the health, safety, and physical environment of the city. Hopeful that eliminating graft might end the corrupt bargain between some businesses and government and instead offer a complement to the reform initiatives of civil rights activists, black organizations in Grand Rapids, such as the local chapter of the NAACP, the Grand Rapids Urban League (GRUL), and the Grand Rapids Study Club (GRSC), put their support behind the Republican reform movement. These organizations understood clearly that boss control resulted in the negligible distribution of resources for an underrepresented black community. Seen as one of the greatest stumbling blocks in the path of democracy, bossism's predicted demise in the face of "good government" paralleled the black community's hopeful aspirations for equality following World War II.[2]

Those hopes were to be dashed. Although the Citizens' Action movement did usher sweeping changes into the city's political structure, it primarily benefited the middle- to upper-class whites who formed the core of the movement. Most of the white reformers displayed minimal interest in addressing the impact of white racism. Instead, members of the Citizens' Action movement replaced a citywide policy of overt discrimination with a complex system of managerial racism. The duplicitous nature of the "progressive" movement concerning the black community was especially evident in the lack of local support for the statewide Fair Employment Practices (FEP) bill of 1955, which was designed to ban discrimination in employment based on race, religion, color, or national origin.

During the forties and fifties, fair employment occupied a central place in the struggle for freedom rights at the state and national levels.[3] Building on Franklin D. Roosevelt's Executive Order 8809, which prohibited employment discrimination in the defense industry, the GRNAACP sought more employment opportunities for blacks. But its views on how to end job discrimination differed from those of the GRUL. While the GRNAACP supported FEP legislation outright, the GRUL pushed for an "open-door" policy based on equal-opportunity hires for qualified black applicants. The GRUL's strategy was developed in part to work within the business structure of the pro-business reform movement, which had a significant influence on the GRUL Board. To protect "freedom of enterprise," the business community rejected FEP proposals, which it considered "an infringement on managerial prerogatives over hiring, promotion, and firing." Indeed, progressive Republicans formed the first barrier to freedom rights in Grand Rapids, and the reform agenda had profound consequences for blacks in the postwar era.[4]

Committed to reinventing Grand Rapids, businessmen and politicians in the reform movement promoted business expansion as a solution to racial problems. Like the New South movement in such cities as Atlanta, the Citizens' Action committee championed laissez-faire as a panacea for metropolitan development and touted Grand Rapids as the consummate example.[5] Under the rubric of progress and public interest, the reform movement practiced a paternalistic approach that rewarded blacks amenable to white interests. This tactical adjustment represented a crucial shift in the hegemonic control of metropolitan space in the postwar era.[6]

Determined to build a city image of middle-class respectability, reform city officials and business leaders routinely sacrificed blacks' needs and interests for the "good" of the larger community. Despite the crackdown on inefficient government, a noticeable absence in substantive racial equality overshadowed the changes made in city government. Although thousands of reform-minded citizens joined forces to topple the political machine in Grand Rapids and seize the political reins of the city, the overall structure of white supremacy blinded them from viewing blacks as equals on any level. It is revealing that Julius Amberg, the chief legal counsel in *Bolding v. Grand Rapids Operating Corporation,* which tried to uphold separate seating for blacks and whites at the Keith Theater, was a key participant in the reform movement. This lack of response by the reformers to appeals from the black community for equality suggests that managerial racism was central to the white progressive movement.[7]

"It Is Awakening"

In April 1942, a group of young businessmen in Grand Rapids assembled informally to discuss city politics and the "responsibilities of self government." It was not long before each conversation touched on the level of corruption in city politics under the control of "a few politically ambitious people who were in many instances guided by the influence of the machine politician."[8] W. B. VerMeulen, a Grand Rapids dentist, was one of the key organizers for what became known as the Republican Home Front. He selected Chamber of Commerce men, such as Stanton W. Todd, a political scientist and graduate of the University of Michigan who had a passion for reform, to battle the "boodling" and "grafting" common in the Grand Rapids city government.[9]

The Republican Home Front, which met weekly beginning in April 1942 at the homes and offices of members, stood for the "principle of representative and good government" at the city, county, state, and national levels.[10] By August, it mounted a campaign to win the position of precinct delegate to the Republican County Convention. It recognized that the precinct delegate, who registered people to vote, provided key information for voters, identified important concerns for candidates, and helped turn out the vote on Election Day, stood at the heart of Boss Rule. According to Home Front correspondence, "Public opinion is slowly awakening . . . and the place to start is at the source of all political power, the county precinct."[11] Despite stiff resistance from McKay and his machine, including outright attempts at intimidation, and early election defeats, the members of the Home Front persisted, and in June 1944, the group "succeeded in wresting control of the convention from the forces which had dominated Republican politics in Kent County for the previous twenty years."[12] In a letter to Todd, Republican County Chairman Oscar E. Waer stated:

> It is just too bad that you could not have been here to witness a triumph for which you were in no small way responsible. The work that you and four or five others have done during the past two years finally brought results. You fellows just refused to stay licked. Instead of quitting two years ago or from time to time since, you kept everlastingly at it and now, for the first time in twenty-five years, Frank McKay cannot go to a State Convention with Kent County in the palm of his hand ready to be used for trading purposes.[13]

One Home Front member, Gerald Ford Jr., was elected to Congress on November 2, 1948. He served the Fifth Ward from 1949 to 1973.

The Home Front weakened the political machine, but it did not overtake it. McKay's financial wealth still made him attractive to his political contacts, and he relished negotiating key backroom deals.[14] He owned thousands of real estate lots, a tire business, lumber and coal ventures, an advertising agency, and industrial companies,[15] and this wealth ensured a presence in city government and state politics that stretched well into the 1960s.[16] He retreated from the spotlight, leaving another Grand Rapids machine politician, Mayor Welsh, to absorb the political blows of the reformers.

Citizens' Action

On May 12, 1949, a sea of people assembled at Fulton Street Park (now Veterans Memorial Park) to protest the McKay-Welsh political machine. Young and old protestors stood side by side to denounce the city's corrupt political bargain. Calvin College students walked through crowds while holding signs that read, "TOSS THE RASCALS OUT."[17] The nearly five thousand aroused citizens in attendance at the public rally demonstrated a strong show of support for change in city governance. One speaker asked, "Whose taxes are we paying?" Irate members of the crowd yelled back, "Frank McKay!" "Who is pulling the strings?" "McKay!" the audience shouted. Jack Stiles, land investor and former campaign manager for Representative Ford, coined the slogan that evening: "Four must go." The crowd listened to remarks from several speakers, including Dr. Duncan E. Littlefair, pastor of the Fountain Street Church, who told the audience members they were getting "kicked around" in City Hall. Coming from Welsh's pastor, the public criticisms leveled by Littlefair were particularly jarring. The result was that audience members demanded the swift removal of Mayor Welsh and three city commissioners. They also voted to organize as a "Citizens' Action" group, and almost unanimously members selected attorney

Amberg to serve as president of the newly established organization. By early June, recall petitions against Welsh included the names of twenty-five thousand registered voters, far exceeding the number required for a recall election.[18]

The Fulton Street gathering resulted from the firing of City Manager Frank Goebel by the mayor and the City Commission, because he would not go along with their choice for city assessor. According to the *Grand Rapids Press*, "Under the old assessment system . . . ward political appointees put a rule-of-thumb value on houses and business buildings, resulting in discrimination between property owners in various part of the city." The dissension over assessment had brewed below the surface for nearly a decade between Welsh and members of the reform organization.[19] With Amberg at the helm of the new Citizens' Action group, members went to work and secured roughly twenty-five thousand signatures in favor of a recall. When Welsh learned that the State Supreme Court had validated the authenticity of the recall petitions, he resigned. Welsh ran again in the municipal primary of 1950, but Paul Goebel, Frank Goebel's brother and a former member of the Republican Home Front group, defeated his bid for mayor. Additionally, two Citizens' Action group candidates won, providing a 5–2 majority in favor of the new Citizens' Action group.

Even though blacks voted in support of all the changes in municipal government and the emphasis on progressive reforms, they remained unsure how this development would impact their community. Realizing that bossism produced minimal gains, blacks supported the progressive movement, but they were leery of the new leadership group. Many of these Chamber of Commerce men owned the stores, shops, restaurants, industries, and companies that effectively prohibited blacks as employees and, historically, as consumers in some cases. Thus, blacks wondered how much forbearance or militancy was needed to achieve tangible signs of racial progress. The GRNAACP and the GRUL had two very different ideas of how to proceed. Those approaches were personified in the actions of Paul Phillips, Hillary Bissell, and Helen Claytor.

Racial Politics and Progressivism

Paul Phillips and the Grand Rapids Urban League

Despite the progressive currents in the city, not much had changed for blacks in the 1940s when Phillips arrived and began his twenty-nine-year tenure as the executive director of the GRUL. "When Mr. Phillips came to Grand Rapids in 1946," the *Western Michigan Catholic* reported, "most restaurants refused to serve him because he was black."[20] Despite Emmett Bolden's victory in the Keith Theater decision of 1927, discrimination in restaurants and other public accommodations did not cease; rather, it just became more subtle. Fountain Street Baptist Church Rev. Littlefair informed his congregants, even in the face of civil rights law and the absence of discriminatory signs, that in "some places they [could not] enter at all." As fewer businesses openly advertised prejudicial practices, he noted, it became "a situation of nervous embarrassment. Permission hinge[d] upon the delicate good will and condescension of the owner."[21]

When Phillips arrived, only a handful of the nearly four thousand blacks living in Grand Rapids had skilled or white-collar jobs. According to *Grand Rapids Press* reporter Tom LaBelle, "Blacks were the last hired and first fired." He added, "They got the low jobs and stayed there."[22] Lillian Gill remembered that when she came to Grand Rapids in 1944, "no blacks could work anywhere except foundries and of course maintenance work in hotels. You couldn't even go in the front door of the hotel downtown in those days."[23] Phillips recognized that as a result of discriminatory hiring practices, the majority of blacks could only find work in occupations where they were subservient and overlooked by whites. In place of earlier overt prejudice, Phillips noted a new form of discrimination that was "manifested by the ignoring of nonwhites, who were not recognized as fellow human beings."[24] As businessmen and politicians attempted to make the city appear more progressive, they employed a new form of managerial racism to retain the status quo.

Phillips had had an intimate relationship with racial bigotry since his early childhood. Born in Omaha, Nebraska, in 1914, the son of a hotel waiter, he grew up in an era of racial violence. During the "Red Summer" and fall of 1919, more than twenty-five race riots occurred in urban centers throughout the country, including Omaha.[25] The memory of violence meted out to blacks during the riot haunted Phillips. However, like many other black youths, Phillips found ways to remain poised and constructively vent his discontent with the existing racial order. The track provided him with the opportunity to prove his ability and challenge the notion of white supremacy. As a shoeshine boy in Omaha, on Saturday nights before the segregated school dances, he shined the shoes of his white classmates, but then on "Monday, I got out on the track and beat the hell out of them."[26]

He had an illustrious track career at Marquette University in Madison, Wisconsin, where he "tied several world sprint records then, as did a couple of peers and friends, Jessie [*sic*] Owens and Ralph Metcalfe."[27] The accolades often veiled the sacrifices and struggles of these premier pioneer athletes. Behind the scenes, Phillips endured immense humiliation. "When he traveled with the Marquette track team," the *Western Michigan Catholic* reported, "he was not allowed to enter restaurants with the other members but had to eat in the kitchen or in another section of town."[28] Phillips had to face the off-track reality of being black.

After graduation from Marquette, Phillips was unable to find appropriate employment. So with degree in hand, he swallowed his pride and worked on a cotton plantation to save enough money to pay for graduate school at Fisk University before returning to Milwaukee as a steel-mill laborer and community organizer. These experiences motivated Phillips to take an interest in getting jobs for blacks in the skilled trades, which remained in large part closed to minorities in Grand Rapids. "Do you know there are more blacks with Ph.D.s than there are black plumbers?" he lamented. The *Western Michigan Catholic* also recognized that many of the black residents in the city with "college degrees were carrying bags at the Pantlind Hotel."[29] Roughly 3,800 minorities, most of them black, lived in the city in 1947. Yet, Phillips recalled, you "could count on one hand the number of minority-race people with skilled jobs or white collar jobs."[30]

As the executive director of the GRUL, Phillips devoted his first ten years in the city almost exclusively to expanding job opportunities for blacks. "There were no civil rights laws then," he recalled. "All we had to work with was our persuasive powers."[31] Without question, Phillips possessed exceptional persuasive skills, and he put them to work in a door-to-door campaign for racial justice. Working within the new structure of white power, his approach required persistence and patience. He visited factories, banks, and hospitals as well as the employers' associations and, most importantly, the Chamber of Commerce to search for black employment opportunities on a daily basis. Strengthened by the number of overqualified black applicants, Phillips implored the chamber and its many white businessmen to incorporate racial fairness into their hiring practices.

"We appealed to their pocketbooks, talking about what a good worker could do for them regardless of his color, and to their decency and morality," Phillips remembered. If that failed, he usually managed to wear down employers with his continued "visits to wrangle jobs for black clients," which, according to LaBelle, "must have seemed like the Chinese water torture."[32] Claytor, president of the YWCA and former GRUL Board member, sensed Phillips's dogged approach and zeal during the interview process, and it prompted her to emphatically support his hiring. Claytor recalled, "We realized what a fine person he was then and he proved us right."[33] As Phillips grew more accustomed to the pulse of the town, in the eyes of some accommodationists, he "slowly became the single most important force for racial justice Grand Rapids has ever known."[34]

In 1942, Bishop Lewis Bliss and Dr. Robert Claytor, the cofounders of the Grand Rapids Brough Community Association, moved the organization closer to the National Urban League before officially changing its name to the Grand Rapids Urban League and Brough Community Association in 1943. In 1947, the Board of Directors shortened the name to Grand Rapids Urban League but expanded its mission to "develop healthy patterns of inter-group relations throughout the community." For obvious reasons, the role of mediator between blacks and whites corresponded nicely with Phillips's attributes and personal ambition to improve race relations as well as with the new managerial process for handling race relations in the city, which used paternalistic logic to determine suitable levels of racial progress.

As a community service organization devoted to intercultural relations, the GRUL prided itself on employing a nonconfrontational approach as its strategy for social change. Through an assortment of didactic and promotional programs, the GRUL endeavored to improve the conditions under which minority group members lived and worked. For example, the GRUL offered young adolescents an opportunity after school or on the weekends to "model clay, weave, play games, dance, sing or gather around for a 'coke.'"[35] The organization also offered "a recreation program designed to meet the recreational, cultural and social need of the community"[36] for adults. Other programs brought together "women of several races sewing, taking educational courses or discussing the community affairs and problems."[37]

These benign programs and Phillips's accommodationist approach permitted him to gain the trust of prominent white businessmen and politicians. Instead of publicly airing grievances, he negotiated behind the scenes to end discrimination in the city. In particular, he recognized that face-to-face visits were necessary to navigate the political matrix of the community, not the earlier GRNAACP approach of public lawsuits. If he failed to achieve results directly, Phillips often knew someone who could. Snubbed by executives at Michigan Bell, Phillips cleverly decided to discuss the problem with the minister of a top Michigan Bell executive. With no hesitation, the "minister took the executive aside, told him that if blacks couldn't be hired for anything except menial jobs at Michigan Bell, there was something wrong with American democracy and he would have to address the topic from the pulpit."[38] The executive heeded the not-so-subtle admonition and hired a black woman with a college degree as a secretary at Michigan Bell Telephone Company.

Phillips's peaceful yet persuasive tactics enabled him to achieve his measures without the use of boycotts or sit-down strikes. Despite the publicized use of pickets, boycotts, and marches to establish civil rights in other areas, such as Detroit and Chicago, Phillips elected to proceed with caution in the 1950s. His diplomacy initially appealed to blacks and whites. Early successes made Phillips the "leading spokesman behind efforts to force the city and county to adopt equal opportunity hiring clauses."[39] The patient crusader "was never overexertive, but at the same time he kept plugging," said M. Howard Rienstra, Third Ward city commissioner and former president of the GRUL. In his first decade, Phillips managed to place "the first minority factory workers, nurse trainees, hospital workers, teachers, sales people, clerical workers and bank employees in jobs."[40]

Yet for every success story of Phillips and the GRUL, another tragedy would offset the scales of progress, and as the influx of blacks continued to rise during the "Second Great Migration," black unemployment rates also continued to rise. As a result, Phillips's moderate leadership approach raised the ire of several established activists in the black community.

Hillary Bissell and the NAACP

Bissell, a white civil rights activist, was born in Greenville, Michigan, located about thirty miles northeast of Grand Rapids.[41] She attended the University of Michigan and graduated in 1934 with a degree in sociology. Bissell subsequently married Wadsworth Bissell, heir to the well-established Bissell Carpet Sweeper Company of Grand Rapids. As a caseworker with Kent County Emergency Relief, Bissell worked to help needy families during the Depression, which put her in contact with poor blacks suffering at the lowest levels of poverty.[42] Her concern for blacks greatly increased when she joined the NAACP in 1943 while living in Sioux City, Iowa. There, Bissell labored to desegregate area schools. While in Iowa, Bissell met the chief counsel of the NAACP, Thurgood Marshall, and the two became regular correspondents.[43]

The Bissells returned to Grand Rapids in 1949 and joined the GRNAACP. She was one of only a few active white members in the organization. "We have members but not active participants—or even people who attend except the *party liners*," she wrote to Marshall. Bissell immediately observed that although the GRUL, the Michigan Civil Rights Committee, and other interracial social service groups had active white participants, these same whites declined to be associated with the GRNAACP. She described this situation to Marshall: "I think it is fine that these groups exist; they perform functions; they can enlist certain support that we couldn't get in NAACP, but to our way of thinking there isn't any substitute for NAACP."[44] According to Randal M. Jelks, "Politically, Bissell fell to the left of most white civic leaders in the city. The established white community was far more at ease in supporting the social work efforts of the Urban League than endorsing the advocacy efforts of the NAACP."[45]

Whereas Phillips was able to accommodate white businessmen and politicians in the city with a moderate approach to change, the GRNAACP's more direct approach fell outside the managerial paradigm. In 1951, the Detroit edition of the *Pittsburgh Courier* labeled the GRUL a Jim Crow affiliate based on the organization's unwillingness to openly challenge the practice of gerrymandering school boundaries.[46] The same year, Bissell's report to *Crisis Magazine* on the local activities in Grand Rapids expressed GRNAACP President Floyd Skinner's position: "We are serving notice that this branch will wage an uncompromising attack on the *Uncle Toms* and *appeasers* as well as jim crow elements in the community. We will justify the faith of those who have so generously sacrificed their time for the NAACP cause."[47] This direct language typified the difference between the GRNAACP and the GRUL. The Chamber of Commerce, politicians, and the new progressive Citizens' Action group preferred to side with Phillips and the GRUL.

White membership in the GRNAACP was "one of the trickiest and most dangerous questions that can be discussed," Bissell stated. "We have 4 white board members out of 25; 3 of these are very active. We have no white officers.

Perhaps half a dozen white members who on occasion can be called upon to contribute real effort in the organization. I doubt whether we have more than 75 white members and most of these are *token*." The local NAACP branch, she wrote, was a "completely *grass roots* organization and its success depends not on the whites but upon the support of the Negro community. We don't even get the complete support from the *Gold Coast* Negro community because this type of Negro tends to give support to the Urban League, which carries a sure social status, which we neither seek nor desire in the NAACP. We are truly a little man's mass movement here."[48]

Bissell emphasized that successful activism was "due to our size, the quality of our Negro leadership, our program of activity, and should not be attributed to the role of our white members."[49] In particular, she referenced Skinner's unwavering leadership: "He really is a positive genius at seeing to that all areas and all economic and social groups feel that they are being given representation and recognition in the organization." Making a clear distinction between the civil rights tactics of Phillips and Skinner, she added that the NAACP was

> not considered one of the nice *do-gooders* groups that it is safe to join. The people who work with us are the ones who are willing to go all out on the entire NAACP policy and program.... [T]he role of our branch here is a rugged one and we are a long way from total community acceptance. The gains we make here, we make because we fight for them.[50]

The obvious tension between the two organizations continued to mount. The GRNAACP took issue with the Urban League's Pilot Placement program, which Bissell stated was "being used as a tool to justify opposition to the FEPC [Fair Employment Practices Commission]." She charged that the businessmen "sitting on the Urban League Board [had] personally refused to hire Negroes in their plants. At the present time, the husband of the president also fits this category." Bissell understood the shifting tide of discriminatory customs, and she recognized that the GRUL's accommodationist strategy comfortably suited the racial paternalism of the new progressive leaders. She wrote to NAACP Executive Director Roy Wilkins, "As you well know segregation in a northern community doesn't usually arrive full blown, it [is a] creeping paralysis, which often appears in the guise of special favors to the Negro community."[51] Moreover, the GRUL strategy allowed new city officials to dictate the rate and pace of racial progress while building the city's progressive reputation in the absence of conflict. Thus managerial racism relied on "good race relations." With David M. Amberg, Julius Amberg's son and fellow chamber member, serving as president of the GRUL, progressive reformers closely monitored the GRUL agenda.

Skinner and Bissell understood the preemptive strategy of the Chamber of Commerce members. By endorsing Phillips's Pilot Placement Program, business owners could exert control over the hiring process and lessen the impact of possible criticism levied against them for employment discrimination. By supporting such programs, the Chamber of Commerce declared that FEP legislation was unnecessary,[52] arguing instead that "to correct one injustice a greater one is committed as the law would infringe the right of employers . . . to choose their associates." Putting forward the contention that the "state cannot by law change social customs and individual concepts of right or banish bigotry with a policeman's billy," the chamber stated that the FEPC legislation would "socialize employment under a sprawling super-bureaucratic control agency."[53] Instead of legislation, in 1950, the chamber urged "industry to continue to face the problem voluntarily." It argued that manufacturers were addressing the problem by "employing minority groups—percentage-wise."[54] These voluntary solutions were clearly designed to maintain the paternalistic nature of race relations in the city.

Offering further confirmation, chamber member David M. Amberg and Phillips coauthored a GRUL "Balance Sheet on Race Relations" from 1950–1953. The GRUL report appeared in the *Grand Rapids Press* on December 19, 1953, presenting a "credit" and "debit" balance sheet of race relations in the areas of employment, housing, public accommodation, health, and education. On the "credit" side of the ledger, according to the report, "a number of firms which previously did not hire non-white workers have adopted the 'open door' policy of hiring on ability, regardless of race. Some plants have also initiated the democratic plan of upgrading within the firm according to ability to perform on the job." Despite the "debit" side acknowledgment that "many employers still refuse to hire non-white workers," the report contained more "credit" than "debit" when it assessed the city's employment outlook. The report additionally listed a number of "first employment" opportunities for blacks to highlight the gains blacks were making. During 1953 alone, the report asserted, twenty-eight companies hired their first black laborers. Only five companies listed hired more than one employee, but never more than four, while the remaining twenty-three hired just one black employee each.[55]

The Grand Rapids Chamber of Commerce communicated with chamber affiliates in Detroit, Boston, New York, Minnesota, Wisconsin, and other locations to compile information regarding the FEPC legislation. Northern Republicans mobilized across state lines in a very organized fashion to oppose FEPC regulation.[56] In Michigan, many leaders of the Republican Party, which controlled both legislative houses, accepted arguments like that provided by Ford Motor Company Vice President Benson Ford: "You cannot legislate good human relations."[57] The Grand Rapids Chamber of Commerce echoed this sentiment:

> The promotion of the minority group idea is fundamentally un-American. Likewise [it is] un-American to encourage organized minorities in [the] belief they can receive special consideration from [the] government

or economic system if they make enough noise. . . . One of the prime necessities for success in business [is] the ability to judge men and determine which was most capable. No Federal or state employee can do this for the employer.[58]

The conservative bloc in Michigan managed to deny FEPC legislation until 1955. At that point, Democrats obtained enough representatives to pass a state-wide FEP bill prohibiting discrimination in employment based on race, religion, color, or national origin.

In this light, Bissell contended that the Urban League was the *"safe organization* and officials and community leaders tend to turn to that group for information and confirmation rather than to [a] militant group like the NAACP." She pointed to membership lists of the two organizations: The Urban League had "only 150 members here and I would judge that over 50% are white. In contrast we have 1,711 and reach a complete cross-section of the community." Yet the GRUL clearly held the most influence with members of the progressive reform movement, because it placated the concerns of the business community. Bissell worried "that through their agency we will find ourselves in the position of being further frozen into the ghetto and that officials will justify their activities by having consulted with the Urban League leaders."[59]

The Citizens' Action group preferred to work with Phillips. He posed no threat, and in return he received important concessions for the black community. After working with Phillips on various community issues, Bissell determined that he was quick to settle for whatever reward white leaders provided. Adding further frustration for Bissell and the GRNAACP, Phillips was elected to the City Charter Commission in 1952, making him the first black elected official. In that capacity, he voted for a new city charter, sponsored by the reform movement, which eliminated ward representation and instead made the City Commission election a citywide vote. Bissell believed that this move weakened the political agency of the black community. She confided to Wilkins that Phillips "was Exhibit A of the forces supporting at-large election up until now, because he sat as a Negro elected at large *representing the Negro community.* Now against the Negro community, he is only *incidentally a Negro* and the Negro community has no right to criticize him because he is simply *a citizen.*" He ran for office so "that a *Negro American could serve upon that distinguished body.*" However, she stated, "One wonders whether the Negro American was to be there simply for decorative purposes or to represent the needs and desires of the Negro community, which Mr. Phillips has not done."[60] William Wilberforce Plummer, Skinner's successor as GRNAACP president in 1958, expressed this confrontational approach:

I believe that the NAACP must have an aggressive and active program. We must be a social action group; we have neither the funds nor the trained personnel to be a social work group. We must take the lead in the community in protesting and denouncing all forms of racial segregation and discrimination.

I firmly believe that the Bus Protest Movement of Montgomery, Alabama, demonstrates the power of protest. I do mean that the NAACP should work with constructive social-work programs, but we must never allow these organizations to modify our program as we see it. If we allow ourselves to be put in a position in which we cannot speak freely for fear of offending our so-called "friends" or if we hesitate to speak, lest we suffer political, social or financial set-backs, then the effectiveness of our unit is severely damaged.

We can believe in a gradual program, providing the delay is necessary to plan a constructive program working toward the end of segregation and discrimination within a reasonable length of time. We do not believe in gradualism if it represents the stealing and denial of Civil Rights because of the violence directed toward Negro-Americans by those that believe in racial superiority. We believe that education will aid solving our problems, but we do not believe that Civil Rights should be denied any citizen while another is being educated. We believe that America cannot afford any more "Little Rocks" for the inter-national stakes are too high for the Land of Freedom to become known as the Land of Race Hatred.

Some members of the black community tried to adopt a strategy somewhere between the accommodationist position of the GRUL and the confrontational one of the NAACP. Claytor exemplified this intermediate approach.

Helen Claytor and the Human Relations Commission

Traveling to Grand Rapids for the first time in 1942, Claytor recalled, "I'd never heard of Grand Rapids, particularly. I didn't even know it was the furniture capital and I didn't think I would ever be back. I came to do my job." Claytor was employed as the secretary for Interracial Education for the national Young Women's Christian Association (YWCA), and she arrived in Grand Rapids to deliver a speech at a local convention. "Apparently," she said, "the YWCA of Grand Rapids had been very bad in its relations with black people. Of course, there was no branch here but they had separate clubs for the black girls." Thinking back on the issues that confronted the local YWCA, Claytor remembered that "they did not allow the black girls to swim in the pool nor live in the residence on College nor I think they did not allow blacks to eat in the cafeteria. It had been a very bad situation." Unforeseen circumstances would cause Claytor to play a much more pivotal role in the history of Grand Rapids race relations than she initially imagined.[61]

She was born in Minneapolis, Minnesota, in 1907. Her father built a home for the family in a predominantly white neighborhood close to the University of Minnesota. "He thought if he built his house as close to the University as was possible . . . we could have room and board at home and go to school and that's what he did." Initially, she recalled, whites "tried to buy him out and they kept offering him more and more money 'til he finally said to them that 'you do not have enough money to buy my principles. You might as well stop coming because you cannot go up to a price which will induce me to sell this house to you.'" Claytor's family stayed in that house, and she went on to graduate cum laude from the University of Minnesota, where she was one of a handful of black students.[62]

She accepted a job at the YWCA in Trenton, New Jersey, and stayed two years before going to work for the YWCA in Kansas City, Missouri, where she lived for nearly a decade. When her husband died in 1941, his brother, Roy Wilkins, the executive director of the national NAACP, attended the funeral, which was held at Claytor's home, and later recalled that "we had to bury my brother in a segregated cemetery."[63]

Claytor then moved to New York to accept a position as a member of the YWCA National Board. That work brought her to Grand Rapids to participate in a state public affairs meeting and meet with Norma Stauffer, an executive of the YWCA of Grand Rapids, who organized a meeting with leaders of the black community. "[T]he black folks of Grand Rapids were just resisting any overtures she was making to them so she thought that they might come to meet a black staff member," Claytor recalled. At that meeting she met her future husband, Dr. Robert Claytor, who was on the Community Chest Board. A year later they married, and Grand Rapids became Claytor's new home.[64]

Unable to obtain a teaching job in 1944, Claytor continued her service in social work in Grand Rapids. "They tried to get me to come on the [YWCA] Board that year and I wouldn't. I felt that was unfair to the black women who lived here." The following year she did accept a seat on the board; however, her election as president in 1949 produced a racial backlash that offered a sobering reminder of progressivism's limitations: "When I was elected President of the YWCA of Grand Rapids four women who had been on the Board with me [when] I had been the Vice President, four women—one of whom was the wife of a minister, one of whom was the wife of a lawyer, four women resigned from the Board."[65]

Civility in Grand Rapids, Claytor discovered, was dependent on blacks' keeping in their place: "Oh, yes. There was no other reason. . . . [T]hey were perfectly willing to be on the Board with me but they thought that it would be disastrous to have a black person President." Clearly the turn of events shocked Claytor. Although she was aware of racism, the personal nature of this incident hit home: "I knew there was this resistance but when one of my good friends who had been the President and somebody for whom I had the deepest respect brought me home one day and sat in the car in front of my house and said to me that she hoped that I would pull out . . . it crushed me." The reality of her surroundings crystallized at that moment, but so did her resolve to move forward. She said, "Don't think that you can move me from President to Vice President. Just forget it."[66]

"It wasn't easy," Claytor remembered.[67] Even though Claytor, "with her vast leadership skills, was almost immediately able to resolve the controversy between the YMCA, YWCA, and the African American community," she now discovered that the complexity of race relations went well beyond just segregated buildings.[68] Rather, in Grand Rapids, businessmen and their wives carried out discrimination from the top levels behind closed doors. Educated and refined white residents, whom Claytor might have expected to be most progressive, given their leadership positions in the community, had no real intentions to even slightly alter the racial status quo in Grand Rapids. White goodwill also came with the presumption that blacks would work within white expectations.

The board incident broadened Claytor's perspective regarding race relations in her new surroundings. It set the stage for several pioneering ventures in the black community, which aroused a more convoluted response from white leaders in the city. Equally important, her public political associations immediately strengthened the position of black activists in Grand Rapids. Although she became the first African American president of the Grand Rapids YWCA, her most important contribution was still to come.

Despite the acrimonious rhetoric, the lines between black institutions were blurred, because, despite their different approaches, their goals remained similar. Claytor was one activist respected in all circles. Not only did she serve as the first black woman elected to the Board of Directors of the Grand Rapids YWCA, but she also joined the GRUL and the GRNAACP. She worked behind the scenes to keep both groups from forgetting the ultimate goal of total black equality. She also commanded a presence among white officials. Thus when the GRNAACP and the GRUL advocated the establishment of a human relations commission, Claytor became the point person for the establishment of a study committee.

Along with a cadre of activists from the GRUL and the GRNAACP, Claytor pressured the new progressive City Commission to create a formal group to address race issues in the city. Despite the reluctance of the city fathers to support this new civic agency, Claytor managed to have the City Commission agree to appoint a "Study Committee" to survey the need for a Human Relations Committee (HRC). Mayor Paul Goebel, of the "progressive" Republican Party movement, reluctantly appointed a seven-member committee, which included Claytor as the lone black committee member.[69]

Over the course of six months, the Study Committee met thirty-five times to review such issues as housing, education, employment, welfare services, recreation, and civil protection. The primary concern was the impact of the steady increase of the black population on the community. The results clearly identified a systematic presence of discriminatory practices against blacks in each area. Nevertheless, the study was unable to determine how "a municipal commission could effectively solve the racial problems." Therefore, the committee sought help from George Schermer, director of the mayor's Interracial Committee of Detroit for nine years and later director of the Philadelphia Committee on Human Relations.[70]

In March 1954, the Study Committee, with Schermer's assistance, finalized its research and submitted to the mayor and City Commission a formal appeal for a charter amendment to establish an HRC. Based on the finding, every area pointed to high levels of discrimination and established a "definite need for such an agency." With the influx of black residents, the question seemed to be whether the city could afford not to have such a commission.[71] The issue of the authoritative capacity of the HRC remained unresolved. Black activists envisioned it as an official body with "enforcement powers to penalize businesses and agencies for racial discrimination."[72] The City Commission viewed the HRC as "liaison between various departments, such as the Board of Education, the Planning Commission, police and fire departments, recreation and health departments, as well as with the various minority groups or their representative agencies." The City Commission viewed the HRC as a sounding board for racial grievances with no formal means of redress.[73]

On July 31, 1954, the Study Committee submitted its final report to the mayor and City Commission and also proposed an amendment to establish a "Human Relations Commission of fifteen to twenty-one members, with an estimated first year budget of fifteen thousand dollars for salaries of an Executive Director, an Assistant Director, and Clerk-Stenographer." Five days later, the mayor, the city commissioners, and the Study Committee hosted a private luncheon. One member wrote to Schermer regarding the meeting:

> I was naïve enough to believe that we could get an acceptance of our proposal on that occasion, and that shortly we would have authorization to go ahead and look for a Director. I had a carefully prepared Agenda for the meeting . . . but . . . it almost seemed that the City Officials wanted to talk about most everything except the matter at hand. So the meeting adjourned without action, except the Mayor stated that it was a nice meeting, and that he hoped within a short time we could get together again as his guests.

The City Commission, mayor, and the city manager did not meet with the Study Committee again until October 1954. Again, the meeting left the matter unresolved.[74]

For the next seven months, the Official Proceedings of the City Commission contained no reference to an HRC, with the exception of a letter from the

GRNAACP in support of such an appointment. Claytor was one of a small group of influential citizens who refused to relinquish this issue: "I was one of the people that helped to found what we called then the Community Relations Service of the City. . . . Some of the people felt there really was no need for such a commission . . . and they would come to the committee meeting almost every time and move that we disband." However, Claytor believed she had found an unlikely ally in Harry Kelley of the American Seating Company, who served as the chair of the committee. She prepared a report covering the conditions in housing and employment as well as in other aspects of the community. "There was a clear discrimination, and our report showed it," but when it came time to present the report, she and Dorothy McAllister sat back, and "Mr. Kelley made the report and it was wonderful because they thought we were special pleaders but Harry Kelley had come along so that he was an ardent believer too and he was able to get it adopted and put into force as we might not have been able to do."[75]

When asked why she was reluctant to present the report, Claytor replied that Kelley "was a big businessman. And at this point the study committee had gone on maybe 18 months and by this time he believed in what he was doing."[76] She recognized that it would take an insider, such as Kelley, who was a Chamber of Commerce member, to complete the task. He would later serve as a member of the statewide FEPC in 1955, which also faced enforcement challenges. Nearly nine months after the Study Committee completed its report, city commissioners made the HRC official in April 1955.[77] However, as Thomas Sugrue notes, "In its first four years, the FEPC settled 829 cases, and dismissed nearly 60 percent for insufficient evidence."[78] With business leaders at the helm, the HRC faced the same fate. It took nearly nine months to hire an executive director. On January 1, 1956, David J. McNamara, who was serving as the director of the Civil Rights Department of the Chicago Human Relations Commission, began his tenure in Grand Rapids.

From the Study Committee's appointment in 1951 to McNamara's first day on the job in 1956, nearly one thousand additional black students entered racially isolated public schools, the "black belt" continued to swell, and the majority of blacks remained confined to service employment opportunities. In the 1950s, when the nation's civil rights movement began to develop momentum through legislation and direct-action campaigns, progressive city officials in Grand Rapids initiated a system of managerial racism designed to eliminate the type of open racial conflict that infamously put Detroit on the wrong side of the racial map during the 1943 racial uprising. In the early 1960s, black activist organizations in Detroit became impatient with the gradualism of workplace integration. Led by the NAACP, blacks in Detroit decided to openly protest businesses that failed to integrate the city's workplaces. The uprising, boycotts, and pickets represented a more direct campaign to defeat job discrimination.[79]

In Grand Rapids, the passage of fair employment legislation and the HRC diffused any real organized direct response. Instead, Phillips continued to use moral persuasion to encourage employers to abide by FEP regulations, and the HRC became the sounding board for all issues concerning race in the city. Therefore, progressive reformers were able to retain the status quo with long, drawn-out bureaucratic procedures, lengthy studies, and numerous committees designed to limit change as well as avert any form of public discord. With the formation of each study committee, city officials demonstrated their willingness to examine race issues to maintain the city's progressive mystique, but the discriminatory conditions that blacks faced remained. Education was one area where this proved indisputable.

The Campaign Education Reform

The black protest movement in Grand Rapids identified educational inequality as the cornerstone of urban discrimination and segregation. Members of the movement realized, as Carter G. Woodson explains in his 1933 book *The Miseducation of the Negro,* that

> when you control a man's thinking you do not have to worry about his actions. You do not have to tell him not to stand here or go yonder. He will find his "proper place" and will stay in it. You do not need to send him to the back door. He will go without being told. In fact, if there is no back door, he will cut one for his special benefit. His education makes it necessary.[80]

Although education did not guarantee success, the Grand Rapids black leadership understood that an inferior educational opportunity almost certainly resulted in second-class life chances. White-dominated school boards made costly decisions, which failed to consider the curricular needs of a growing black student population. Prior to the Second Great Migration, black students attended integrated schools.[81] The era of school diversity coincided with a period of mixed inner-city neighborhoods, but both were abruptly curtailed after 1945. Campau Area Schools, geographically located in the core of the city, had a combined 27 percent minority enrollment in 1947, but that number soared to 74 percent by 1960.[82]

Home to seven public elementary schools, the Campau Area became the focus of civil rights activists' efforts to eliminate racial problems and promote educational reform in the early 1950s. After a decade, most inner-city black schoolchildren still attended separate schools. Residential segregation, the most common hallmark of northern single-race schools, only scratches the surface of a litany of discriminatory procedures used by school officials to racialize the educational process. The Campau Area Schools bore a striking resemblance to the resource-deficient black schools in the South. Ultimately the distinction between de jure and de facto segregation by scholars and policy makers means little, for the results in both cases were the same. School buildings, teacher staffs, resources, and alienated student bodies reinforced and intensified racial segregation. The Grand Rapids School Board's (GRSB's) related decisions that created these inequities drew the attention of GRNAACP activists during the 1950s. In her evaluation of Grand Rapids, June Shagaloff, national educational director for the NAACP, noted that although black students did not enter schools displaying formal "FOR WHITE" and "FOR COLORED" signs, the obvious fact remained that the city's public school system operated as "one of the most tightly segregated of any city in the North."[83] School inequality remained the unacknowledged engine of segregation and oppression.

The years following World War II added a new challenge to the democratic learning mission of the public school system. With 2,660 black residents in 1940, the GRSB successfully managed a token integrated school system. Despite the small size of the black student population, the fact that the GRSB emphasized "the mingling of the races . . . and wholesome friendly relationships" among its diverse student population seemed to be a good sign for black residents. Considered to be a "model of integration which might well be copied by other cities," it appeared that Grand Rapids stood poised to exemplify the criteria for integration in America's urban schools during the 1940s. Local leaders pointed proudly to a progressive political movement, where community members had battled against a dominant political machine and won. On the surface, then, Grand Rapids seemed an unlikely place for educational injustice. With the rapid influx of black residents, however, a remarkable racial change occurred in the public school system that challenged the GRSB's commitment to educational democracy and the city's commitment to better government.[84]

The Campau area, which included Franklin, Maplewood, Vandenberg, Henry, Madison Park, Sheldon, and Jefferson schools, comprised the core inner-city elementary schools in the developing "black belt" of Grand Rapids. The tide of black migrants had a tremendous impact on the city's student enrollment at these schools. The student population at Lafayette and Sheldon, according to a 1949 Grand Rapids School Survey, or Reavis Survey, had already surpassed "the maximum acceptable in buildings of their size and exceedingly rapid increases . . . [were] indicated." Schools such as Franklin included class sizes that exceeded fifty pupils. In an attempt to handle the overflow of new arrivals, school officials placed students in semi-basement rooms. Based on the high degree of overcrowding, the GRSB determined that the Campau Area Schools represented the "first need in the school building program."[85]

From 1940–1950, the number of black children in the Campau Area Schools had increased from 280 to 836. As black enrollment increased, white student populations decreased, especially at Franklin, Sheldon, and Henry. The appearance of an educational color line concerned several community activists from the GRUL and the GRNAACP. In 1952, Dr. Robert Claytor, Urban League president; Hillary Bissell, GRNAACP member; and Dr. Donald Bouma, profes-

TABLE 2.1   ENROLLMENT OF BLACK STUDENTS IN
CAMPAU AREA SCHOOLS, GRAND RAPIDS

| School | Number and Percentage of Black Pupils | |
	1940	1950
Henry	111 (38%)	191 (80%)
Franklin	86 (19%)	409 (78%)
Sheldon	45 (8%)	339 (61%)
Vandenberg	14 (3%)	135 (25%)

sor at Calvin College, were among those who formed the Campau School Committee (CSC). They joined several race-relations specialists to raise awareness of the existing problems in predominantly black schools. Fearful that racial isolation would lead to administrative neglect and educational inequity, the CSC authored a study that it believed described symptoms of segregation on the horizon of the Grand Rapids public school system. Equally important, the committee enumerated a number of reasons why GRSB members needed to take positive steps to "modify a pattern of increasing separation of the races in schools in this part of Grand Rapids."[86]

In a short time span, the racial composition of the Campau Area Schools changed from predominantly white to predominantly black. According to the CSC report, more than half the public elementary schools had no blacks enrolled, while five contained five or fewer black students: "91% of all colored children enrolled in elementary schools were enrolled in 4 schools: Franklin, Sheldon, Henry, and Vandenberg." The deep concentration of minority students marked an important shift from an integrated classroom experience in center city neighborhoods to a racially isolated learning environment with fewer resources (see Table 2.1). The CSC believed, in the aggregate, that these numbers surely constituted enough evidence to warrant action by the School Board. Moreover, of these four schools, Sheldon surpassed its capacity by nearly 150 students, Franklin had the highest student-teacher ratio in the city, and Vandenberg was filled to capacity. These high numbers resulted in an acute shortage in student resources, excessive student-teacher ratios, ineffective work conditions for educators, and prohibitive losses in educational time for black schoolchildren.[87]

The high number of black students at Franklin, Sheldon, Vandenberg, and Henry posed a serious problem for school officials. The evident trend in each was an increased concentration of black students and a simultaneous decreased enrollment of white students. Henry, for example, had been underenrolled since 1939, despite the influx of black students. Only 17 percent of the white children in the Henry area attended that school, while the remaining 83 percent obtained transfers to other districts or attended nonpublic schools.[88] With Henry School located on the border of the "black belt" and an all-white residential area, the

GRSB refused to make a boundary change that would have required neighboring white students to attend Henry School during the 1950s. Instead, through the establishment of selective geographic attendance zones, GRSB members contributed to the creation of single-race schools. Board boundary decisions allowed white parents living near Henry to send their children to such schools as Congress and Hillcrest Elementary, both of which had zero black enrollment. Schools contiguous to the Campau area, such as Congress, Oakdale, Dickinson, Buchanan, and Kensington, had no black students. Black schoolchildren in two schools, Fountain and Ottawa, composed less than 1 percent of the students. The GRSB's manipulation of school boundaries, drawn with the purpose of maintaining racial isolation, rejected the earlier commitment to integrated classrooms and demonstrated the board's unwillingness to take responsibility for achieving school desegregation.

The issue of zoning raised the concern of CSC members. In addition, the GRSB's postwar building pattern showed a complete abandonment of prior promises and an obvious neglect for the needs of the black community. Despite the 1949 Reavis Study, which listed Campau Area Schools as the first building priority, GRSB officials instead decided to build new schools at the periphery of the city. A generation earlier, the financial crisis of the Depression prevented the GRSB from building a single new school for twenty-five years. Postwar prosperity resulted in a suburban housing boom and the need for new school facilities. The citizens of Grand Rapids approved a special school tax designed to provide $10 million for new school-building efforts and improvements in 1950. From these funds, the GRSB constructed sixteen new schools, fourteen in the burgeoning suburbs and two in the inner city. Board members disregarded the CSC study regarding overcrowding and the poor conditions of the Campau Area, where only two of seven schools were classified as "adequate," three were listed as "old" with no room for expansion, and the remaining two were simply listed as "inadequate" because of age and structural deficiencies. Furthermore, the play area surrounding all seven schools was listed as "severely limited."[89]

To increase capacity at existing black schools, the GRSB instead converted activity rooms used for fine arts and practical arts into classrooms. GRNAACP activists objected to the GRSB's blatant contempt for the needs of a rising black-student enrollment. "We find it comparable to putting beds for the family in the living room and dining room," noted Bissell. She continued, "It adds to the sleeping space as the Board has added to class space, but it does not reduce the overcrowding." Although the GRSB dismissed the impact of substandard conditions, such as overcrowded black schools and higher pupil-teacher ratios, the GRNAACP issued a statement that declared, "We believe that 8 years of overcrowding at Franklin and 6 years of overcrowding at Sheldon and Vandenberg means that nearly 2,000 children have been denied an opportunity to gain a sound elementary education in healthy school surroundings."[90] The GRNAACP realized that the educational inequalities between black and white schools in

Grand Rapids resembled the segregationist educational policies commonly associated with Jim Crow states.[91]

Although the Supreme Court's *Brown v. Board of Education* decision of 1954 determined the unlawfulness of intentional segregation, this decision appeared applicable only to southern schools. The emphasis on de jure segregation allowed northern school board members to have a momentary sigh of relief. However, concerned school district officials worried how the Court would proceed regarding de facto segregation cases. On January 24, 1961, Federal District Judge Irving R. Kaufman provided insight into one possible response. He ruled in *Taylor v. New Rochelle* that the School Board had gerrymandered neighborhood school boundaries and that school officials had declined to remedy the racial imbalance. Thus, Grand Rapids learned that gerrymandering also fell under the national microscope. In addition, the State Board of Education in Michigan and the State Civil Rights Commission issued a joint statement declaring that "creative efforts by individual school districts were essential in reducing segregation." The statement proclaimed that "local school boards must consider the factor of racial imbalance in making decisions about selection of new school sites, expansion of present facilities, reorganization of school attendance districts, and transfer of pupils from overcrowded facilities, since 'each of these situations present an opportunity for integration.'"[92] Aware of Judge Kaufman's decision, the GRSB recognized the similarities in its public school system.

The facts of the *Taylor v. New Rochelle* case closely resembled the pattern of segregation in the Campau Area Schools of Grand Rapids. Lincoln School, in New Rochelle, was built in 1898. For more than thirty years, white children attended Lincoln. When black students began arriving, a "policy of gerrymandering was instituted which led to the confining of Negroes within the Lincoln School district by redrawing the district lines to coincide with Negro population movements." In addition, the School Board provided transfers for white students to neighboring elementary schools. As a result, by 1949, Lincoln had become nearly 100 percent black. Similar to GRSB members, the New Rochelle School Board failed to make boundary changes even after a number of civic groups demanded that the board redistrict. For eleven years, the School Board "discussed the problem, hired experts, made surveys, and constantly reiterated its belief in racial equality and the necessity for equal opportunities," but the end result produced no substantial action to alter racial imbalance at Lincoln School. The Court discerned the fraudulent intentions of the School Board and ultimately decided that "it would not permit the school authorities to confine integration to a bare token under the guise of a neighborhood school plan."[93] This decision sparked a renewed commitment among local activists in Grand Rapids, and it also prompted concern within the administration of Grand Rapids Public Schools.

Throughout the 1950s, the GRSB ignored the concerns of the CSC report and maintained racially imbalanced schools. Like the New Rochelle School

Board, the GRSB hid behind the concept of neighborhood schools and inaction. Initially the GRSB offered to build a new school on the same site of an already racially imbalanced school to ensure that blacks would not attend neighboring white schools. The GRNAACP refused to accept this recommendation. Bissell wrote to the director of branches for the NAACP national office:

> We are fighting the location of a school in the heart of the Negro community, which would inevitably be all Negro. Through a study on projected enrollments in the area which I did, we were able to dispose of that school but now we are going further to attempt to bring about redistricting for better integration and because of the distribution of our Negro population this is entirely feasible, although at present we have one school 88% Negro, one 75%, and one 52%.[94]

Although pressured by the GRNAACP, members of the GRSB refused to make boundary adjustments to alleviate overcrowding in the Campau Area Schools. Instead, the School Board highlighted the benefits of Grand Rapids schools compared to schools in Detroit. For example, Grand Rapids never implemented the "platoon system" that involved marching little schoolchildren from room to room. In addition to the "platoon system," Detroiters complained about the absence of a cumulative record for each child from kindergarten through high school. Grand Rapids had kept such records for years. Furthermore, whereas Detroiters did not have regular parent-teacher conferences, Grand Rapids had incorporated such practices in its "reporting to parents" system for many years. And although Detroiters objected to the thirty pupils per class standard, Grand Rapids classes had three fewer students on average. Notwithstanding these progressive educational achievements, the GRSB was unable to hide the school system's racial imperfections.[95]

The absence of a single black GRSB member ensured that the issues most important to the black community would not receive consideration. For decades, black organizations ran candidates for seats on the Board of Education. With GRNAACP candidates, such as Bolden, Study Club candidate Ethel B. Coe, and GRUL candidate Phillips, blacks tried to exercise change through traditional politics. Instead, during the 1950s, white businessmen and their wives dominated the GRSB. Often these members viewed racial change with suspicion and appeared more concerned with preserving the white schools surrounding the Campau area. It was no coincidence that several board members resided in high-risk areas near boundary lines contiguous with the "black belt." Instead of opening up school district lines and creating integrated school communities, GRSB members regulated the existing lines to retain segregated schools while approving the construction of new schools farther away to relieve white families of the burden of sending their children to predominantly black schools.

Board members were elected from a citywide pool of candidates. Unlike Jeffrey Mirel's description of Detroit in *The Rise and Fall of an Urban School System,* which details how the "liberal-labor-black coalition" that formed in the late 1940s "took control of the school system" in the 1950s, the GRSB consisted of a tightly knit business coalition committed to a segregated building program.[96] Melvin D. Anderson, who served as manager of the Westinghouse Electric Corporation and president of the Kent County Board of Education, lived in the southeastern section of the city, near Hall Elementary School. In 1955, he was seeking his fourth two-year term on the board, and during his tenure on the GRSB, he approved the Campau Elementary School in the "black belt" and successfully avoided scattering black students to predominantly white schools, such as Hall, Buchanan, and Burton. William H. Beaman, the GRSB president, was seeking his third term the same year. Beaman was the vice president and treasurer of F. Raniville Company and a father of three children attending the city's public schools. When he first ran for the board in 1949, Beaman claimed he "advocated careful consideration of an integrated school system plan."[97] That soon changed. Beaman lived within the exclusively white Ottawa Hills Elementary School boundary. He was a member of the Ottawa Hills Elementary and Senior High Parent-Teacher Associations and knew of the impending movement of black families toward Ottawa Hills.[98] The neighboring schools, Sigsbee and Alexander, experienced black student increases in a short time span. In 1952, Sigsbee's black population was 5.5 percent; it reached 18 percent by 1955, and in 1960 it was 41 percent. Similarly, Alexander went from 0.3 percent in 1955, to 3 percent in 1957, and then to 12 percent in 1960. Given these trends, Beaman abandoned his initial position and instead approved the construction of Maplewood Elementary School in the "black belt" to provide temporary relief from black overcrowding and redirect the black student population back toward the Grand River instead of pushing it southward.[99]

Along with the entire GRSB, which consisted primarily of Chamber of Commerce members or their spouses, such as Amberg's wife, Callie S. Amberg, Anderson and Beaman read the CSC report that stated, "The Committee is concerned that there exists so serious a situation of concentration of Negro children in a few schools. Further studies by the committee indicate that if trends continue unchanged, Grand Rapids will have a complete separation of races in a number of schools a few years hence."[100] Nonetheless, the all-white GRSB paid no attention. In fact, after hearing a CSC presentation, GRSB member Robert S. Tubbs declared, "We are here to provide an educational system. You are trying to compel us to take action that is not our business to take. Boundaries are set on the basis of total population. But we are not a social institution. Buildings do not segregate; people segregate."[101] Tubbs failed to accept that GRSB members were the individuals segregating the city's schools. Indeed, many of the GRSB members were the most concerned with getting their children and the white students in their area through the public school system without having to encounter black students. The CSC "recommended the building of additional classrooms at existing schools [Vandenberg, Jefferson, and Madison] and drastic boundary line changes and open enrollment in all underutilized schools regardless of location," but the GRSB ignored its request.[102] The *Taylor v. New Rochelle* decision threatened the GRSB practice of gerrymandering. It shifted the emphasis from residential patterns to the board's own actions and inactions in intensifying segregated schools. Therefore, the initiatives by GRSB members, such as Amberg, Anderson, and Beaman, now faced greater scrutiny. Moreover, the fact that Judge Kaufman demanded that New Rochelle develop and submit a school desegregation plan added to the urgency for the GRSB to find a new way to address the issue of racial imbalance. Perhaps unsurprisingly, the black community managed to make a substantial breakthrough the following year.

"Yes sir, we've made a giant step forward," proclaimed a beaming teenage inner-city resident. The youngster looked up to Phillips and congratulated him with a smile after the 1962 citywide election results ensured Phillips a seat on the GRSB. Defeated twice before, Phillips became the first black elected to the board and only the second member of his race to hold a major elective position in Grand Rapids.[103] Ten years after the Campau report and nearly a year after the follow-up study, the election placed the business community's foremost black official in a position to effect positive change. As a result, the heightened expectations from within the black community rested squarely on the shoulders of the one black man in a political position to alter their adverse circumstances.

A leader who relied on enthusiasm, charm, and, most importantly, patience to create change seemed to accommodate the GRSB's manner of educational reform. Many times Phillips's unassuming demeanor and leadership style as a representative of the Urban League guided the black community toward increased social justice. Now Phillips diligently employed civil rights activism during his eight-year tenure as the first black on the GRSB to improve educational opportunities for black children. It was during his GRSB service, beginning in 1962, that Phillips stood at the center of the struggle for school integration in the city. Throughout the turmoil over school integration, Phillips found himself in a position in which "board members and white parents berate[d] him for being impatient and not realistic" about integration, while he defended "those very whites to less tolerant blacks."[104]

Upon joining the board in 1962, Phillips highlighted several areas of racial concern. He wanted the GRSB to "approve hiring Negro counselors," because none worked in the public schools. Phillips also requested that the board look into reestablishing a vocational training school to better address the employment needs of minority students after graduation. In addition, he encouraged the board to facilitate talks between the Grand Rapids Real Estate Board and Federal Housing and Home Finance Administration officials to "work constructively to try to alleviate Negroes' housing problems." Finally, Phillips demanded that discriminatory hiring practices end.[105]

Former School Board member Vernis Schad, in her lecture "Revisiting Racial Segregation in the Mid-1960s," concluded that Phillips wanted to formally establish that the policies of school officials "encouraged prejudice" as well as evaluate what methods the city school system could employ to "discourage prejudice." Despite his many requests, Phillips's humble approach opened up lines of communication regarding race without appearing overbearing. He gently prodded the GRSB to make an inquiry of the issues as an attempt to forestall any dire consequences. The board complied and appointed a committee to look into the concerns that Phillips raised.

After meeting with the state attorney general regarding racial discrimination in the schools in 1963, Phillips reported to the School Board that he felt it necessary to conduct a self-inventory of the city school system. He proposed examining de facto segregation, overall hiring policies, teacher recruitment and placement, and school boundaries. His persistence won the GRSB's consent, which again produced a committee to evaluate the racial practices of the school system.[106] He managed to pivot the center, or center the black experience, within the structure of daily operations of the GRSB. With a history of tactical resourcefulness in negotiating rights for the black community, he understood the realities of white power, and he addressed "the people who had political, civic, and economic power in the city to bring pressure to bear on their peers."[107] The GRSB presented Phillips with the forum to apply his own pressure.

Of the nine School Board members when Phillips arrived, "seven were businessmen, including the president of the local Chamber of Commerce," who tended to favor the status quo. But Phillips did not seek radical change, nor did he employ radical methods; rather, he provided white officials with the means to avert the drastic changes occurring around them. Phillips served as a barometer by which prominent white community members could safely gauge the temperature of the black community, and monitoring the black community became increasingly important during the 1960s. Equally important, Phillips enabled the GRSB to safely navigate racial imbalance with a proactive business approach that avoided the form of scrutiny experienced in New Rochelle. Yet the GRSB managed to obstruct progress just enough to impede the desegregation process.[108]

The apparent shift in the changing structure and momentum of the civil rights movement caused awareness and alarm among white GRSB members. National as well as local circumstances heightened responsiveness among committee members regarding the problem of segregated schools. Locally, the black community persistently kept educational justice on the School Board docket. Seven years after a group of black principals in Grand Rapids presented the GRSB with a study of the severe deprivation of isolated inner-city schools in

1952, Dr. Bouma delivered two lectures at Fountain Street Church in Grand Rapids on "Democracy in Grand Rapids" and "How Far Is It from Little Rock to Grand Rapids?" whereby he "challenged the board of education to explore its responsibility to find some answer to that question."[109]

Phillips entered the brewing controversy over school segregation at a pivotal time. He warned prominent whites of the dissatisfaction among the black community. Mounting pressure from the GRNAACP and the startling 1962 school population figures, which revealed that nearly half of black youths dropped out of school prior to graduation, increased the appeal of Phillips as a GRSB ally. Moreover, the fact that the percentage of nonwhite pupils in the elementary schools of the city, as reported by former GRSB member Schad, "had risen from 7 percent in 1950 to over 20 percent in 1966" and that "over 98 percent of all nonwhite elementary children attended only ten of the sixty elementary schools" certainly added value to Phillips's insights. The School Board could clearly see that a problem existed within the city system. Moreover, Phillips's methods did not immediately clash with the tacit gentlemen's agreement on race relations in the city, because he understood that "sitting down, talking and trying to persuade" often produced piecemeal resolutions.[110] However, the pressure applied by members of the GRNAACP must also be taken into consideration. Much like William Chafe's findings in Greensboro, North Carolina, the "two traditions of caution and activism—both responses to the realities of white power—played off against each other"[111] in Grand Rapids. What appeared to be polarized approaches to equality simply formed two sides of the same struggle to bring about racial progress.

In Grand Rapids, these two traditions existed simultaneously. Although job discrimination and employment would linger, blacks in Grand Rapids began to challenge the educational policies more directly in the coming years, with Phillips maneuvering within the board. But inextricably linked to the problem of segregated schools was the biased housing structure that limited the ability of blacks to purchase homes outside the growing "black belt." Rather than simply being a product of de facto segregation, housing patterns in Grand Rapids were tied closely to discriminatory practices of local bankers, lenders, real estate agents, business coalitions, and political officials. In particular, at the local level, the growing housing crisis in Grand Rapids exemplified the effectiveness of managerial racism as city reformers executed a building campaign that left blacks confined to decaying inner-city neighborhoods.

3

THE SUBURBAN OASIS

The Origins of Segregated Space

The Housing Dilemma

With the second ghetto virtually intact in Detroit, Chicago, and New York by 1960, the absence of a clearly defined first black ghetto was conspicuous in smaller cities, such as Grand Rapids, during the postwar era. The overwhelming emphasis on urban shifts in larger cities tends to mask the fact that smaller black communities developed differently. As late as the mid-1950s, blacks and whites lived in a number of interracial neighborhoods in Grand Rapids. During the postwar housing boom, however, white residents capitalized on a suburban growth market that excluded blacks. Simultaneously, as part of the "Second Great Migration," nearly eight thousand new blacks entered the city between 1950 and 1960.[1] Yet as the black population increased, their housing options did not. Pervasive racism in the Grand Rapids housing market helped confine the majority of the black population to homes in one section of the city. As a result, the core black residential area continued to grow larger and more concentrated. Bolstered by the Federal Housing Administration's (FHA's) racially restrictive practices, local builders, real estate brokers, bankers, and white homeowners ensured the majority of blacks had minimal access to homes outside the developing "black belt" near the center of the city.[2] As business reformers and progressive reformers concentrated on bettering city services, building suburbs, and developing the downtown area, the growing black community neighborhood needs went left unattended.

This chapter examines the spatial transformation of Grand Rapids. It challenges conventional notions of de facto metropolitan development and illuminates how the construction of segregated space in Grand Rapids materialized not as a natural result of housing migration patterns but instead as a consequence of organized white efforts to combat black suburbanization and to maintain white-only neighborhoods in the post–World War II era. By examining acute structural barriers, established at the municipal level, and active efforts by white individuals to confine minorities to a circumscribed geographical location within the central city, this chapter maps the metropolitan terrain to reveal how Grand Rapids evolved as a city within a city, with a black core and white periphery. The discriminatory practices of FHA programs, local builders, real-estate groups, banking institutions, and white protest attempted to restrict black home ownership to the inner city. Additionally, this chapter illustrates how black agency also transformed the metropolitan landscape. As Robert Self correctly notes in his book *American Babylon,* "It is too often overlooked that black Americans too imagined the city and its possibilities."[3] Rather than marginalize their efforts to contest spatial inequality, this chapter demonstrates that housing segregation represented an ongoing struggle for the black population of Grand Rapids.

Around the kitchen table in 1944, Helen Claytor's American suburban family gathered to eat and to share the day's experiences. Filled with excitement, Roger Wilkins, her twelve-year-old son, spoke of his latest exploration of the family's newest Grand Rapids suburban neighborhood: "I suppose I talked more than I had at any time since we moved to Michigan. I told my family everything I knew about Jerry and about where we had been and where we would go the next day." Brimming with innocence, the young schoolboy mentioned to his stepfather and mother, Dr. Robert and Helen Claytor, that "Jerry had said that everyone in the neighborhood knew where we lived and had talked about it." The seemingly innocuous statement prompted his stepfather to give a head gesture to Roger's mother that indicated the appropriate time had emerged. Now was the moment to discuss the reality of being black in the Grand Rapids suburbs.[4]

The casual dinner conversation materialized suddenly into a formal history lesson in race relations. "When Pop bought the house here, the seller didn't know he was a Negro," his mother explained. "Your Pop didn't say whether he was or he wasn't and the man didn't ask."[5] When the neighbors found out that a black family owned the home, they started to meet to discuss buying the house back. The white resistors "told him they thought he would be happier with 'his own people across town,' but he told them that he hadn't found a house across town good enough for his family and that he assumed that the people around here were Americans and that those were 'his own people' so he didn't feel uncomfortable."[6] In an attempt to intimidate the family, one white suburbanite suggested burning a cross on Claytor's front lawn. But Dr. Claytor purchased the house for the benefit of his family; he did not intend to sell it.

Light skin, green eyes, and straight hair enabled Claytor, on occasion, to transcend the racial boundaries created by Michigan's second-largest city. Dr. Claytor's wife, Helen, remembered, "He did not have the physical characteristics that people usually associate with black people so Realtors would show him houses but it would seem as though very quickly they would find out."[7] Notwithstanding his color, Claytor's socioeconomic status made him an ideal suburbanite. Initially Claytor's physical features even managed to dupe real estate brokers into showing him "houses outside the 'Negro District' until they found out he was [black]. He was then told that all the houses they looked at were sold."[8] "The word seemed to have gotten around in real estate circles that a doctor who did not look like a 'Negro' was looking for a house."[9] As a result, she continued, "what one day would be available to him, the next day he would be told that this had already been sold." Claytor's futile negotiations with real estate brokers persuaded him to deal directly with the home owners. This strategy proved successful, as Claytor found a house on the northeastern side of Grand Rapids.

"So he was in this neighborhood looking to make a house call and saw a sign in the front yard that said 'For Sale By the Owner' and he realized by then the runaround by the real estate people so he stopped in to look for the house and . . . although he didn't think it was ideal, it was a house big enough for the family he was acquiring and he bought it."[10] But the antiblack suburban campaign began once his white neighbors discovered that a black man had purchased the suburban home. According to Helen Claytor, "Finally the woman in the family burst out and said to him, 'You know you're a Negro.' And he said, 'Oh, yes I do. So that's what this is about.' And they pled with him to sell the house back to them but he didn't." "There was a lot of protest," she remembered, and it took "a few years" before her neighbors became more agreeable with the presence of a single black family in their neighborhood.[11]

Claytor's family was one of only five black families who managed to move to suburban Grand Rapids by the late 1940s. Why had so few blacks in Grand Rapids managed to fulfill their suburban dream? How did this territorial arrangement reinforce the racial inequity of metropolitan resource distribution in the postwar era? And to what extent did the policies of the new progressive business leadership facilitate the uneven metropolitan growth patterns in and around Grand Rapids?

According to Michigan's *1961 Report to the Commission on Civil Rights*, the denial of blacks of the right to "live where their economic and educational status would enable them to live, remain[ed] the greatest single barrier to equal opportunity in education, and to integrated participation in other aspects of community life" not only in Grand Rapids but elsewhere in metropolitan America.[12] Although the Claytor family overcame disgruntled neighbors, Roger Wilkins could not help but reflect on the peculiar irony of his family's situation. He said, "That night I thought about the Stuits and the other people on the block. Our house was just about the biggest in the neighborhood, and we had a nicer car than anybody on the block." He added, "I was pretty sure that none of the other men was a doctor and that the women probably hadn't even gone to college, much less been Phi Beta Kappa. And, though that bit of social calculus was somewhat comforting, when it was all done, the other people were still white and I was still a Negro. There was no getting around it."[13]

The incredible suburban growth that occurred during the post–World War II years helped establish many new neighborhoods in and around Grand Rapids, but nearly all these communities refused to accept black residential candidates, such as Claytor and his family. People living in the suburbs rarely openly discussed protecting suburban space from "undesirables." Rather, as noted by sociologist Donald H. Bouma in a public lecture delivered at the Fountain Street Church during the fall of 1958, suburbanites wanted "nothing to do with the city—those smelly, crummy slum areas." If the immediate concern centered on distance from the slum, why did so many whites object to black neighbors in the distant suburbs? Bouma indicated that the real problem stemmed from the fact that people living in the suburbs "wash[ed] their hands . . . to avoid responsibility for a problem one has had a real part in creating."[14] The problem was racial segregation and the signs of poverty that accompanied inner-city disinvestment.

As one white home owner stated, "I'd like to sell a house to a Negro in this neighborhood, but my white clients would either move out or boycott my business."[15] As a result, whites benefited from the postwar housing boom as well as enjoyed greater flexibility in their ability to exercise social and economic mobility. Mrs. Q. S. Tregre, a white resident of the Alger Heights suburb, recalled that "when we moved here we thought we were moving out into the country. There wasn't a house around us and we were the first to build on this street."[16] In 1939, with only five other houses located on Alger Street, the area certainly resembled a quiet countryside. The economic prosperity of the postwar era converted Alger Heights into a bustling Grand Rapids suburban community in the short time span of one decade. By 1950, Alger Heights evolved into a district consisting of nearly "2,500 homes with an average valuation of from $10,000 to $12,000 each, and a quarter of a million dollar shopping district that offer[ed] most of the accommodations found in downtown Grand Rapids."[17]

Although no ghetto existed in such cities as Grand Rapids and Lansing prior to the 1950s, a definite trend of black segregation in the postwar era became apparent to black residents. As evidenced by the mushroom growth in metropolitan areas, such as Alger Heights, whites idealized suburban life more than ever during the postwar years.[18] Mrs. Raymond Martens, also a white resident of Alger Heights, said, "We liked the neighborhood so well . . . that we decided on that one visit this was the neighborhood for us."[19] Each of these residents, however, understood that the FHA and municipal-level race restrictions on dwellings located in Alger Heights afforded the promise of stable home ownership. The white suburban exodus united the search for new homes and greener pastures with a secure investment in racial homogeneity.[20] In addition to the federal guarantee of homogeneous metropolitan spatial arrangements, Human Relations Commission (HRC) records revealed that white residents also established segregated communities through numerous "gentlemen's agreements" between property owners and real estate brokers, which barred blacks from white neighborhoods.[21] These racially bonded agreements crafted by key Chamber of Commerce members proved critical in the formation of the first Grand Rapids ghetto by the 1960s. So too did the official neglect of the progressive reformers, who chose to consciously ignore the needs of the black community. However, black residents, such as Claytor, continued to demand access to suburban space. Individually and collectively, blacks contested segregation, and their activism invites further consideration, because it elucidates the black urban experience in the postwar era.

Twenty Acres of Equality

"No progress has been made with the housing problem" in the city, exclaimed Paul Phillips in 1960. Considered the one "ambassador" able to "break down racial barriers" in the city, Phillips struggled to understand why blacks made so little progress in the area of housing. He said, "Housing is the number one problem," and the city would soon face "serious problems if we [were] to continue to enforce housing segregation policies."[22] Just one year prior, the final report of the Fourth Annual Housing Conference of the Michigan Committee on Civil Rights stated, "Where, in 1940, the minority population of Grand Rapids lived in a comparatively integrated community with a considerable percentage of white neighbors, today we find block after block without a single white resident. What was at first a restriction to certain residential areas has developed into a pattern of totally segregated Negro neighborhoods."[23]

Phillips realized that not only did "deeply prejudiced" whites move to "escape arriving Negroes," the majority "want[ed] to maintain the status quo to keep Negroes from their areas."[24] But what infuriated Phillips and so many other black residents was the fact that "all new construction, and hence VA and FHA housing [had] been restricted to white purchasers," according to a report prepared by the HRC for the State Advisory Committee on Civil Rights. Records indicated that in addition to the federal policies, there was "a general practice among land owners and their agents, subdividers, builders and developers to restrict land sales to white residence."[25]

In the absence of an open housing policy, Grand Rapids Urban League (GRUL) officials relentlessly pressed the City Commission to adopt a comprehensive housing ordinance in 1956, which replaced the housing measures passed in 1914 and later amended in 1915 and 1922. The old housing ordinance contained low standards that made it virtually impossible to eliminate blighted conditions. The old ordinance, for example, only required one toilet per two families. Furthermore, baths, kitchen sinks, inside toilets, and hand lavatories were not mandatory. Phillips and the GRUL, along with several community organizations, such as the GRNAACP and the Allied Construction Council, helped Health Department Director Dr. W. B. Prothro revise the ordinance. The revisions included improved sanitary conditions, water-heating facilities, and minimum space requirements. However, given that a staff of only two men also handled schools, public swimming pools, new construction, rodent control, and other environmental health inspections for the entire city, enforcement proved difficult.[26]

Despite the limited success of Housing Ordinance No. 1425, blacks in Grand Rapids continued to defend their rights and interests. Aware of the limitations and benefits of living in a small community, blacks pragmatically assessed their options and responded in myriad ways to racial segregation. While some took on real estate brokers, others challenged city officials to live up to the strictures of the 1956 Housing Ordinance, and some sought to develop inner-city neighborhoods. Often unrecognized in the grand development of metropolitan space during the postwar era, blacks established viable neighborhoods, contributed to the maintenance and improvement of stable neighborhoods, and fought against neighborhood disorganization and decay with meager resources.

Relegated to the oldest section of a racially divided city, blacks inherited neighborhoods on the brink of decline where homes were in desperate need of repair. Despite limited resources and racial discrimination, Robert Barber, an assessor for the city, stated, "There [were] areas that Negroes have moved into that [were] 100 per cent better now than they were 30 years ago." In particular, the 600-block of Pleasant Street Southeast illustrated the types of improvements blacks made within their neighborhoods. From neighborhood cleanup efforts to individual repairs, paint jobs, and landscape enhancements, black home owners were committed to raising their property values. Barber believed that "a large share of the blame" for the deterioration in housing quality in the inner city lay "with absentee owners," not black home owners.[27]

In addition to individual efforts to improve the community, such organizations as the "Chest Improvement Club," which consisted of white and black city residents, and predominantly black groups sponsored by the Urban League, such as the "Neighborhood Block Clubs," worked to improve and stabilize neighborhoods in the "black belt."[28] A 1958 report by the Grand Rapids Health Department indicated that "many families were taking a serious interest in improving properties and living conditions" in the inner city.[29] Determined to establish a decent living environment, blacks invested in the neighborhoods in which they were allowed to reside and made repairs to their homes.

According to the 1950 census, roughly 60 percent of the nonwhite housing units were owner occupied in 1950.[30] Thus home ownership reflected black agency and the purposeful attempt to establish community. Black home owners, such as Ezell Brown, who lived in his inner-city home for more than twenty years, believed they could improve their neighborhoods. Their human agency produced a community of their own, an investment that blacks did not take lightly. Forced to buy in declining areas, in many cases blacks paid more for their homes in the "black belt" than the homes were worth. Furthermore, the limited available space meant that blacks could not build new homes; rather, the prohibitive policies restricted them to purchasing old homes. The result was that some blacks, such as Floyd Skinner, challenged the white supremacy of suburbanization. "We've got to scatter," Skinner urged the black community. "We've got to go where they say we can't go. We've got to show them black men are people like themselves and we can't do it all concentrated in one spot." Heeding his own advice, Skinner moved his family from the "black belt" into "a two-story home on a corner lot in a fine but not fancy neighborhood in East Grand Rapids" in 1952. They were the first black residents the outlying suburban residents had seen. Although Skinner's transition to the suburbs took courage, black demand for access to suburban home ownership, however, was met with tough resistance.[31]

This was certainly true when four blacks—Dr. Julius Franks Jr., Joseph W. Lee, J. E. Adams Jr., and Samuel Triplett—attempted to purchase a twenty-acre residential tract along Fuller Avenue from the city's Sinking Fund in 1962. Despite overwhelming odds, blacks still desired better homes. "We've been talking for years about how to get new houses for Grand Rapids Negroes," Franks recalled in 1962. According to a report prepared by the City's Study Committee on Human Relations, black residents, such as Franks, faced restriction not only in the locality in which they lived but also in the kinds of housing available to them. Moreover, the study revealed "that Negro families economically able and desiring to move into other areas have been unable to buy or rent north of Wealthy Street, east of Fuller, or south of Franklin."[32] Nonetheless, blacks routinely challenged the racial barriers of segregated neighborhoods in Grand Rapids. In their effort to achieve housing equality, blacks in Grand Rapids pursued a variety of options to contest the sustained opposition to spatial integration. From individual attempts to penetrate the suburban shield to collective efforts to challenge discriminatory housing legislation, blacks in Grand Rapids made efforts to dismantle the spatial color line that separated the inner city from the surrounding suburbs.

The city rejected the first bid of $20,500 from the "Auburn Hills Corporation" and subsequently set the minimum purchase price at $54,250 and the terms for paying off the balance for five years. The four black investors, however, surprised the city's Sinking Fund trustees with a second bid of $60,000 and "a firm belief that all men are created equal." As Franks explained to a *Grand Rapids Press* reporter, "We want people to think of a new well-kept home in another section of the city when Negro housing is mentioned—not the old rundown buildings in that southeast area." The four men did not want to build an all-black suburb; rather the investors promised to build a community "where White and Negro persons both will have an opportunity to buy our homes."[33] With a down payment of $12,000 and a bid $5,750 over the asking price, Franks, Lee, Adams, and Triplett hoped to turn their lofty aspiration into reality.

Located nearly three miles to the northeast of the emerging "black belt," the twenty acres extended to a newly developed white subdivision just beyond Sweet Street and Fuller Avenue. When news of the proposed housing project became available, white residents from the Second Ward formed the White Citizens Committee to protest the legality of the housing deal.[34] At a meeting with the members of the HRC Housing Committee, the organization's spokesmen, Richard Kall and Harold Hatherly, stated that white neighbors opposed the "creation of an 'all-negro' settlement because of fears that property values in the surrounding area [would] decline." According to Kall and Hatherly, residents "regard[ed] as financially unsound the plans of the Negro group."[35]

Despite the White Citizens Committee's emphasis on property values, its escalating anxiety had everything to do with race. Virtually synonymous, space and race maintained an inextricable relationship throughout the postwar era. The metaphoric identification of ghettoes, slums, and suburbs comparatively positioned black and white populations spatially and racially. These distinctions functioned to represent "natural" and "appropriate" metropolitan spatial segregation in northern communities during the postwar era. Identified as independent spaces, suburbs represented the antithesis of inner-city communities often depicted as dependent spaces. Through the metalanguage of race, striking physical characteristics of neighborhood space reinforced notions of blackness and whiteness. Consequently, blacks and whites assumed a spatial definition that made race the defining feature of space.[36]

According to Franks and Triplett, "The old houses in the 'ghetto' [sold] for unusually high prices and without having been refurbished by the seller." Lee added, "There [was] a seller's market in homes for Negroes," but nobody really knew how many black families could afford to move to new homes "because they [had] never had the opportunity." Triplett commented, "We look[ed] at this as an act of citizenship. We [were] assuming duties as citizens of Grand Rapids and as men."[37] Thus, through the land purchase, the four men hoped to offer the kind of housing that "people of all colors desire for themselves and their children."[38] Located three miles from the "black belt," the twenty acres purchased by the black investment group represented a small piece of equality.

Hatherly, who lived in an adjacent neighborhood, considered the establishment of an integrated suburb "a step backwards and therefore ill-advised."[39] He was not alone. Hundreds of other white residents in the neighboring areas protested openly and organized the White Citizens Committee. The group's spokesmen, Hall and Hatherly, said that they were not opposed to "token" integration, but the group vigorously pressured the City Commission to persuade Franks and his partners to drop their investment. Robert and Ruth Krueger, area residents, sent a letter to the *Grand Rapids Press* that stated their displeasure with Frank's plans. "We don't want our neighborhood to be a slum area in a few years," they explained. They asked, "How many neighborhoods in this city can you name which have been taken over by colored which have not become slum areas?" They concluded, "We object to the manner in which this project has been forced down our throats. In these United States we are all supposed to have civil rights—where are ours?" Ironically, the Krueger family lived in an area that originated and expanded as a result of restrictive white segregation and the suppression of black rights.[40]

Despite strict opposition, the investment group had supporters among the white community. In a letter to the Grand Rapids City Commission on December 28, 1962, Stanley and Nanette Schneider wrote:

> We, as white citizens, would like to take part in this opportunity to get to know and to have our children know and appreciate and be friends and neighbors of people of all races and backgrounds. We have told Dr. and Mrs. Franks . . . that we wish to purchase one of the lots in the new 20-acre development. We hope our family will have the chance to participate directly in this important progressive venture in democratic living.

Apparently Mayor Stanley Davis also felt this was a necessary step forward. Having approved the land purchase, Davis said he "would prefer private initiative to overcome the lack of adequate housing for . . . Negroes." However, he asked, "how much longer can we wait for private enterprise to do it?"[41] This infuriated residents in the Second Ward, who believed Mayor Davis was unfairly sacrificing their neighborhood. Irate residents in the adjoining area placed their City Commission representatives in a precarious position: Either support segregated space, or move forward with integration against constituent consent.

With a primary election only a few months away, Evangeline Lamberts and Robert Jamo, Second Ward commissioners, felt the heat from their constituents to obstruct the land purchase. A well-known Citizens' Action activist and community organizer, Lamberts became the first female city commissioner in Grand Rapids in 1961, when she defeated Robert Blandford. Lamberts often challenged many of the initiatives posed by Mayor Davis, and the land pact would prove no different. After several meetings with members of the White Citizens Committee, Lamberts attempted to avoid open conflict, and she urged "Dr. Franks's group [to] delay the project pending further study." "For Sale" signs popped up in the area of the proposed housing development, and it appeared that panic had set in. Lamberts appealed to her constituents not to make hasty decisions and acknowledged the financial factor was "a legitimate concern to you and me." Lamberts stressed that the City Commission had no responsibility in the land sale but promised to investigate the legality of the sale by the Sinking Fund trustees.[42]

Lamberts and Jamo "clashed sharply"[43] with Mayor Davis, who served as the president of the Sinking Fund and signed the land contract. Mayor Davis and First Ward Commissioner Bernard Barto then tried to have the opinion filed without debate, but the Second Ward commissioners demanded that execution of the sale had to come with approval from the City Commission. It appeared that the Second Ward commissioners tried to change procedure concerning this deal because of the objections of their constituents. Historically, the Sinking Fund had the right to accept or to reject bids without commission approval. Now Lamberts and Jamo attempted to interpose and to pass judgment regarding the validity of Sinking Fund projects on an individual basis. They requested a resolution from former city attorney James Miller, but Miller, to their disappointment, ruled that "a land contract sale [was] legal and in line with city policy."[44] However Lamberts and Jamo refused to accept the decision and delayed ratification of the integrated planned housing project. Mayor Davis charged that the city commissioners who were "trying to make an issue of this should hang their heads in shame."[45]

Nearly a week later, the controversial sale hit another roadblock. Attorney Jack M. Bowie, who represented the white residents in opposition to the sale, charged that at least part of the proposed land tract had been reserved for a park under the city's master park plan of 1950. Despite the fact that the tract was not included in the 1957 adopted plan and the new master plan of 1962, Bowie contended that the Sinking Fund illegally sold land designated for public park use. Refraining from comment, the purchasing quartet allowed their legal representative, attorney Benjamin Baum, to speak on their behalf: "They, as well as I, recognize that no matter what they do to follow all the laws, somebody will raise a point to try to upset their valid transaction." He explained that the real issue prohibiting the conclusion of the sale was "the color of their skin." He reminded the commission that his clients legally participated in two bidding procedures and ultimately settled on a price $5,000 over the asking price set by the trustees. F. William McKee, acting city attorney, agreed and determined the sale was valid. However, Bowie's charge allowed the Second Ward commissioners to postpone its decision another week.[46]

When the City Commission finally ended weeks of procrastination on Tuesday, January 22, 1963, and ratified the twenty-acre sale during a special closed meeting, it refused to back the title. Thus instead of providing a "Deed C" conveyance, which was originally promised to the purchasers, the commission voted to issue a "quitclaim deed" when all the conditions were met by Franks, Lee, Adams, and Triplett. With the "Deed C," Franks and his partners would have had a guarantee from the city: "The Deed C conveyance the buyers had been promised would provide a 'warrant' that the city had done nothing to place a 'cloud' on the title."[47] This would have left the city open to a possible lawsuit over the condition of the title and a damage suit by the quartet. However, the "quitclaim" came with no such assurance. Thus, it served as one last attempt from municipal officials, Lamberts and Jamo, to stop the sale or at least to provide a hollow victory for the purchasers.

In the end, Lamberts, Jamo, and members of the White Citizens Committee did all they could to block the sale. With minimal caution, the Second Ward commissioners in particular discounted the potential financial loss of Franks and associates. The "undesirable elements" that Lamberts and Jamo were trying to protect the Second Ward from proved to be doctors, teachers, and social workers who happened to be black.[48] The initiative by the four men boldly defied the dominance of segregated suburban space and facilitated the passage of the Fair Housing Ordinance on December 23, 1963. Their efforts represented one example of a stable integrated suburban neighborhood in Grand Rapids.

Despite the success, however commendable, the fact that approximately 98 percent of the black population still remained tightly situated in the "black belt" should not go unnoticed. Aside from the Franks's sixty-four-unit development in Auburn Hills, which housed white and black residents, two new black families were living in East Grand Rapids, fewer than a dozen in Wyoming Township, and fewer in the northeastern or northwestern sections of the city.[49] Skinner died in 1962, at the age of sixty-two, and he never had the chance to see the purchasing groups, in his own words, "scatter" and "go where they say we can't go." However, the expanded impact of segregation would not become evident beyond the black community until the late 1960s, when businesses packed up and tax revenue precipitously declined.

"For Whites Only"

Except for East Grand Rapids, the suburbs around Grand Rapids did not exist prior to the 1950s.[50] Instead, the outlying area of Grand Rapids consisted of sparsely inhabited villages and townships. Grand Rapids Township and the city of East Grand Rapids shaded the northeastern and eastern borders of the city. To the south and southwest were Paris (present-day Kentwood) and Wyoming townships along with the village of Grandville, and Walker and Plainfield townships rounded out the circumference of exterior suburbs to the west and north. By 1950, none of the townships, with the exception of Wyoming, had more than ten thousand residents. But the enormous residential expansion that took place during the postwar years quickly transformed these former farmer regions into functional districts.

The building boom that began with interior suburbs, or suburban neighborhoods inside the city limits, such as Alger Heights in the 1940s, expanded so rapidly that the *Grand Rapids Herald* reported that Alger Heights was 80 percent full and quickly nearing its capacity by 1950.[51] According to Grand Rapids city historian Gordon Olson, businessmen and clerical workers with an average age of forty-five responded to the "attraction of inexpensive lots, quick availability, and ready financing."[52] Even without paved roads, sales teams convinced buyers that "the dirt streets and treeless lots would soon be transformed into comfortable subdivisions with paved, tree-lined streets."[53] The real estate firm of Simerink and Duthler sold this promise to entice prospective white home-buyers to Alger Heights and the surrounding suburban areas. These undeveloped regions appeared far less risky as financial investments with the guaranteed backing of the FHA.

As new residents arrived, however, the need for improved services, such as sewage, fire, and water provisions, followed. The influx of people necessitated the development of a new "ultramodern shopping district" in Alger Heights. Also, the population growth compelled the Grand Rapids School Department to build two new additions at the area neighborhood schools, which cost more than $200,000. Likewise, churches were needed within the immediate vicinity. The new $150,000 South Congregational Church was still under construction, and Seymour Christian decided to undergo a $110,000 expansion program. A 1950 state highway department survey confirmed the dramatic shift from a five-home countryside quarter to a full-fledged "hustle and bustle" suburb that "within a 12 hour period had approximately 8,000 cars and 1,175 pedestrians pass the corner of Alger Street and Eastern Avenue."[54]

Small interior suburban communities, such as Alger Heights and Burton Heights, evolved overnight in the postwar era as developers' mass-produced homes modeled after those built in Levittown, New York. According to an HRC study, it seemed as if "unseen 'For White Only' signs" existed on for sale or for rent homes in the suburbs of Grand Rapids. Like most Levittowners, white residents in Grand Rapids understood the relief suburbs afforded them from the dramatic demographic shift caused by the northern movement of blacks during the "Second Great Migration." An article in the *Grand Rapids Herald* declared that "the population growth of urban centers in the past eight years [was] one of the most significant developments of our time."[55] When black residents moved into the city, they created a domino effect as white residents migrated to the suburbs. But few mechanisms were in place to prevent the rapid spread of segregated areas in the metropolitan region from becoming larger and larger.[56] Instead, the process of stratification accelerated as people's prejudices and economic and social aspirations fed on each other.[57] The mass exodus produced a dramatic change in the pattern of development, as the "stage was set for builders to construct street after street of suburban cookie-cutter homes."[58]

In 1958, Dr. Bouma highlighted this growth rate when he stated that "the difference in the rate of increase during the last six years between the city and the surrounding areas [was], of course, spectacular." He noted, "While the city grew about 7%, the fringe grew about 40%."[59] Wyoming, located south and southwest of the central city, represented a remarkable suburban development of the exterior suburbs that were established outside city limits. It evolved from a largely agricultural region in 1930 that consisted of 211 farms to a sprawling suburban community in 1954, which was touted in *The City of Wyoming:*

A History as a "better place to live and work"[60] than the central city. Thanks to the new General Motors (GM) plant, Wyoming consistently outranked Grand Rapids in building permits issued throughout the 1950s. The population rose to thirty-six thousand by 1954 and increased to approximately forty-one thousand by 1956.[61] Although Wyoming led suburban development in the surrounding areas, Olson reported that the outlying populace "often looked to Grand Rapids to help supply basic needs. Calls for improved services were heard from many quarters as housing developments and a growing population accelerated the demand for water and sewer-lines, paved streets, and adequate fire-fighting and police protection."[62]

Developers, who understood the relationship between city and suburb, aggressively purchased tracts adjacent to the city. They attempted to model residential development as "a continuation of the urban grid pattern of the central city so that the boundary between the two units [was] crossed without any perceptible change in the urban environment."[63] Advertisements by real estate firms, such as Bremer Realty Company, Fletcher Realty Company, and Simerink and Duthler Realty, inundated local newspapers with advertisements that proclaimed, "We're Looking Back to a Gratifying Past and Forward to a Useful Future."[64] That "gratifying past" would bring roughly 55 percent of the suburban male workers and nearly 75 percent of suburban families in social organizations that convened in the city back to Grand Rapids regularly.[65] These middle- and lower-middle-class suburban families also returned to "capitalize on the diversified cultural and educational opportunities abounding in metropolitan Grand Rapids," but the "useful future" belonged to the racially homogenous spaces of the suburbs.[66]

Connected to Grand Rapids by the I-196 expressway, the exterior suburban residents of Grandville and Jenison also used the city for work, play, and entertainment. Both communities experienced tremendous development in the 1950s and 1960s. According to John W. McGee, editor of *The Story of Grandville and Jenison, Michigan,* although "Grandville and Jenison may fringe on a large metropolitan area and profit from this advantage . . . tomorrow's citizens of these communities should still be able to enjoy the same blending of old with the new that makes each one today a good place to live, work and raise a family."[67]

Indeed, the residents of suburban areas benefited from their segregated position relative to Grand Rapids. Many Jenison residents commuted to Grand Rapids for employment. McGee discovered these residents decided to live in unincorporated Jenison, "with its many lovely homes sprawling out into thirty-three square miles of Georgetown Township." He also noted that although Jenison residents worked in Grand Rapids, "most shopping needs of the residents [were] met within the confines of Jenison. Supermarkets, a dime store, jewelry shop, furniture store, pharmacy, appliance store, fruit market, barber and beauty shops, and service stations [were] all in close proximity."[68] This form of lopsided investment held true for a number of exterior suburbs.

TABLE 3.1   PROPORTION OF GRAND RAPIDS METROPOLITAN
AREA POPULATION LOCATED WITHIN THE CENTRAL CITY

Year	Percentage of Population within the City
1920	86.2%
1930	79.5%
1940	76.8%
1950	71.0%
1956	65.0%

Grandville sits on the southwestern corner of Grand Rapids. According to a metropolitan report entitled "When One-Third of a City Moves to the Suburbs," the suburban city, carved out of the northwestern crook of Wyoming, "was incorporated in 1933 but until the Second World War a small village atmosphere for the most part prevailed and the city lay separated somewhat from the bustling metropolitan center."[69] In the 1940s and 1950s, "Grandville's area exploded more than three hundred percent," and the rapid growth "distinguished Grandville as the fastest growing community in Kent County during the fifties." To accommodate the new residents, developers built a central shopping district, which contained "a variety of businesses and services that [met] the shopping needs of the community." Services ranged "from accountants to truckers while the diverse business community include[d] everything from a dry land marina to a superior baby shop."[70]

By 1956, noticeable trends existed in the population growth of the Grand Rapids area in the form of how quickly the growth developed and where in the metropolitan area the growth occurred. From 1940 to 1956, the central city's population declined by nearly 12 percentage points (see Table 3.1). It should be noted that "this steady drop occurred even though the city increased its population by 51,538 (37.4 per cent) over this period." Stated in a different way, "38.8 per cent of the 36 year growth settled in the city, 61.2 per cent in the suburban fringe." These figures elucidate the scattered population growth throughout the Grand Rapids Metropolitan Area. In fact, every peripheral area community "at least doubled itself in 36 years." The data reveal that the majority of metropolitan development occurred in the suburban areas, yet the brisk pace of development in these former countryside areas required high-level urban services. Unable to provide for themselves, initially the suburban communities relied exclusively on the central city and a host of government services to ensure development of their newly founded neighborhoods. Thus, we must shift the focus onto government intervention to better understand the intricate connection between federal policies, local investors, and suburban growth around Grand Rapids.[71]

Segregation, a Not So "New Deal"

As described by historian Kenneth T. Jackson, in his *Crabgrass Frontier,* the FHA, founded in 1934 for the purpose of guaranteeing long-term residential mortgages, created and maintained segregated urban-growth patterns throughout metropolitan America. As the most important government-housing agency of the New Deal era, the FHA "solidified the government's new responsibility to finance private housing for millions of Americans."[72] The FHA made use of Residential Security Maps designed by the Home Owners' Loan Corporation, which outlined each metropolitan area on a four-scale color-coded grade.

Designed to map the "trend of desirability in neighborhoods," the Residential Security Maps provided real estate brokers in Grand Rapids with valuable information regarding safe investment areas. Residential Security Map developers collaborated with field agents, local real estate brokers, and mortgage lenders in Grand Rapids to determine neighborhood desirability as well as offered a map for smart growth based on race. The four-point evaluation grid established neighborhoods marked "A" as "well planned sections of the city . . . they [were] homogenous in demand as residential location in 'good times' or 'bad.'" In contrast, areas labeled "D" "represent[ed] those neighborhoods . . . characterized by detrimental influence in a pronounced degree, undesirable population or infiltration of it."[73]

The FHA utilized the Grand Rapids Security Residential Maps as the latchkey for safe loans, which furthered suburban growth. This government agency, therefore, distributed financial support on a discriminatory basis. The FHA endorsed the use of restrictive covenants and actually provided a higher positive rating to areas that enforced regulations and where "effective restrictive covenants [were] recorded against the entire tract, since these provide[d] the surest protection against undesirable encroachment and inharmonious use."[74] The application of racial covenants, therefore, ensured builders and owners that the FHA would insure their property and investment. The function of this policy was extremely beneficial to white home buyers after World War II, but especially so during the first five years preceding the war, when more than nine hundred thousand units of FHA housing were produced.

The racialized housing principles of the federal government appeared visible in the *Federal Housing Administration Underwriting Manual,* which for decades warned against the encroachment of "inharmonious racial groups"[75] into neighborhoods occupied by families of another race. Everywhere present in the underwriting manual, race was the determining factor in the success or failure of neighborhood compositions. According to the *Federal Housing Administration Underwriting Manual,* change in the "racial occupancy" contributed to instability and decline in property values.[76] The FHA even described the wording for a sound restrictive covenant essentially designed to strengthen and supplement zoning ordinances. According to the underwriting manual, a thorough restrictive covenant, among other verifications, should prohibit the re-subdivision of lots, control the design of all buildings, and enforce the "prohibition of the occupancy of properties except by the race for which they are intended . . . and should run for a period of at least twenty-five to thirty years."[77] Mortgage appraisers penalized areas without such written protections and rewarded areas that contained what the government considered to be sound segregation policies.[78]

The ideology and practice of the FHA underwriting manual policies were not limited to a single suburban neighborhood. Instead, the impact was felt throughout the entire metropolitan region in both urban and suburban spaces as loan policies facilitated the development of new housing as opposed to already existing homes. To secure a comfortable living environment, the FHA advised that its policies be enforced in the use and development of structural organizations, such as schools. According to the FHA, institutions of learning "should not be attended in large numbers by inharmonious racial groups."[79] These policies contained important implications for the future of public education during the postwar era. It effectively eliminated the notion of an integrated school system and explicitly condemned the existence of integrated schools as hazardous to a community. Moreover, the FHA underwriting guidelines defined race as the primary signifier for urban and suburban schools. The language naturalized the association of white students and suburban schools, as juxtaposed with an antagonistic characterization of blacks and suburban schools. Thus the notion of de facto segregation loses its luster when one considers how the federal government endorsed overt racial discrimination and rewarded communities that legitimated segregation.

The FHA manual addressed the importance of racially homogeneous schools as a critical component of the success of any healthy neighborhood composition. As foreseen by the FHA, schools were the fundamental building blocks in the development and maintenance of desirable communities. Prestigious schools or school districts served as essential lifelines for communities. The FHA believed that homogenous neighborhoods produced community vitality. According to the FHA underwriting manual, if "the children of people living in such an area are compelled to attend school where the majority or a goodly number of the pupils represent . . . an incompatible racial element, the neighborhood under consideration will prove far less stable and desirable."[80] It was further suggested that in such situations, white parents might well consider paying a fee that would allow their children to attend another school with similar students. Therefore, the FHA considered race the critical variable in developing housing and schools that determined the success or failure of a neighborhood.

The FHA attached greater importance to "zoning protection in and near large metropolitan centers than in places having smaller populations and less rapid rates of growth."[81] This growth-control ideology was established by several methods. When zoning ordinances, restrictive covenants, and deed restrictions—the most effective mechanism—were not in place to check racial occupancy, the FHA believed that "natural or artificially established barriers [would] prove effective in protecting a neighborhood and the locations within it from adverse influences. Usually the protection against adverse influences afforded by these means include[d] prevention of the infiltration . . . [of] inharmonious racial groups."[82] FHA representatives encouraged local appraisers to make a "thorough study" of landscapes to ensure the presence of natural and artificial barriers. The role of the state in achieving stratified neighborhoods in the North effectively extended beyond definitions of de facto segregation.

The growing influx of blacks in northern cities subsequent to World War II deepened and widened metropolitan ghetto areas. White families in the North and West resisted and protested the in-migration of minorities by escaping to underdeveloped areas located on urban fringes. The government provided the economic and legal springboard that allowed white families, rich and poor, to formulate racially homogenized utopias. As a single government entity, the FHA provided government insurance for mortgages on "4.4 million homes, totaling nearly $29 billion" from its inception in 1934 to 1957. Of this total, "2.5 million were new homes." FHA-insured mortgages actually accounted for nearly "20 and 30 per cent of the new homes built each year."[83]

This proved true in Grand Rapids, where developer growth patterns mirrored national trends of suburban expansion. But the design of Grand Rapids metropolitan growth also resembled closely the Residential Security Map recommendations for smart growth put forward in 1937. Sections of the city marked "A" offered residents "good transportation, park, playground and good schools." Moreover the "Area Description" forms of the Home Owner Loan Corporation cited "A" areas as well as "restricted" communities whose inhabitants were "native white, white-collared" with a zero "Negro" population. For instance, the Residential Security Maps marked the suburban locale of Ottawa Hills as an "A" section and dubbed it the "best residential area within the city limits," because it remained "highly restricted" and devoid of "Negro's [sic]." Protected by the same "restrictions," Alger Heights and Burton Heights also received high ratings in part by having a zero black population.[84]

Situated "far from schools" and limited by a lack of "some city services," outlying suburbs, such as Wyoming Township, received a mark of "C" on the Residential Security Map in 1937. However, postwar suburbanization and the development of new schools eventually turned Wyoming Township into a fertile area for growth. By the 1950s, both issues were resolved as developers took note of the most important building influence—race—and Wyoming Township was remade into yet another "restricted area" with no blacks. Such places as South Central, which evaluators determined to have "all city facilities, close to south end industries," received the lowest grade of "D," because the "types of inhabitants" or the "few Negro's [sic]" who lived there represented an undesirable population. It only took 1 percent black occupancy for a neighborhood to receive a "D" rating, even if the area had favorable influences, such as "good transportation" and location "close to school." Therefore, whites sought out all-white neighborhoods, which ensured them financing opportunities as a result of racial segregation.[85]

The history of these surrounding suburban areas linked closely to the growth and development of Grand Rapids. The Comstock Park settlement area, located north of Grand Rapids on the southern boundary of Alpine and Plainfield townships, experienced accelerated growth and development as a spin-off effect of the central city. Located on the fringe of Grand Rapids, small towns and villages, such as Comstock Park, received economic advancements and prosperity during the post–War World II boom. Formerly little more than a ghost town, Comstock Park endured several industrial losses that brought the community to a standstill during the Great Depression of the 1930s. The tanning activity that served as the economic engine of the community came to a halt with the "loss of government contracts" over the course of the 1920s and 1930s. Initially, the Old Mill Creek Tannery closed in 1924. The Michigan Tannery followed a decade later in 1934. As a result, Comstock had to develop new economic relationships to survive.[86]

According to David Wier, author of *Comstock Park: Mill Town to Bedroom Suburb*, small communities, such as Comstock, "Thanks to New Deal programs, acquired schools and libraries and museums and roads they had long put off out of traditional parsimony." Wier noted that with World War II at hand, many Comstock Park "blue collar workers went to Grand Rapids to find employment in war industries." In many instances, "women began to leave the household and join their husbands working in the factories." Thus a new economic relationship forged between Comstock Park and the central city of Grand Rapids, as Comstock became almost "totally dependent on Grand Rapids industries and the state and national governments for financial support."[87]

Such villages as Comstock found growth opportunities in urbanization. One Comstock Park community member, Edgar Lee Masters, proclaimed:

> Go into any community of the kind I am speaking of and you'll find this process going on. The town is being made into a ganglion of the city. Telephone and telegraph wires make it part of the metropolis, the radio, the automobile, the airplane, the city newspaper . . . the standard grocery stores, the standard drug stores, machine gas stations, everything that the city can boast of, the small town of today can boast of. The privately owned canning companies, lumber mills, are taken over by large corporations who run them more cheaply and more efficiently.[88]

The changes in Comstock Park were apparent, as the community was flanked with commercial opportunities along Alpine and Plainfield avenues, where local residents purchased goods in a convenient manner. As stated by Wier, such stores as "K-Mart, Meijers Thrifty Acres, Family Foods and the North Kent Mall provided" goods and services "at a lower cost and in a more attractive environment."[89]

The postwar years in Comstock Park "also witnessed community residents looking to the outside for employment. With the passing of the tannery . . . men traveled to the industrial and commercial areas of Grand Rapids to seek their livelihood." A community survey conducted in 1969 revealed the long-term connection: "Comstock Park is a typical suburban type community. There is practically no farming and very little industry. Residents are employed in the metropolitan area of Grand Rapids as factory workers, in the professions, and in the various services industries." Therefore paychecks earned in the central city were often spent outside the inner-city boundaries. The ability to work in the city and live in the suburbs appealed to city residents seeking to "escape the city life and to seek cheaper housing as well as land for home gardens. But with being located so close to the metropolitan community, these former city residents [sought] the advantages of both worlds, the small village and the large city."[90]

Thus, Wier could assert that within a thirty-year period, Comstock Park evolved "into a bedroom suburb of Grand Rapids," as "developers purchased land and constructed homes." The largest "development, Westgate, dominate[d] the community and house[d] the middle-aged and the middle-classed."[91] The Westgate neighborhood, which began in the late 1950s, contained nearly seven hundred homes that ranged up to $50,000 by the early 1970s. However, the greatest change in Comstock Park was the continued and dramatic alteration of the town's landscape. New additions, such as the freeway built through the area in 1966 and the continued development of homes, allowed the residents of Comstock Park to reap the benefits of its parent city without assuming any responsibility in turn.

The Comstock description of suburban growth was typical in each of the outlying areas as concentrated efforts of development poured into unsettled areas neighboring metropolitan Grand Rapids. Additionally, many of these outlying suburbs were becoming industrial centers. Walker Township, which bordered the inner city to the west, represented such a suburb. A study on Walker Township by the local Historical Committee noted the relatively slow growth until the early 1950s. "At that time," according to the study, "the once small township blossomed into a population of approximately 16,000 people and sixty million dollar state equalized valuation." With 65 percent of its valuation consisting of industrial and commercial-type corporations and only 35 percent made up of residential contributions, Walker afforded the "taxpayer the advantage of a very competitive, if not lower tax rate than other communities which [were] made up principally of residential units and very little commercial or industrial development."[92]

The federal government's involvement in the housing industry widened in the early 1930s. As a part of Franklin Roosevelt's New Deal, the government initiated programs to counter the housing collapse experienced during the Great Depression. The government intended to use incentives to alleviate effects of the Depression and stimulate the housing market. The efforts of the federal government enabled private businesses to provide relief for individuals to retain current homes as well as purchase new ones.[93] Touted as a tremendous social engineering program that assisted needy citizens during a time of crisis, the New Deal housing program instead operated as a racially sanctioned welfare initiative that further segregated landscapes across the country and disproportionately provided white citizens with government handouts, indicating that suburban homeownership was not intended for all citizens.[94]

The federal government, through various institutions such as the FHA, the Veterans Administration (VA), and the Federal National Mortgage Association (FNMA), satisfied the home-buying needs of white residents in the suburbs. The FHA greatly diminished the total down payment required for suburbanites. As reported by the Department of Housing and Urban Development:

> It is difficult to comprehend what the housing credit market was like before these institutions were created. Today, Americans take for granted a private mortgage credit market that offers 30-year low down payment loans on homes and that recently has been supporting the construction of over 2 million new housing units annually.
>
> In the 1920s when the population was about half of today's, annual production averaged about 600,000 units per year, and the family mortgage constituted a major financial burden. Until the Federal Laws of the early 1930s, the typical home mortgage was for 1 to 5 years—and seldom longer than 10 years. Loans for half the value of the property carried a high interest rate and had to be repaid in full or refinanced at maturity. The prime mortgage was often accompanied by second, third, and sometimes fourth mortgages, at still higher interest rates due to their lesser claim on the property."[95]

As a result of the racially motivated federal programs, blacks disproportionately remained confined within the boundaries of inner-city spaces. Conversely, FHA underwriting policies ensured that white residents, in unprecedented numbers, profited from race-based housing guidelines.

The phenomenal housing growth during the two decades following World War II provided all white citizens, regardless of class, an opportunity to own homes mainly at the edges of the central cities and into the extended suburbs. This social movement, which occurred as millions of blacks moved north and west between 1940 and 1970, was often erroneously linked to white citizens' thrift, hard work, and morality. The celebratory union between whites and the suburbs had less to do with morals and more to do with racially designed gov-

TABLE 3.2 NEW HOUSING UNITS STARTED IN THE
UNITED STATES, BY DECADE, 1930–1959

Year	New Housing Units Started
1930–1939	2,734,000
1940–1949	7,443,000
1950–1959	15,068,000

Source: U.S. Bureau of the Census, 1966, 18.

ernment-welfare policies. Government legislation effectively decreased home down payments, provided significant incentives through mortgage guarantees, and offered income-tax deductions and write-offs to ensure the development of "white-only" suburbs.

Indeed, this was true in Grand Rapids and nationally, as the federal government bankrolled white suburbanization through discriminatory housing subsidies, and the actions of real estate agents, individual home buyers and sellers, and neighborhood associations enforced spatial segregation and racial prejudice. Thus, government agencies, such as the FHA, made it possible for many white Americans to turn inward and solve social problems with individual solutions by abandoning urban space and retreating to the confines of elaborate, but still subsidized, suburban space.[96] Through ideology and policy, the federal government promoted racial discrimination in housing that, as historian Benjamin Kleinberg argues, had "significant implications not only for the growth of suburbs but also for the future of central cities."[97]

One major reason, which is often overlooked, was the fact that New Deal federal housing policies were executed at the local level by so-called competent local real estate brokers and mortgage lenders that the federal government believed would "represent a fair and composite opinion" of spatial patterns. Business leaders, such as Harold T. Fletcher, Charles B. Gardella, James F. Harris, Peter Hoek, and Walter S. Palmer of Fletcher Realty Company, along with Henry W. DeBoer and John G. Emery of DeBoer Brothers Realty Company, represented seven of the twenty-three local persons trusted by FHA field agents to decide spatial desirability in Grand Rapids. This small cadre of men, not the FHA field agents, essentially designed the local Residential Security Map and subsequently engineered the racial guidelines for segregated growth in Grand Rapids. The group, which included Chamber of Commerce members, determined desirability of neighborhoods by their various business interests. Indeed, political and business leaders established a consensus of the greater public good based on a shared notion of white property consciousness. This broad-based arrangement in Grand Rapids pivoted on the security of private property. It ultimately allowed businessmen, at the local level, to appropriate New Deal housing policies to service business ends. Moreover it became the underlining principle for post–World War II urban development (see Table 3.2).

A representative from the HRC who studied the housing crisis in Grand Rapids stated:

> The bulk of new housing in the Grand Rapids area since the war has been constructed with the aid of FHA and VA mortgage insurance. All (or nearly all) of this housing has been limited to whites by the policy of builders and real estate groups. FHA and VA have taken no stand on the question of availability of this housing to minority groups; the local attitude favoring containment of non-whites in older housing have prevailed, and as a result Grand Rapids is more segregated than ever before. Although all groups support these government programs, only whites have been allowed to benefit from them in Grand Rapids. FHA and VA continue to subsidize segregation here with the knowledge that builders are practicing racial discrimination.[98]

Not surprisingly, secondary cities, such as Grand Rapids, disproportionately felt the effects of stratified race and space. The growing discrimination and segregation in the city of Grand Rapids caused complications in the public educational system. School-district boundaries often coincided with municipality borderlines, and the Board of Education assigned students to the schools within their neighborhoods. As a result, segregation between municipalities in a metropolitan locale created segregation in schools. In 1952, no schools in Grand Rapids contained more than 90 percent nonwhite students. By 1961, three schools had nonwhite populations of more than 90 percent.[99] Moreover, in 1952, only two schools contained minority student bodies of 70 to 89 percent, but by 1961, four schools fell within this percentage range.[100] The increased concentration of minorities within the inner city, coupled with the exodus by white residents to the suburbs, strained inner-city school funding and often forced overcrowded black student populations to attend aged school facilities with limited resources. Housing became inextricably bound to the process of public education.

Thus black inner-city dwellers were casualties of the metropolitan problem, not the cause. According to the National Commission on Urban Problems, blacks were "virtually imprisoned in slums by the white suburban noose around the inner city, a noose that clearly signified, 'negroes and poor people not wanted.'"[101] Discriminatory fiscal and zoning practices denied blacks access to the full range of housing opportunities. The consistent refusal of these rights during the post–World War II years ultimately set the stage for a tumultuous growth period, one saturated in bitter racial hatred that ultimately resulted in violence. But to understand the process and effect of residential segregation in Grand Rapids, it is necessary to assess the impact that the unequal development of suburban growth had on the metropolitan region.

The Center City Plantation

The racial restrictions on housing limited the 7,841 new minority residents to areas that traditionally housed nonwhites. The GRUL noted that the bulk of the minority population, 88.6 percent, lived within five census tracts positioned squarely in the heart of the inner city.[102] But restriction or residential confinement served as a critical issue even before the 1950s. A 1940 study of Grand Rapids, conducted for the Interracial Committee of the Council of Social Agencies, reported on 319 black families and found that 4 of every 10 tenant families tried to improve their living conditions by accessing quarters that offered more for their money. However, doing so outside the prescribed minority boundaries was virtually impossible. In a good number of cases, white landlords practiced discriminatory behavior by posting higher rent prices for blacks. Despite the possibility of paying more, the large majority of black renters claimed that it was impossible to obtain better accommodations, because "agents would not rent to Negroes in certain areas."[103] The same held true nearly twelve years later, when the average city rent was $36, but blacks paid an average of $41, or nearly $5 more than whites paid per month. Yet discrimination prohibited blacks from accessing lower-priced available rental units outside the "black belt."[104] Records revealed the experience was similar for black owner occupants who desired to upgrade their housing conditions but "felt that they were definitely restricted as to where they could live in Grand Rapids . . . because of their racial identity."[105]

The study also revealed the poor condition of the minority dwellings. The Westside area survey exposed the reality that many of the homes were "recommended for demolition." A number of the units were listed as being among the condemned for nearly two years. Only three of the homes on the list received repairs, and of those three, "only one showed signs of having been actually placed in condition for decent living."[106] Blacks who rented experienced inferior living conditions. The majority of black residents were situated in single-family homes converted into two-family dwellings. These dual-family units enabled landlords to collect rent from two groups of renters, but the result was to provide facilities unfit for both families. Generally these structures needed major repairs and lacked basic facilities, such as toilets or private baths. More than half the black tenants lived in "cold water flats where they must furnish heat from small stoves, there being no central heating plant."[107]

In August 1952, the GRUL offered a detailed block examination of interracial neighborhoods to illuminate the city's housing problems. Claytor, chairman of the GRUL, witnessed firsthand the city's discriminatory housing practices. Faced with systemic opposition from the Grand Rapids Real Estate Board (GRREB), which handled 95 percent of all housing transactions in Grand Rapids, Claytor penetrated the racially stratified suburbs of Grand Rapids because his fair-skinned complexion appeared white. Passing the suburban color prerequisite, Claytor purchased a suburban home through a private sale in 1944 on the northeastern side of town.

Yet the economic ability of many black residents in Grand Rapids did not transcend their racial orientation. Instead blacks were limited by a renewed commitment to racial prejudice, which was inextricably linked to property rights. The increased investment in whiteness assured that the urban crisis would fall squarely in the lap of the collective black community. As Claytor's wife, Helen Jackson Claytor, recalled, "[In Grand Rapids] there were two distinct African American neighborhoods then and . . . you could almost count on the fingers of your hands the black people who lived outside of these particular areas."[108] Consequently, the Claytors worked tirelessly to undermine racial housing restrictions.

The GRREB, which declined to admit the six black real estate brokers in Grand Rapids, supervised the majority of the housing "gentlemen's agreements." Thus, even the GRREB clearly sanctioned discrimination based on race by adhering to the National Association of Real Estate Board (NAREB) Code of Ethics policy article 34, which stated, "A realtor should never be instrumental in introducing into a neighborhood a character of property or occupancy, members of any race or nationality . . . whose presence will clearly be detrimental to property values in that neighborhood."[109] Real estate brokers enforced this policy on a daily basis. A president of a local realty company straightforwardly admitted that his realty group "dealt with a prejudiced public and that popular censure [made] it impossible, as a business proposition, to sell to Negroes except in the delineated areas." The bias actions of local real estate groups, laws, and restrictive covenants, the 1952 housing study committee concluded, created "an ugly scar in the center of the city."[110]

The GRUL concluded that few mechanisms existed to prevent "the rapidly spreading segregated areas"[111] in the center city from becoming larger and larger with the flood of black migrants. The influential Chamber of Commerce seemed more occupied with supporting the development of the downtown area then with the elimination of redlining in mortgage lending policies. No legislative campaign was comparable to the chamber's attempt to thwart FEPC measures, nor did progressive reformers descend on Fulton Park to rally against neighborhood segregation. Instead, the dynamic business leadership opted to pass on equalizing property rights. Rather the numerous complaints issued to the newly formed HRC implicated local businessmen. In 1956, for example, a black real estate agent issued a formal complaint that his client "had applied for a mortgage at three banks, two mortgage companies, and a savings and loan association, without success." Four institutions, he said, "told them they did not have sufficient funds to make the loan, and two places reported they were making loans only to their own customers." Unable to secure a mortgage loan locally for his client, he turned to the Voluntary Home Mortgage Credit Program. In what became the typical progressive reform response, the "Committee instructed the Director to discuss it with representatives of lending institutions in the City." The HRC director, despite his progressive reputation, was Chamber of Commerce member Harry J. Kelley. Thus diplomatic resolutions seemed linked to finding people who hardly jeopardized the prevailing controllers of economic power.

Instead of setting a bold precedent, managerial racism formed the heart of the progressive reform movement. This proved true, in part, because Chamber of Commerce businessmen, such as the president of Union Bank and Trust Company Edward J. Frey, the Old Kent Bank and Trust Company Vice President Glenn A. Ferrey, and the Executive Vice President of the Michigan Trust Company Howard C. Lawrence, had no desire to frustrate business interests. Like Lawrence, who had conducted a wide variety of activities in politics, banking, and industry, the Chamber of Commerce desperately sought to strengthen its economic position. Lawrence, a Republican, served as state treasurer from 1931 to 1932, as state banking commissioner from 1936 to 1937, and as executive vice president and director of the Michigan Trust Company from 1937 to 1944. Perhaps it should come as no surprise that five of the twenty-three local representatives who collaborated with the FHA field agent were from Lawrence's Michigan Trust Company. Thus the city's commercial leadership cultivated an uneven playing field in the city's housing struggle.

With no proposed solutions except official neglect, the Chamber of Commerce was complicit in the construction of a divided city. The process of stratification "accelerated as people's fears, prejudices, and economic and social aspirations fed upon each other."[112] Many white citizens of Grand Rapids watched their neighborhoods turn racially mixed and "fled" as a result to the more appealing and racially homogenous suburbs. Their departures opened vacancies for more minorities, and this in turn "convinced the whites who were still in the city that fears of racial inundation were justified, and they, too, left."[113]

This was true in the Franklin School District, according to the GRUL study. Located in the heart of Grand Rapids, the GRUL research revealed "many of these white families [were] selling their homes to Negroes," as the "young white families [were] anxious to purchase homes elsewhere" to avoid the domino effect at Franklin School. Railroads consumed much of the total landscape of the district, which consisted of roughly sixty blocks: thirty-six residential and twenty-four industrial. Blacks lived on twenty-eight of the thirty-six residential blocks. These minority families lived in 259 dwelling units, and nearly half these units consisted of apartments. Often landlords "converted single dwelling units into small apartments" and received "as much as $225.00 per month from their renters."[114] Yet the landlords made no modifications to establish separate gas and/or electric facilities for their tenets. Moreover, building owners only provided gas and electric services to 10 percent of the renters, and landlords furnished fewer than 8 percent of all the minority tenant families with heat. Yet by the 1950s and 1960s, builders were making these amenities standard features in the new suburban homes.

In response to the problem of inadequate minority dwellings on a national level, President Dwight Eisenhower declared in 1954 that "many members of minority groups, regardless of their income or their economic status, have had the least opportunity of all our citizens to acquire good homes."[115] This was clearly the case in Grand Rapids, where many of the dwellings occupied by minorities in the Franklin School District were overcrowded and substandard. The GRUL revealed that the Franklin quadrant contained homes with "families consisting of twelve and fourteen persons . . . housed in four rooms."[116] In two cases, black families "consisting of eighteen persons were housed in a five-room house."[117]

In addition to the problem of overcrowding, nearly one-fifth of the facilities were cold-water flat homes that did not contain provisions for running hot water. Basic conveniences, such as heat, were often nonexistent. In 31 percent of the housing units, space heaters were used as the primary means of warmth. Overall, according to GRUL research, "one out of every five dwelling units was considered in poor condition." The majority of these substandard residences were located in the northwestern area of the Franklin district, where numerous black families interviewed stated that they would not enhance their dwellings because of "the rapid encroachment of industry into residential blocks, and . . . the proposed expressway which may take a considerable portion of the residential blocks."[118]

Nearly seven thousand families lived in substandard conditions in 1950, according to the census. Roughly 1,500 homes did not have refrigeration and 800 had no kitchen sink. These unsafe and unhealthful housing conditions affected the physical health of the residents in the "black belt." According to the Michigan Committee on Civil Rights, the poor living conditions made blacks more susceptible to "tuberculosis, pneumonia, rheumatic fever, and social diseases." The inadequate conditions proved especially detrimental for children living in the "black belt." In 1952, nearly 22 percent of all deaths in the black community in Grand Rapids occurred before the age of five, as compared to 6 percent of white deaths.[119] Thus deteriorated, overcrowded, and hazardous conditions adversely affected the well-being of the occupants living in the "black belt."

For obvious reasons, a number of blacks chose not to invest in dilapidated facilities. Given the fact that more than 65 percent of the homes located in the northwestern section utilized space heaters and nearly 80 percent lacked running hot water and the obstacles facing these minority residents crystallizes. Yet as the racial numbers shifted within the Franklin School District, so too did the housing conditions. The number of inadequate housing structures that used space heaters in the southeastern section dropped to 19 percent, while only

7 percent of the dwellings did not have hot water. The majority of the units farther east in the southeastern section, home to the largest number of white residents, were considered in fair condition, as every nine of ten families had hot water, while fewer than 16 percent of the dwellings relied on space heaters. Black residents in Grand Rapids faced barriers not posed to whites in the quantity of housing available to them, and the most evident difficulty remained the concentration or segregation of their neighborhoods from white metropolitan residents.

The Sheldon School District also demonstrated early signs of racial stratification. According to the GRUL, the "Negro population ha[d] increased tremendously in this area. . . . [T]he trend point[ed] toward the moving out, of more and more white families, and the moving in, of Negroes." Bounded by Division, Buchanan, Franklin, and Hall streets to the east and Division, Sycamore, Jefferson, and Highland to the west, this section consisted of thirty-two blocks. The majority nonwhite population lived in 172 dwellings located in the eastern portion of the district. Apartments represented 58 percent of all dwelling units. This was also true in the Henry and Sigsbee School Districts, where the entry of new minority families was small and tightly restricted. This area, bounded by Union, Wealthy, Eastern, and Sherman streets, served as the cutoff point between the black and white worlds of Grand Rapids, because no black families lived north of Wealthy Street. Movement toward the white occupied areas sparked reaction, as it was reported that "several white families [were] disturbed with the rapid influx of Negroes" into the neighborhood.[120]

A closer look at the condition of the houses located in the five highest black populated census tracts further highlights the disparity in the quality of housing between whites and blacks. For instance, according to the 1960 census, census tract 22 contained 255 minority housing units, of which 113 were considered deteriorating, 87 dilapidated, and 3 sound. However, sanitary facilities were lacking for a total of 203, or 80 percent, substandard dwelling units. Census tract 23 contained 808 nonwhite housing units: 352 were considered deteriorating, 92 dilapidated, and 34 sound but lacking sanitary facilities. Here again, more than half the nonwhite homes were considered substandard. In census tracts 24 and 26, at least 20 percent of the housing units occupied by minorities were considered substandard, while 19 percent of nonwhite homes in census tract 25 maintained the same designation.

Black families that lived in a five-to seven-room home did so at a rate of eight to ten persons, compared to the average of three to five white occupants living in the same size dwelling. Nearly 66 percent of the nonwhite population shared the living quarters of a multifamily dwelling, whereas 70 percent of Grand Rapids white families lived in single-family homes. This number accentuates the racial disparity in housing, as a nonwhite family could not select from the "many single family homes located in areas which [were] not available to them."[121] According to the GRUL, by and large, the dilemma of overcrowding in Grand Rapids stemmed from the "the inability of the Negro family to exercise freedom of movement or choice in type of home . . . , the crowding of more people into an inflexible area because of the influx from the South . . . , and the increased application of 'restrictive covenants' or of comparable action."[122] A housing crisis existed in the center city of Grand Rapids, and although the black community understood this truth, white residents continued to ignore the issue of discriminatory housing practices.

Grand Rapids lacked a suitable supply of low- and moderate-cost dwellings. Concentrated largely within the Campau district, minority overcrowding continued at a rapid rate throughout the 1960s. The black population of Grand Rapids increased nearly one thousand persons per year from 1960 to 1970. Because of the existing racial discrimination in the sale and rental housing markets of Grand Rapids, the majority of these new minority migrants moved into an all-black region called the "Model Neighborhood," or "black belt." Despite the influx of black migrants, "absolutely no new homes [were] built in the area for at least 30 years."[123]

Instead, in an effort to alleviate overcrowding, city officials permitted the conversion of numerous single-family homes into several smaller units. Although this process provided a roof top for some black migrants, it did not offer a more suitable living space. Moreover, according to the GRUL, the "number of units created this way" remained "offset by those demolished as a result of condemnation."[124] In 1967, city officials demolished nearly one hundred buildings located in the all-black Model Neighborhood area. The figure given probably doubles in actual family units due to the frequency of converting single-family homes into two-, three-, and sometimes four-family units. The inadequacy of these dwellings surfaced in an intensive code-enforcement inspection conducted by the city covering nearly 1,200 units in the "Model Neighborhood" area.

The report "showed that three-quarters of the units had housing code violations, and one-quarter were dilapidated or required major repairs even to meet minimum housing code standards."[125] This figure represented an increase in dilapidated housing units within the minority neighborhood since 1960. Furthermore, the results of the substandard homes accounted for in the survey also represented an increase from a study conducted in the same area five years prior, which clearly demonstrated the decline of these dwellings and the absence of policy initiatives to rehabilitate the neighborhood by providing newer homes.

The problem of discrimination did not settle or level off in the 1960s. Rather, by 1968, "less than 5% of the city's Negro population live[d] outside the all-black ghetto." Economic capabilities did not ensure justice in the Grand Rapids housing and rental markets. The few times black residents in Grand Rapids acquired expensive homes outside the prescribed black ghetto area, the rare transactions occurred from the "sale by the owner rather than through a realtor, and often the Negro buyer acts through a white intermediary and [purchased] the house sight unseen." The concentration of black residents into a confined territory actually "increased rather than decreased in the last 30 years."[126]

Even when lower-income families possessed enough money to afford rental housing, white landlords still "consistently denied [blacks] opportunity to rent."[127] White landlords preferred to keep their sizable apartment complexes vacant instead of renting to black people. One Grand Rapids landlord stated firmly, "I don't rent to colored in that apartment."[128] His statement confirmed the fact that two markets existed in the city. The discriminatory process and lack of "open occupancy" effectively limited opportunities for black residents. The housing structures, which ranged from thirty to one hundred years old, served as reminders to minority residents of the inequality present in their community. Although homes sprang up all along the urban fringe area and outlining suburbs during the postwar era, blacks did not receive a new home-mortgage loan within their "Model Neighborhood" until 1967. Even fire and home-owner insurance remained elusive in the "black belt" until 1968. How could black residents of Grand Rapids insure the future preservation of home items? Considering these facts, it made more sense not to own, especially because black residents who did own their "homes in this area [were] unable to get home improvement loans from banks, even where their credit [was] excellent."[129]

As southern black migrants began to occupy housing vacated by former inner-city ethnic whites moving to the suburbs, the ghetto area expanded. Black occupants left to exist in the deteriorated spaces of the inner city could not access the elusive suburban dream or participate in the racialized form of equal opportunity housing in the suburbs. Generations of blacks tried in vain to move outside the ghetto area as Floyd Skinner had prescribed, but corrupt real estate brokers, racist home owners, biased city officials, and prejudicial governmental policies restricted black access to the suburbs. Because of racial conservatism, the unmet promises of equality, veiled by de facto rhetoric and northern liberal auspiciousness, continued to retard the social and economic mobility of the black community. To better illustrate this point it is necessary to assess the racial outcomes of the American dream and reality in Grand Rapids.

Suburban Dream, Urban Crisis

A sign reading "Grand Rapids—All-American City" greeted drivers as they entered the metropolitan limits of Grand Rapids in 1961. A little farther down the road, in the central business district, pedestrians could view "car bumpers and sidewalk refuse cans, flags on buildings, floral displays—all heralding the home town." Even police donned their uniforms with shoulder patches that acknowledged the Grand Rapids municipality as an "All-American City." The prestigious award "was presented to Michigan's second largest city because of outstanding citizen teamwork in meeting major civic problems in a way that would benefit the community as a whole."[130]

The city of Grand Rapids received the award from the National Municipal League and *Look* magazine in 1961. It represented the second coming of the coveted award for the city. The first honor occurred in 1949, after the Citizens' Action group fight for good government managed to overthrow George Welsh and topple the McKay machine. This time the city was recognized for the basic improvements made to community living established through good government reforms under the leadership of reform mayoral candidate Paul Goebel. On both occasions, the city received the right to display the ubiquitous shield for promotional purposes, and on both occasions, the business leaders pushed the agenda. Ironically, beneath the shield, Grand Rapids was instead a city laden with racial difficulties that met the needs of the larger metropolitan area but failed miserably to address the concerns of the central part of the city. While accommodating the peripheral needs of Grand Rapids during the post-war economic boom years, city officials neglected to remedy the economic and social needs of inner-city residents. Racism continued to hinder the growth and development of central urban spaces. White racism intensified in "the discrimination and segregation of Negroes in employment, education, and in their enforced confinement in segregated schools and housing."[131]

Although the "white middle class, not wanting to be associated with the Negro, had begun to move to the suburbs,"[132] the forced concentration of blacks in the city widened the "black belt" and created more blighted areas in the city. The attempt to build outside Grand Rapids without investing in the central city proved costly, as racial isolation returned to haunt the metropolitan core region. The "All-American City" of Grand Rapids was hit with the cruel irony of financing the city's demise. As municipal officials lauded the distinction, which placed Grand Rapids as the "first city in the country to complete its freeway system,"[133] the hub of the city was increasingly in disarray and despair. Twenty-four miles of interconnected freeway spanned the city limits and supplied outlying areas with access to Grand Rapids.

With the assistance of federal funding, the expressways transformed the urban and suburban landscape, as these new arteries allowed masses of the white population and industry to reside comfortably outside the city. The arterial highways were only one of several structural forces that affected the center city.[134] The automobile, water and sewer development, utility-line extensions, and mortgage money for suburban expansion all facilitated the transformation of outlying pig farms into burgeoning suburbs complete with malls and industrial parks, with a nearby center city suburban dweller welcome to enter and exit leisurely. These suburban amenities produced "major commercial and industrial flight from the city," as peripheral growth also meant the "retail core contracted."[135]

Grand Rapids resident Ronald Vanderkooi recalled in the late 1950s how downtown Monroe Avenue was then a busy thoroughfare, and that there were no expressways "rushing us around town to provide 'free' parking at some shopping mall." He continued, "I do remember that crowds shopped in down-town stores and rode buses to get there. Other folks came from Kalamazoo and Muskegon eager to shop downtown Grand Rapids."[136] But with the advent of strip malls on the suburban periphery, fewer visitors frequented the shops downtown. Rogers Plaza, located beyond the suburb of Alger Heights, opened its doors in 1961 and sparked a suburban retail movement that "would establish 28th Street as the second busiest thoroughfare in state."[137] Shopping centers, such as Kentwood Mall, Woodland Shopping Center, and North Kent Mall, quickly facilitated an urban sprawl that enticed downtown businesses, such as Sarrat's, to relocate to the newly built suburban malls. Even "hotels closed as they lost out to motels along the expressway."[138] Thus, suburban development left the inhabitants of center city Grand Rapids with decaying buildings and shrinking economic opportunity.

Grand Rapids city officials began to grasp the dangers of suburban growth in the late 1950s. City Planner John Paul Jones "realized that downtown could not compete with the suburban retail centers."[139] Concerned about the financial exodus, Grand Rapids officials "sought a way to combat the problem of a shrinking tax base."[140] City officials considered the "New City" annexation plan, championed by the Chamber of Commerce, as a natural resolution. As a third-term Citizens' Action mayoral representative, Goebel sought to fulfill the expansion mission of the business coalition. With key reform advocates, such Dorothy Judd, at his side and the Chamber of Commerce at his disposal, the progressive mayor agreed to back the recommendations of the Grand Rapids Metropolitan Area Study (GRMAS) group, which advocated a total merging of services, including water, fire, sewers, parks and recreation facilities, police protection, health facilities, and schools. Thus the 1958 final plan promoted the unification of Grand Rapids and a large portion of the outlying suburban area, including Wyoming, East Grand Rapids, Walker, Paris, and Grand Rapids townships.

Edward Frey, president of the Chamber of Commerce, noted that "there isn't one person, one organization that can isolate itself and survive in our present, complex economic society." Backing the plan wholeheartedly, he argued that the merger would spawn an "atmosphere of confidence that will attract all types of businesses." Frey's assessment stemmed from past experiences, when Grand Rapids successfully employed annexation to preserve the city's tax base. But city services (i.e., water, sewer, and fire protection) no longer attracted established outlying suburbs, such as Wyoming, which had successfully managed to create their own infrastructure. Many of these suburbs had developed into industrial centers with employment opportunities that now attracted Grand Rapids residents. Thus the strength of the central city was waning. In fact, the results of the December 8, 1959, vote on the New City Plan made it clear that suburbanites ardently supported home rule over joining with Grand Rapids. Suburbanites rejected the proposal at a rate of nine to one, while residents of Grand Rapids favored expansion by nearly two to one. The results had confirmed a new reality: that perhaps the outlying suburbs now had more to offer than the city by the Grand. The newfound autonomy afforded suburbanites the luxury "to enjoy all the cultural benefits of the city-funded programs while only paying for the services that would specifically help their smaller community."[141] The underdevelopment of the central city suddenly placed Grand Rapids in a much more precarious position.

Blight raised maintenance costs and lowered the valuation of property. For example, according to the *Grand Rapids Press,* in 1966, "the city, county and Board of Education collected $93,691.98 less in tax revenue . . . than they'd collected five years before." The valuation of property dropped roughly $1,828,650.[142] Predictably, downtown Grand Rapids became a virtual ghost town by the 1970s, as "downtown stores, theaters, shops, and restaurants were closing, and downtown cruisin' had become an almost solitary exercise." Suburban flight had taken its toll on the inner city, as "19th-century buildings that had once been the pride of the city fell into neglect and disuse." Although Grand Rapids still stood as the predominant metropolitan player, the sobering reality surfaced that "the central city was now the largest in a cluster of municipalities that counted as many people living outside its borders as within."[143]

Individual and group prejudice successfully combined with legal and political sanctions to transform ethnic neighborhoods into racially stratified landscapes that produced a suburban oasis for whites. Moreover, a negative stigma developed regarding urban space, and the cost of racism became all too obvious by the mid-1960s. In 1967, City Manager Henry B. Nabers contended that "part of the problem here lied with certain ethnic groups' insistence on living separately," which "divide[d] the community." Therefore, in the years immediately following World War II, a disproportionate number of white suburbanites managed to live the "American Dream." Suburban havens afforded white residents with the prospect of newer, more spacious homes in less-congested residential space. The benefits of the suburban oasis extended beyond spatial aesthetics, as suburbanites managed to accumulate generational wealth through home equity, access to greater educational resources through newer school facilities, and more sanitary environments that produced fewer health conditions.

Despite the fact that many black residents "desire[d] to purchase homes elsewhere,"[144] or outside the spaces of the ghetto, restrictions were placed on their movement within and especially outside the city. The racial discrimination and ultimate segregated design of the Grand Rapids housing industry existed in varying degrees but extended into the sale, rental, condition, and location of the housing units. The housing industry excluded the majority of black home buyers from suburban residential areas outlying Grand Rapids and firmly limited their dwelling opportunities to the older and blighted areas of the center city with access to equally depleted resources. Inner-city neglect by city officials caused the taxable values of many properties to decrease. Thus given a shrinking revenue stream, increased blighted areas, and fewer businesses, blacks were left to manage an urban crisis while whites lived in an oasis amid the prosperity of the suburban dream.

Despite the emphasis on ethnicity in some areas, access to the "American Dream" hinged on the acceptance of a shared understanding of black inferiority established by segregationist policies and reinforced by individual discriminatory actions. However, for most residents in Grand Rapids in the postwar era, "ethnic difference among whites became a less important dividing line in American culture, while race became more important. The suburbs helped turn European Americans into 'whites' who could live near each other and intermarry with relatively little difficulty."[145] With the newfound construction of whiteness, based on property rights, racism in the post–World War II era effectively doubled its hegemony. Rather than decline, as sociologist William Julius Wilson had argued would be the case, race was redefined and solidified to establish and preserve suburban spaces. The rearticulation of racism manifested itself daily in the restriction of minorities to suburban landscapes, while the "possessive investment" in whiteness afforded whites' access to the "American Dream."

Despite protest and initial prejudice, a small number of blacks, such as the Claytor family, Dr. Franks, Triplett, Adams, and Lee, managed to penetrate the racially stratified suburbs of Grand Rapids. Whereas Franks and associates won the Fuller-Sweet Street battle against the City Commission, Claytor eluded the suburban eye test, because his skin complexion appeared white. Passing the suburban complexion prerequisite allowed Claytor the opportunity to live the "American Dream" like so many of his white skin-toned neighbors. A home in the suburbs allowed Claytor's stepson, Roger Wilkins, the opportunity to attend a resource-rich suburban high school and subsequently graduate and receive a college education from the University of Michigan. Similarly, according to historian Randal M. Jelks, Franks's Auburn Hill development demonstrated that "a neighborhood can be integrated, and can stand the test of time."[146] Yet the economic ability of so many black residents in Grand Rapids did not transcend their racial orientation. Instead blacks were limited by the renewed commitment to racial prejudice in the postwar era. The increased investment in whiteness assured that the urban crisis would fall squarely in the lap of the collective black community.

Therefore, situated in the inner city, the majority of blacks in Grand Rapids did not have access to the "All-American City." Stranded in the central city, these blacks sought to carve out rich lifestyles to help brighten the bleak condition of the increasingly apparent urban crisis. Unwilling to allow the circumstances of the inner-city crisis to define them, many of the members of Grand Rapids black community battled daily, both individually and collectively, to change their plight and chip away at the relentless internal and external forces of discrimination. Despite their efforts, the damage of post–World War II suburban development and simultaneous underdevelopment of the inner city forever changed the face of the larger metropolis. As blacks consistently attempted to grasp the elusive American Dream, racism assured that they would have to do so from the disadvantaged position of a city in crisis. Unwilling to withstand another generation of broken promises, young blacks began to make their voices heard. Their discontent with the city's racial structure emanated from within the school structure, but it soon overflowed into the community at large. The influence of black youth expression began to expose the regulatory function of managerial racism.

Sarah Glover, n.d.
(Grand Rapids History and Special Collections, Archives, Grand Rapids Public Library, Grand Rapids, MI.)

Grand Rapids Study Club ladies, n.d. *(Grand Rapids History and Special Collections, Archives, Grand Rapids Public Library, Grand Rapids, MI.)*

Emmett Bolden, South High School
Yearbook, 1919. *(Grand Rapids History
and Special Collections, Archives, Grand Rapids
Public Library, Grand Rapids, MI.)*

Chamber of Commerce,
Federal Square Building, n.d.
*(Grand Rapids History and Special
Collections, Archives, Grand Rapids
Public Library, Grand Rapids, MI.)*

Frank D. McKay, June 26, 1958.
*(Grand Rapids History and Special
Collections, Archives, Grand Rapids
Public Library, Grand Rapids, MI.)*

George Welsh, circa 1939.
*(Grand Rapids History and Special
Collections, Archives, Grand Rapids
Public Library, Grand Rapids, MI.)*

Helen Claytor, n.d.
(Grand Rapids History and Special Collections, Archives, Grand Rapids Public Library, Grand Rapids, MI.)

Dr. Robert Claytor, n.d. *(Grand Rapids History and Special Collections, Archives, Grand Rapids Public Library, Grand Rapids, MI.)*

Paul Phillips, Brough Community Center, February 5, 1947.
(Grand Rapids History and Special Collections, Archives, Grand Rapids Public Library, Grand Rapids, MI.)

South High School, Vocational Information Institute, August 12, 1957. *(Grand Rapids History and Special Collections, Archives, Grand Rapids Public Library, Grand Rapids, MI.)*

Ella Sims, n.d. *(Grand Rapids History and Special Collections, Archives, Grand Rapids Public Library, Grand Rapids, MI.)*

Lyman Parks, circa 1972. *(Grand Rapids History and Special Collections, Archives, Grand Rapids Public Library, Grand Rapids, MI.)*

4

THE MUSTACHE SAGA

The Rise of Black Youth Protest

South High School

During the 1960s, public schools were vibrant arenas of political and cultural contention, providing an open environment where children of various religions, races, and social classes interacted without parental guidance or supervision. For many Grand Rapids residents, the gap between what children were learning in schools and the values their parents embraced at home led to deep concerns. This cultural clash heightened their anxiety that the country was changing culturally and socially, and their fears were not unfounded.[1]

The high school students' rights movement became a nationwide phenomenon by the late 1960s. From hair debates, clothing styles, and dress codes to censorship and the First Amendment, students challenged the democratic principles of school officials. Theoretically, these students were adults-in-training. Yet school administrators seemed willing to endorse this notion only when student sensibilities conformed to the expectations of respectability established by the school administration and community. Students who deviated from the "norm," however, faced draconian sanctions.

In most cases, as noted in Gael Graham's *Young Activists*, school officials sought to "impose any rules they wished, including rules that had little to do with education and reflected instead the class, race, and ideological biases of the authorities."[2] Indeed this was the case at Brooklyn Technical High School, where the white principal, Isador Auerbach, routinely sparred with the black study body. Although black students represented only 20 percent of the school population, their political views often became the object of contention. Auerbach "ripped down a picture of Black Panther Eldridge Cleaver that students had posted in the cafeteria, claiming that Cleaver was a 'fugitive from justice,' not a positive role model." In a separate incident, the following year, Principal

Auerbach "called the police to remove a Black Nationalist flag from campus." He justified his action by claiming the law "forbade schools from flying any banner except the American flag." However no such law existed. According to the New York Civil Liberties Union, it simply represented "the lawlessness of principals."[3]

In 1969, at Owego Community High School in Illinois, the School Board decided "since there is so much similarity in the dress of male and female students who wear slacks and sweaters, there should be some way by which teachers could easily distinguish the boys from the girls." To achieve this distinction, the board banned "the wearing of a girl-style hair-do by boys."[4] In response to the dress code at Mariemont High School, in Cincinnati, former student Geoff Burkman remembered, "We pushed things as far to the limits as we could without actually trashing those limits. For instance, if the code said no sideburns below the bottom of the ear, then we all made sure we grew our sideburns (those of us who could) right down to that line."[5]

On occasion, adults failed to control their emotional response to student challenges. Marsh' Fenstermaker recalled "an art teacher taking scissors and personally trimming a girl's bangs after repeatedly asking the girl to do this herself."[6] Similarly, emotions ran high at Wellesley High School, in Massachusetts, when school officials failed to censor a portion of LeRoi Jones's play *The Slave*. When a large crowd of parents attended the subsequent School Board meeting to denounce the performance, one student-athlete began reading lines from the play that contained profanity. Some adults at the meeting became outraged and "went ape" as they proceeded to attack the student, yelling "kill him!" Confirming the bond between school and community authority, the police arrived and promptly arrested the high school student, not the riotous parents. Perhaps apropos, another student commented, "Here was America right before our eyes. . . . This is what America really is."[7] Unable to avoid this harsh and often problematic reality of school policies and politics, a similar incident at South High School would transform school-community relations in Grand Rapids.

The rich history of South High School produced such graduates as Michigan State University President John Hannah and, even more notably, U.S. President Gerald R. Ford. By the 1960s, the glory days of South High as the "flagship" of the Grand Rapids public school system had slipped into a distant memory. The changing demographics of Grand Rapids transformed South High into the most populated minority school in the city. For many whites, the influx of black students at South caused the meaning of "place" to take on a new racial and spatial definition. White residents remembered South High as a terrific school. It was considered the elite school to go to when Ford graduated from South. However with the influx of black students, South High developed a reputation as a disciplinary school, and residents labeled the students as difficult children. Thus, the changing racial demographics from white to black had contributed to South's being known throughout the city as a "tough school."

The memory of South was contested terrain. Blacks hardly embraced the same memory of South as did many whites. Such concerns as the absence of black teachers and the formation of a Ku Klux Klan "club" at South High during the so-called flagship era that whites spoke of fondly caused blacks to construct their own memories. For example, two former black South High sports stars, Emmett Bolden and Roger Grant, were litigants who helped desegregate the Keith Theater in 1927. Milo Brown, a GRNAACP member and former president of the Grand Rapids Urban League (GRUL) who attended South High, became the first black mortician in the state of Michigan outside Detroit. Brown unsuccessfully ran for mayor and city commissioner in the 1930s, but despite these two political losses, he continued to work feverishly for equal rights in the community and eventually cofounded the Progressive Voters League (PVL).

Bolden, Grant, and Brown were only a few of the South High graduates who were known throughout the black community for making contributions beyond their school days. Yet the intersection between place, memory, and identity for blacks who looked to South High as a source of pride remained a hidden chapter in the larger history of Grand Rapids. Whites failed to recognize the harmful contaminants of their whitewashed memory of South and simply expected blacks to embrace long-standing racist customs. Similarly, whites paid minimal attention to the rich tradition of South's history that many blacks in the community relished. South provided alternative heroes for the black community within a memory of inequality. As a result, the meaning of South High often underscored controversial community issues, and the school became the public theater for several acts of the black freedom movement.

The impetus toward increased racial tension heightened during the 1960s, as the South High School neighborhood developed a sizable black population. In 1965, roughly 1,037 black students and 945 white students were enrolled at South High School, which, of all the Grand Rapids high schools, had the greatest number and highest percentage of minority students. Following South's 52 percent were Central High with 23 percent, Ottawa Hills with 13 percent, and Creston and Union High with roughly 1 percent each. These were also the only high schools assigned additional assistant principals to institute a "tight rein on disciplinary problems."[8] But the School Board's increased emphasis on discipline often translated to members of the black community as a form of racial bias and a general cultural chasm between white educators and black students. The perception of random disciplinary acts by the School Board coincided with a notable decline in the academic reputation of South as the flagship high school of Grand Rapids.

Even many inner-city white families whose children attended South High contended that "the school had been permitted to fall behind."[9] In letters to the Grand Rapids school superintendent in 1960, white parents complained that the School Board had accepted a reduction in South's high academic standards because of "an influx of some students from other areas who have not had the opportunity of adequate education." As members of the Parent-Teacher-Student Association proclaimed:

> South High School is an integrated school. Its past history as a fine educational institution is a matter of record, but the community is changing and it is feared that the Board of Education and its staff have failed to make South High School an outstanding example, locally and nationally, of what can be done to make both White and Negro families proud of the school and proud that they live in a community that practices racial tolerance which is part of our American heritage.[10]

The merits of this claim gained additional strength, as it coincided with the GRNAACP's discovery of white teachers in Kent County who continued to routinely request transfers out of integrated schools. School administrators, the GRNAACP argued, minimized racial biases of white teachers that resulted in the subsequent miseducation of black students and instead highlighted adolescent conduct.[11]

The academic abandonment of South troubled white and black parents, but the prison atmosphere bothered students who experienced the conditions daily. Initially, few could conceive of a viable response, and the School Board relied on student silence to continue the escalation in school discipline. The School Board chose to make South High an example to assuage the rising concerns of parents in other schools that might find their minority populations on the rise. But the problem of containment became a community concern when reports in 1962 revealed that nearly half the black students in Grand Rapids quit school before graduating. This staggering statistic increased the fears of white community members beyond the South High neighborhood, as the ominous imagery of idle black youth lurking in the streets became cause for alarm. No longer was the ascension of chaos limited to the walls within segregated schools; instead, it posed a threat to the entire Grand Rapids community.

Education, Jobs, and Freedom

The complexion of school education changed dramatically in Grand Rapids during a short period of time. Dropout rates rose steadily, as black children elected to leave school at the minimum age of sixteen, which left them, according to the *Grand Rapids Press*, "ill-equipped to provide for themselves and to cope with the problems of American society." There was a time, according to the *Press*, "during the school-building boom of the '50's, when a popular illustration had would-be students standing before closed schoolroom doors, unable to get in because of overcrowded classrooms and inadequate facilities." At that time, black community members in Grand Rapids rang the bell of "equal opportunity" and "more schools"; however, the "Negro boys and girls who deliberately [did not] avail themselves of the educational opportunities for which the race has waged an unceasing fight" posed a unique and complicated dilemma within and outside the black community, the article noted.[12]

Black dropout rates from 1951 to 1958 rose steadily, and by the end of the decade only forty-nine black seniors graduated in 1960.[13] The increase in minority dropouts appeared to represent a discernible change in the mind-set of black youth. Dr. William Plummer and Rev. John V. Williams, president and Education Committee chairman of the NAACP, respectively, linked the drop-out issue to the systemic discrimination in the public schools in 1958. They voiced "deep concern" over the segregated assignment of teachers and noted, "Students are aware that there is a pattern of discrimination in the assignment of Negro-American teachers. This is damaging to the Negro student because he sees in his own educational system the segregation pattern; it is damaging to the vocational aspirations of students when those whom they should look as status symbols are victims of this pattern."[14] The Grand Rapids School Board's (GRSB's) inability to solve the predicament of racial imbalance allowed nega-tive circumstances to reach a boiling point, and in most cases the option of receiving a paycheck while facing discriminatory circumstances appeared more beneficial than remaining in school and enduring racial bias moneyless. There-fore, the racial inequity that accompanied racial stratification, along with a combination of factors, caused a number of minority youth to select employ-ment over education.

Dropouts posed a problem not only for educators but also for the commu-nity at large. When combining rising unemployment compensation and welfare budgets with low tax bases in black housing areas, it became evident, the GRUL argued, that "discrimination becomes an extravagance that society can no lon-ger afford." South High School counselor Tony LaPenna did not view the drop-out problem as an issue related to racism. Instead he attributed the rise in drop-out rates to "a backlog of drifting, misbehavior and lack of motivation" among black students. The School Board also cited behavior patterns, social problems, and home environments as the critical factors driving the current problem. Although the black community was less likely to agree with the perspectives of the school officials, "tough talking Paul Phillips, a Negro himself and executive secretary of the Urban League," the *Press* noted, "has one answer: 'It's moti-vation, or rather, the lack of it, that creates this I don't-care-attitude.'" Phillips challenged the black community to assume responsibility for the current prob-lems among minority students. He claimed, "The youngsters are not being motivated by the Negro community to improve themselves."[15] Instead, accord-ing to Phillips, black parents failed to define goals and encourage the ambitions of their children.

But the influx of black migrants generated a labor challenge for Phillips and the Urban League that was directly related to the dropout problem. Despite efforts by Phillips to secure employment opportunities for black youths through the "Skill Bank" program (a program designed to provide job training skills and seek employment opportunities for black youth), a report of sixty-seven other Urban League cities revealed that only four cities ranked worse than Grand Rapids in 1960. Although the city's total unemployment rate was 5.3 percent in 1960, the unemployment rate for blacks reached 14 percent.[16] Moreover, the available jobs relegated blacks to menial service positions, such as busboys, dishwashers, janitors, or elevator operators. Dissatisfied blacks in Grand Rapids complained that the moral persuasion methods employed by Phillips were often "too gentle, not to mention slow" and that they helped only a select few.

Many southern black migrants soon considered Phillips an "Uncle Tom" because of his alleged lack of forceful radical politics. Despite this criticism, Phillips "sympathized with the black impatience." However he resolved to dismantle racial barriers by invoking the politics of moral persuasion. Although on the surface many blacks interpreted his tactics as accommodationist, Phillips maneuvered within the white power structure. Political savvy allowed Phillips to operate behind-the-scenes with noteworthy success. He never ignored the unequal conditions separating blacks and whites, but the early success in Grand Rapids reinforced Phillips's commitment to moral persuasion, and, despite criticism, he remained faithful to that strategy throughout the 1950s and much of the 1960s.

As Grand Rapids entered the 1960s, Phillips recognized that his methods had fallen out of favor with the black community. He warned prominent whites "that black people were growing edgy and that an explosion could be expected."[17] The white community of Grand Rapids ignored his warnings, partly because of its own divided opinions of Phillips. The moderate tactics Phillips used found a favorable response among white community leaders. The managerial form of racism practiced by Chamber of Commerce members and business politicians placed whites in the role of patron and blacks as client. Designed to filter each racial issue, managerial racism ultimately sought to locate a "middle ground," as long as it was situated squarely on the interest-side of the "race managers."[18] Thus the application of managerial racism relied on strict procedures designed to bog down racial change while effectively presuming a position of compliance. Phillips's appeals satisfied the paternalistic prerequisite for advancement in Grand Rapids, because he operated within the traditional framework. Orderly black progress could occur at a piecemeal rate so long as the "managers" of race in the city approved and set the terms of agreement.[19]

Unsurprisingly, many whites on the opposite end of the economic spectrum, working-class Dutch and Polish residents, in particular, considered Phillips's aims and tactics radical and accused Phillips of being a "communist." Blue-collar whites believed that blacks needed to work, not bargain or negotiate, to obtain advancement within the community. Increasingly, in the early 1960s, whites throughout the nation associated civil rights with handouts for blacks, and the white community in Grand Rapids was no different.[20] For example, in a letter to Congressman Ford, Grand Rapids resident Charles R. Collins denounced President John Kennedy's agenda to expand civil rights, saying he did not "believe the colored people should have that much equality until they substantiate the right to it."[21] Another Grand Rapids resident, George Spruyt, added, "We cannot prevent the Negro in our Modern times to eventually be a part of our American way of life but it must not be done by putting the white race under a law of force."[22] These letters expressed the growing displeasure and resistance to black advancement within the white community of Grand Rapids. John Lamse, a real estate agent, summed up the voice of white opposition in a letter to Representative Ford:

> I do not believe that the earned "rights" of any minority are in danger. I sincerely believe that the ethical and legal rights of the majority are definitely in danger. Many of those in a position of great power and influence "stir in these racial waters," but most of them use such a long stick that none of the results spill on them personally. They have sufficient means to avoid the "fallout."[23]

Whites in Grand Rapids were convinced that the city's social structure was in jeopardy because of politicians conspiring with black residents to acquire their vote.

Black residents recognized that moral persuasion could not address the needs of the burgeoning community. The difficulty Phillips had encountered in acquiring jobs for a few dozen blacks meant that obtaining employment for thousands of new black residents through a piecemeal strategy of appealing to the social, moral, and ethical principles of the business community would be a Herculean task. Legislative politics in Grand Rapids decidedly favored a conservative majority, and the powers of moral persuasion proved slow and ineffective for the black masses.

Although Phillips's self-help ideology resembled the conservative sentiments of the school officials in their attempt to direct blame toward new black migrants, he acknowledged that Grand Rapids was "greatly affected by prejudice and discriminatory hiring practices." He also conceded that "even completing high school is not going to make things easy"; however, he believed "too many are taking the quick way out, blaming their own lack of initiative on external forces."[24] Phillips worked vigorously, however, to secure industrial employment for standout high school students. Although placed in jobs below their qualifications, these black youngsters sporadically obtained employment, which enabled them to develop some semblance of a working-class life.

All black community members did not share Phillips's viewpoint. Rather the efforts of the first black Human Relations Commission (HRC) executive director, Alfred E. Cowles, hired in 1961, and Charles Sims, a welfare caseworker, provided some different insights. A study conducted by the HRC revealed that in many instances, black students left school to support family members, while others dropped out because they could not "afford the cost of renting cap and gown, printed announcements and other expenses considered minor by their fellow students."[25] The report identified a number of critical factors listed by the actual dropouts. Regardless of whether the reason was a financially overburdened home or the inability to afford graduation items, it seemed apparent that economics played a critical role in students' decision process. Thus the "external forces" that Phillips and like-minded white Grand Rapids officials dismissed evidently played a more critical role in the everyday decision-making process of most black secondary students.

The surface reasons varied among each individual dropout. For instance, one black student, described as a "well-mannered Negro," decided to leave school after failing the tenth grade. The student, referred to only as Nathan, recalled, "I got a car that year; it wasn't the car's fault, it was mine." After repeating the tenth grade, Nathan chose to leave school just a few months prior to graduation. Reassessing the decision to drop out, Nathan entered night school to make up the final three credits he lacked and still hoped to participate in the June graduation. Nathan maintained aspirations for higher learning. He planned to attend the apprenticeship program in Junior College upon graduation. His vocational courses in high school demonstrated promise of becoming a good mechanic."[26] But Nathan understood, as did many black high school students, that obtaining a degree did not provide results in Grand Rapids. Rather, Nathan mentioned that "if and when [completed], he will go to Chicago. 'I can get work there and learn my trade. They're funny about that here.'"[27] Apparently, Nathan understood the racially influenced employment "score."

Ostensibly, black students did not see the value in graduating from high school. A degree did not equal economic and social mobility for many black students graduating from high schools in Grand Rapids. Rather the students who did remain in school simply found themselves a few paychecks behind the dropouts who left ahead of them to obtain the needed but menial wages to survive. In many instances the two students, "drop-out and high school graduate," worked side by side. This was the case with Nolan Groce and George Lowe.

In 1962, Groce, nineteen years of age, was employed at the Butterworth Hospital. After graduating from high school and spending a year and a half at the local Grand Rapids Junior College, Groce found work as an orderly for the hospital. His coworker, Lowe, twenty-one years of age, completed only the tenth grade before making the decision to leave school and start work. Lowe labored in the housekeeping department at the hospital. Their paths brought them both to the same organization, and, although in different capacities, both made the same wages. The aspirations held by both centered on returning to school someday. Lowe, married and the father of one, mentioned that he could not afford school, while Groce expected to return to Junior College and go on to obtain his medical degree. Yet the reality for both students was that education failed to translate into increased economic mobility. Thus race did not provide a distinction between a black graduate and a black dropout; rather, the structural barriers of race denied them both meritocratic opportunities and regularly positioned minority dropouts and high school graduates equally at the lowest level of society.

The crisis did not stem from lack of motivation as coined by Phillips, or even misbehavior as expected by the School Board. Instead the problem was much more basic. The HRC declared, "[The] problem is job discrimination." The figures from its study reported that the average salary for black high school graduates working in Grand Rapids was below $43 dollars per week, or "barely a living wage," mainly because the jobs consisted of unskilled positions and offered minimal opportunities for advancement (white high school graduates' average salary was $63). Black graduates from 1960 and 1961 illustrate this point. A study conducted at Aquinas College revealed that in two years, only 124 black high school students graduated and that of those, only 5 black women received jobs outside the service industry. Three were listed as sales clerks, and two worked as nurses' aides.[28] Additionally, a comparative study of white and black high school graduates for the same years indicated that black graduates faced greater difficulty obtaining work, were more likely to be unemployed, and secured fewer white-collar positions.[29] Therefore many black secondary students questioned why it was necessary for black youth to stay in school two years past the mandatory age of sixteen while family members at home suffered and the dropouts who left school ahead of them made just as much in wages without the high school degree, if not more.[30]

The discriminatory barriers facing black children inside and outside the school facilities within Grand Rapids increased the level of hopelessness. The consequence of being black in Grand Rapids offered limited opportunities. Discriminatory practices that failed to justly evaluate the talents of black youth often effectively dried up the potential life chances of the black youth. Realizing the futility of the present circumstances, many black youngsters simply opted to work now in a menial post rather than be disappointed later by working in the same tedious job with a degree in hand. One black student stated that there "are a lot of places in this town that won't hire colored folks. What good is it to go to school and get education if you can't use it when you get out?"[31]

The HRC research validated this concern. Its study on dropouts revealed that "finances, rather than racial problems, appeared to be the chief reason for leaving school, education seemed less important than the improvement of employment discrimination." The HRC resolved to address this issue and held a "drop-out conference" in October 1963. However, only fifty black parents showed up, primarily representing students who were not at risk. In planning the seminar, the HRC failed to consider its target audience. For example, the meeting was held on a Saturday, when most black parents worked. Communication regarding the conference was not sent through the school, nor did the

HRC contact parents directly. It failed to provide transportation and decided to hold the meeting in a church that most blacks never entered. Lewis B. Clingman notes, "The entire day was in fact aimed at a white, upper-middle-class audience of reformers and offered no real practical answers as to how concerned parents might influence their children to remain in school until graduation." Learning from these missteps, the HRC held another dropout conference at South High School on April 30, 1964. It asked black preachers and school administrators to notify parents, and despite a severe snowstorm, many of the "unreached" parents attended. But despite the solid turnout, the remaining five scheduled gatherings were canceled, and the "official records fail to explain why."[32]

White community members berated black dropouts and labeled them as a communal liability, and many whites argued that the dropouts would be ill prepared to "accept the responsibility of improving [themselves] and the community." Making a connection between the increased numbers of complaints of disruptive behavior in city parks, the police department "reported a direct ratio of Negro crime incidents with the percentage of Negro drop-out students," but it "provided no supporting evidence for this claim."[33] Yet many whites failed to acknowledge the abundance of black high school graduates from 1960 and 1961 who still faced unemployment as well as low compensation. Job discrimination, as a social problem, forced numerous black students to leave school early to "support large families," and many of these dropouts, as cited in the *Grand Rapids Press,* realized that "even completing high school [was] not going to make things easy."[34] The white community of Grand Rapids paid little attention to the economic dislocation of black residents within the community. Moreover, whites failed to realize the connection between joblessness and black student dropouts.

Rather than focus on economic inequities and biased hiring practices, whites in Grand Rapids emphasized the behavior and culture of black residents, particularly black youth. The solution offered to remedy delinquency within the school system further reinforced the treatment of integrated and predominately black schools as sites of crime, rather than sites of learning. It also vividly illustrated the shift from the perception of South High as an academic institution to a custodial facility for black students. But with nearly 48 percent of the population white, school officials emphasized conformity to minimize disruption caused by black students in school.

One tactic used to contain cultural intermingling was the implementation of dress codes, which were, in reality, a heavy-handed response to perceived threats associated with the mixing of races, classes, and cultures within the community. Schools across the country invoked dress codes as a means to "delimit fragmentation, to foster centripetal energies, and to provide students with a sense of commonality."[35] In other words, public schools endorsed conformity as a means to downplay individualism. Uniformity, or at least the appearance of uniformity, was designed to undermine cultural diversity while ignoring economic disparity and social injustices. Clothing, hairstyles, facial hair, and various dialects, however, were forms of identity and status that often served as a means for students, especially black students, to challenge the prevailing cultural norms.

Students

The fear over dropouts heightened in 1964, when two black juveniles recently expelled from school assaulted James Clayton, a white South High School science teacher. The incident occurred when the two students, aged fourteen and fifteen, were found roaming the halls after hours with a broken broom handle. As Clayton "reprimanded them for tapping the floor with the handle," one of the boys struck the teacher. Another South High teacher, Robert K. VanOveveren, went to Clayton's "assistance in the melee." The incident caused Clayton to resign. He referred to South High as an "unworkable situation" and said the attack was the result of "'laxness' on the part of the police and courts and the school administration." VanOveveren added that "he sympathized with his fellow teacher's position but he himself would not quit because 'I was there before these kids were and I think I have the right to stay. They will not drive me out.'"[36]

The incident put not only South High but also the entire black community under a microscope. It appeared to confirm the fears among white residents and to justify their clamor for more discipline. In response to the incident, former South High football coach Kent Esbaugh publicly stated that "morale was low" among South faculty. He pointed to delinquency as a contributing factor for his resignation in 1964. Esbaugh chided the administration for not clamping down on the lawless element. He stated, "If we are going to get to the point where we are ruled by intimidation we will be no better off than some backward countries." VanOveveren shared this sentiment and added, "[It] is a case of a few with bad natures. . . . I believe more teeth should be put into the law to curb the hoodlum element."[37]

The former South High student who had actually hit Clayton with the stick was caught, placed in custody, taken to the courthouse, determined guilty, sentenced, and finally jailed in a matter of a few hours. Furthermore, school officials determined that the former student would face a citywide ban from attending public school. When concerned parents asked the HRC to look into the matter, Dr. Jay Pylman advised the HRC "not to concern itself with the incident since it had been resolved by the court."[38] The HRC agreed. Although the assault took place after school hours, involved two previously expelled juveniles, and was an isolated occurrence, it increased white association of blacks with excessive crime. The swift handling of the teenager satisfied whites; however, Pylman sought to make sure nothing remotely close to this would occur again. He declared that the problem required disciplinary intervention, in which "the community, the schools, and the police all must work together for a solution."[39]

On August 12, 1966, a *Grand Rapids Press* article introduced Superintendent Pylman's plan for uniformity in the Grand Rapids Public Schools, reporting that the intention was to transmute the behavior of what Pylman called "delinquent youth" by changing their mode of dress and appearance. Without any supporting scientific data, Pylman and the School Board posited a direct correlation between "delinquency" and dress. Without further defining "delinquency," Pylman demanded that delinquent students align their social mores with those of the community through a strict discipline and grooming policy. Based on the assumption that boys' long hair and girls' short skirts reflected a lack of discipline and encouraged student resistance to established rules, the policy demanded that boys have "neat" haircuts, prohibited girls from wearing miniskirts, and required all students to tuck in their shirts and blouses and wear socks and shoes at all times.[40]

Pylman had served notice to the Grand Rapids community during the summer of 1966 that "the school system expects to maintain a tough policy this year regarding appearance, grooming and discipline" and that students were expected to "conform with the mores of the community." Superintendent Pylman stated, "99 percent of our children are clean-cut and responsible students . . . but we're not going to let that one-half of one percent lawless element dictate policy." Pylman allowed principals significant latitude to enforce the good grooming policy, declaring that he would "give the strongest backing possible to the principals and teachers."[41]

Certainly few held greater appreciation for a return to discipline than South High School principal and former Marine Charles Davidson. Davidson was very candid about his responsibilities at South. He came to South High as an assistant principal exclusively in charge of student discipline as part of Superintendent Pylman's plan to implement order. Davidson recalled how a top administrator with the Board of Education said to him upon his appointment to South High, "I want you to be known as the 'nigger knocker.'" Davidson agreed that "tough measures were necessary to rid South of a gang of discipline problems."[42] Instituting educational instructional programs was not Davidson's primary task.

Not everyone agreed with the extreme perception of lawlessness linked exclusively with South. Elmer H. Vruggink, assistant superintendent of Grand Rapids, disagreed with the distinct disorderly image of South. Instead he stated, "I don't think South was worse than any other school." Also, Joseph H. McMillan, director of the inner-city schools programs and the only high-ranking black employee with the Board of Education, substantiated this claim and added, "The biggest problem at South is shaping the instructional program to fit the needs of low-income, ghetto kids."[43] Davidson, however, viewed discipline as the chief form of education and pride. He and his fellow principals had been given significant latitude to alter the district's grooming policy as they saw fit, but only Davidson decided to restrict facial hair.

When contacted by the *Detroit Free Press,* Romulus Romani, principal of Central High School, agreed with the "grooming policy" but clearly stated that he had no problems with mustaches in his school. Similarly, Assistant Principal R. Carlson of Ottawa High School publicly agreed with Romani. The tenets of the original grooming plan, which dealt with dress standards and "neat haircuts," elicited little more than grumbling from students at South High when first issued. It was not until Davidson's autocratic enforcement of the ban of facial hair that resistance arose. In mid-October, five black students who refused to comply with the ban were suspended from school. After conferring with their parents, four of the five returned with every trace of facial hair removed, but when one student resisted, the mustache incident was far from over.[44]

Claiming that Davidson's no-mustache rule infringed on his "personal rights," the fifth student, Cleo Cross, chose not to shave, a decision that placed his academic career, his graduation, and a definite basketball scholarship in jeopardy. As a junior the previous year, Cross led South High in rebounding and was also the basketball team's third-highest scorer. Now, with college scholarships at risk, his resolve to remain at home rather than shave pointed to his determination to see the issue through. Cross explained, "I don't know how far I'll have to go, but I'm not gonna shave. If it means that much to them to have me shave, it means that much to me *not* to shave." It was not long before other black students, following Cross's example, also openly resisted with their bodies and a new moral fervor for racial justice. By early November, nearly thirty young men were sent home and told not to return until they were clean-shaven.[45]

Despite staunch parental support, student dissatisfaction had initiated the opposition, and student activism effectively sustained the movement. Still, the growing number of suspensions sparked community unrest. Expressing grave concern over the issue, black parents complained to Superintendent Pylman that the "policy as it related to mustaches was discriminatory to the Negro student."[46] Many supported the personal rights of their sons not to shave. Georgia Atkins, the mother of Melvin Atkins, another senior star athlete, charged, "If they put my son out . . . I'll go back with him. They'll have to put *both* of us out!" Cleo's mother, Lettie Ann Cross, summed up the brewing situation: "Cleo says he's not gonna change his mind and I'm not gonna change mine in backing him, so I guess the battle is on."[47] The School Board underestimated black youth discontent at South. Similarly, the capabilities of secondary students escaped the attention of school officials. Unmoved, Pylman issued an official statement on behalf of the Board of Education "backing Mr. Davidson's decision to prohibit students from wearing mustaches."[48] The battle lines were drawn, and the School Board left black students with only one option: Shave their mustaches or leave public school.

Lettie Ann Cross personally appealed to Davidson to readmit her son, mustache and all, but he refused. Lending support to her position were Ray Tardy, head of the Sheldon Complex, a Grand Rapids social welfare agency that operated antipoverty programs, and his brother, Mel, also on the agency staff. The brothers were among the first adults to publicly maintain that Negro youths grew mustaches to "emulate their fathers," that mustaches were a symbol of the passage from boyhood to manhood, and that wearing them was "part of the black man's culture." Ray Tardy noted that "nine out of 10 Negro men have a mustache," citing among them such notable black leaders as Dr. Martin Luther King Jr. and NAACP executive director Roy Wilkins.[49]

A small number of Cross's supporters, led by Ray Tardy, met with Davidson, Pylman, and two members of the Board of Education behind closed doors to discuss the dilemma. At the acrimonious meeting, Tardy attempted to articulate the cultural significance of mustaches in the lives of black males. Stressing the magnitude of the issue, Tardy proclaimed, "We want the Negro boys to emulate the successful national Negro leaders, nearly all of whom wear mustaches." Several ministers who attended asked if, instead of completely eliminating mustaches, the "order could be rewritten to permit boys with neat shaven mustaches to attend school." Insensitive to the cultural distinctions drawn by Tardy and others, Pylman claimed the "school's total interest was in educating the children and that rescinding the directive would weaken South's program for authority." Ultimately, Pylman backed Davidson's unsubstantiated rationale that "having clean-shaven students was more conducive to the learning atmosphere."[50]

For his part, Davidson scoffed at the idea of mustaches being representative of black cultural heritage. "I can't buy this heritage bit," he said. "My good Negro friends tell me this is nonsense." Disputing Davidson's position, the *Grand Rapids Times,* a local black weekly newspaper, printed the photos of eleven well-known black male leaders—all wearing mustaches. The *Grand Rapids Times* also reprinted a 1953 *Jet Magazine* story, "Why Negroes Wear Mustaches," by University of Chicago sociologist Donald Pearson. Contending that "80 percent of Negro men lean to a hair-adorned instead of a clean-shaven lip," Pearson also included explanations as to why various black men chose to wear mustaches. Famed photographer Gordon Parks recalled that he grew his first mustache as a boy "to apply for a man's job" and had maintained it ever since. Dr. Ira Reid, retired Haverford University sociologist, said he grew his mustache simply "because his father wore one."[51] In short, the cultural argument was well documented in 1953. But Pylman and Davidson either overlooked the supporting documents or possibly understood them well but felt that black cultural practices had minimal value.

Davidson said that he did not want to create controversy but instead to provide a more congenial atmosphere for learning and to make the students of South High "as proud as they can be of our school."[52] But self-expression was a critical source of cultural pride for black students at South High, and a number of them believed that they were being denied the right to exercise control over their own bodies. Although Pylman's grooming policy applied to the entire

Grand Rapids school district, Davidson's no-mustache edict was exclusively enforced in the high school with the largest minority population. At a historical moment when, nationally, more young blacks began to consciously emphasize cultural heritage, employ direct-action protest, and articulate "Black Power," Davidson's policy illustrated the gulf between white school administrators and majority black student populations. According to historian William H. Chafe, the wave of black youth "who came to maturity during the halcyon days of the civil rights struggle . . . remembered history began in 1960, not in 1954 or 1945; thus the sit-ins represented a starting point, not a culmination, of protest."[53]

The reference points for black secondary students in 1966 included the pivotal shift in protest tactics witnessed in the Greensboro sit-in of 1960, the increased youth participation with the founding of the Student Nonviolent Coordinating Committee (SNCC) that same year, subsequent freedom riders, visible urban rebellions in 1965, and the public call for "Black Power" in 1966 by Stokely Carmichael. Ironically, these same crucial national events also prompted white leaders in Grand Rapids to institute petty regulations. According to an article in *The Education Digest,* "Trivial regulation is more damaging to one's sense of one's own dignity and to the belief, essential to any democracy, that one does have inalienable rights"; therefore, restrictions such as the no-mustache policy functioned to "convince youth that it has no rights at all that anybody is *obligated* to respect, even trivial ones."[54] Through managerial racism, white administrators had attempted to delineate proper behavior, define appropriate responses, and dictate suitable negotiations for the black community.

Keeping with the managerial system, the mayor directed the Grand Rapids HRC to help combat discrimination by investigating the mustache situation on October 28, 1966, to determine whether "racial overtones" colored Davidson's no-mustache order.[55] HRC President Eugene Sparrow privately felt that numerous whites remained ignorant of the intimate and implicit symbols shared among blacks.[56] Yet despite his clear opposition to Davidson's policy, Sparrow toed the line; the HRC, serving as another arm for the City Commission, city manager, and mayor, publicly supported the call for discipline and remained muted on the issue of race. The HRC proceeded ever more cautiously after a few members "had become very outspoken in their condemnation of the City Commission" in 1965, and, consequently, the City Commission "reduced the total membership of the [HRC] from twenty-one to fifteen." Although Mayor Christian Sonneveldt argued that the reduction would ensure greater efficiency, the reconstituted HRC did not include any members who publicly criticized the City Commission. A number of organizations "accused the Mayor and City Commission of reducing membership in order to remove 'controversial trouble-makers.'" As a result, Clingman notes, "the majority of the [HRC], therefore, were not, nor did they want to be, involved in what they considered merely a school disciplinary issue."[57]

The *Grand Rapids Times* reported that "the real issue was that the white majority and many self-styled Negro leaders simply have not been in contact with the mass of the people in the Ghetto area."[58] More black community members began to publicly echo the sentiments of the *Grand Rapids Times,* and on November 8, 1966, more than three hundred citizens, including ministers and civil rights activists who formerly supported "gradualism," held a mass meeting at New Hope Baptist Church to condemn the mustache regulation. Although Davidson claimed his position had nothing to do with race, many blacks felt differently. The disagreement was about much more than a disruption in the learning process. Lettie Ann Cross, for one, did not "feel a mustache had a thing to do with education," and, referring to the mounting racial tensions, added, "I am not fighting a mustache issue but a lot of problems."[59] Among them was the fact that Davidson was South's third principal in the past six years. Administrators also found it difficult to find teachers who wanted to work in the integrated high school. Finally, the measures taken to improve academic performance at South High continually focused on increased discipline, as suggested by the hiring of assistant principals with the sole purpose of ordering student behavior. The mustache mandate was just another restriction that many students and parents felt was unjust. The controversy also represented an opportunity to openly express dissatisfaction with the existing conditions within the inner city.

Despite several acrimonious negotiating sessions, the contending sides in the dispute were unable to reach a compromise. Fearing that the issue could quickly escalate into a citywide problem, Mayor Sonneveldt, former Chamber of Commerce president, called both sides together and requested that Dr. Donald H. Bouma, a Western Michigan University professor, facilitate a discussion. Participants in the closed meeting on November 12, 1966, included Superintendent Pylman, Principal Davidson, representatives from the Sheldon Complex and the Urban League, and an unidentified parent of a South student. The two sides managed to draft a formal statement that affirmed "support by the community of the general standards of dress and conduct." The statement also put "school officials on record for the first time as willing to revise the policy," although they did not specify how.[60]

The Walkout

While city leaders debated the issue behind closed doors and Cleo Cross remained suspended from school, black students assembled in basements, houses, and other places to discuss the problem. From mid-October until November 15, the *Grand Rapids Press* repeatedly informed the community that the mustache policy was being appraised and revised but offered no tangible proof to the students that their concerns were being addressed. Managerial racism effectively operated through gradualism, and school administrators along with city officials in Grand Rapids attempted to utilize this approach to handle the school controversy. Traditionally, sitting down and discussing the issue likely would have cooled the dispute and allowed the GRSB time to implement a study regarding facial hair and educational policy. However, frustrated by the lack of action and equipped with a new inner awareness, the students acted in their own interest and staged a demonstration.

On Wednesday, November 16, 1966, approximately four hundred black students marched out of South High School to protest a newly implemented "good grooming" policy put forward by school Superintendent Pylman with the approval of the GRSB. The walkout occurred against a backdrop of civil rights demonstrations in nearly every city. Student-led demonstrations represented a new approach to challenging American racism. Nearly eleven months after the Greensboro sit-ins, more than a hundred towns desegregated lunch counters as a result of student-led direct-action protest.[61] These demonstrations crystallized the precocious political awareness of young blacks and sent shock waves through cities across America.

Significantly, although these black students were the last individuals white leaders imagined consulting to assess racial dissatisfaction within the black community, the students' organized protest at South High offered the first direct-action protest and served as a symptom of the larger black community's discontent with the politics of moderation. It did not take long for black parents to follow in the footsteps of their children's direct-action approach. The students' actions had a transformative effect on parental consciousness. The day after the student protest, a number of black parents demonstrated openly for the first time in the city's history at South High. They "picketed quietly outside the school" and carried signs that read "THIS IS MICHIGAN NOT MISSISSIPPI."[62] Most of the students who walked out the previous day returned to school to avoid additional disciplinary action. The parent protest demonstrated resistance within the black community to Davidson's decree and the procedural format employed to handle all racial grievances. But not everyone in the community had the same viewpoint, and the student protest only enhanced the intraracial divide.

Philips, who was the only black GRSB member, supported the decree imposed by Pylman and Davidson. Phillips had fought to obtain educational rights for the black community just as he had for jobs in his position at the Urban League. But his statement at an emergency School Board meeting that followed the protest demonstrated a conflict of interest between his politics of moderation, political position, and middle-class status and the direct nonviolent strategy employed by politically underrepresented working-class black parents. "This has gone beyond the issue of moustaches and is now in the realm of respect for authority," he said. "The majority of Negroes in the city and at South High School respect law and order. If some decide individually they don't like a law and break it, then that becomes the law of the jungle."[63] The high-brow response toward the actions of black protesting families underlined a growing divergence in the black community over the struggle for equality.

Some black parents rallied to support Phillips's view and defended Davidson's actions. Fred Johnson, a local businessman, and Rebecca Scott, the wife of a Grand Rapids police officer, came forward to "express opposition to the walkout at South High School . . . over the school's ban on student moustaches." About thirty black parents met on a Tuesday night to "support the authority of the school to make and enforce rules."[64] To many middle-class black parents, the issue was not about racial discrimination or about black culture, but about racial uplift ideology, which centered on assimilationist strategies to obtain progress by accepting dominant white definitions of respectability. Hoping to preserve the gains made through the politics of moderation, Phillips even went so far as to offer an apology to the white community and issued a plea for conformity to black residents. As he told a *Grand Rapids Press* interviewer, "I'm very sorry this has degenerated into a racial issue. But even if we don't like laws we must obey them."[65]

Phillips's position on the necessity of obeying the law underscored many of the white perceptions regarding South High. A November 23, 1966, WOOD-TV editorial claimed, "Mr. Davidson probably wrote tough rules because of a minority at South who go to the toilet on the floors, attack girls, assault teachers, and otherwise act like animals. If the involved people will work to control the 'animal' element with the same fervor they attacked the mustache ban, we'll have a better city."[66] The editorial referred to black protestors as "animals" numerous times. Such callous commentary with comparisons of black action to animal behavior caused many of Phillips's opponents to wonder whether room existed for the politics of moderation in such a racially charged community.

Feelings about the controversy ran high, and letters to the editor inundated the *Grand Rapids Press.* Several citizens even went so far as to write to request assistance from Congressman Ford. One black woman, Theresa B. Crawford, wrote, "I consider myself fairly well read; have talked with a number of educated negroes . . . and . . . no one I have talked to knows or has even heard that [a mustache] is a part of our culture."[67] Doris G. Hall, a white parent of a South High student, felt that a good integrated school experience would help prepare her children for the future. In her letter to the *Grand Rapids Press,* Hall pointed out that many families had "deliberately chosen to live in the South High District," and she expressed support for the nearly six hundred black students who chose to remain in school and not participate in the walkout.[68]

With the new direct-action approach of the school walkout and Cleo Cross still remaining out of school, the resolute intention of the students became very apparent. These students began to change the mood of the black community. To apply more pressure, high school students used the resources and materials of the Sheldon Complex to send out news releases on the mustache issue and publish pamphlets on what they saw as the restriction of their rights. With the help of Tardy from the Sheldon Complex, students even initiated a neighborhood petition that resulted in the acquisition of nearly three thousand signatures from local community members supporting the rights of the students to wear mustaches. The incident caused Dorothy Hoogterp, South High School nurse, to lose her job because she authored a poem in support of Cleo Cross that was printed in the local black weekly.[69] The rising publicity surrounding the mustache controversy caused reaction on a statewide level. Bill Gill, the NAACP state adviser, characterized the South High School situation: "This isn't a public school, this is a prison," and he promised to take the matter directly to NAACP State President Albert Wheeler of Ann Arbor.[70] Finally, in late November, the mustache saga gained national exposure with the publication of an article in *Jet Magazine* about the controversy that articulated black student concerns regarding the school policy, explained the cultural meaning of facial hair in the black community, and challenged Davidson's handling of the dress code.

The unflattering regional and national publicity, together with local pressure, finally influenced the Board of Education to intervene. On December 1, 1966, the board announced the formation of a "committee of 15 South High School area citizens, parents, teachers and students . . . to review the good citizenship, good grooming policy at South." With the committee composed of a cross-section of the South High district and not simply the managerial elite members, the political playing field started to level. The South High Review Committee included four black parents, two black community leaders, one black student, and one black teacher along with five white parents, one white student, and one white teacher. Perhaps most important, black students finally had a seat at the table.[71]

Community members, black and white, young and old, now had an opportunity to play active roles in deciding the future direction of their school. With disgruntled students threatening to organize a second walkout, the committee promptly met and wasted no time in returning a verdict. By a vote of 12–1 (the two students had advisory, not voting, roles), committee members recommended rescinding the ban on student facial hair and suggested that the board could "permit a student to have a neatly trimmed, nonconspicuous mustache not extending beyond the extremities of the upper lip."[72] On January 25, 1967, acting on the committee's recommendation, the Board of Education voted in a new policy that said student "facial hair must be neatly shaved without beards, goatees or excessive sideburns."[73] With the ban lifted, Cleo Cross, mustache notwithstanding, was free to apply for readmission to South High after a suspension that had lasted roughly two months. By the time he returned, the basketball season was nearly over, and although he graduated with his class, he could not rejoin the team and realize his dream of a college basketball scholarship because of his decision to protest.

Davidson also found his career dramatically altered. Remaining with the Grand Rapids Public Schools, he was eventually demoted to assistant principal responsible for discipline and activities at Creston High School shortly after an "unauthorized teacher walkout" took place at South High in 1967. He was subsequently fired during the 1970–1971 school year from Creston "because of a larceny conviction . . . that led to a 30-day jail stay and $100 assessment."[74] Reflecting back on the South High walkout, Central High assistant principal Al Jackson recalled that "he disagreed with Davidson's account of the mustache ban that led first to the suspension of a black athlete, later to several other students." According to Jackson, "The ban 'lost Davidson the trust and confidence of most of the black community.'"[75]

It also widened the gap between the black community and the GRSB. The GRSB took note of the events at South High, which had revealed a new form of black political power and the youth standing at the center of the movement. Phillips's prophetic warning fully realized by school officials would need greater attention. Thus the direct-action protest led by the black secondary students at South High served as the defining event that altered the course of civil rights activism in the city. The GRSB members now had to plan for the unexpected and to anticipate incipient movements before they occurred. The rising tide of black disaffection surfaced citywide, and it provided another reason why the GRSB had to finally respond to the recommendations made by the committee of fifty-two and release the School Board's "Master Plan" for the city's public schools.

Black Political Power

The controversial incident of 1966–1967, which centered on the wearing of a simple mustache, broadens the conception of the civil rights movement to include youth participation, daily struggles, and cultural shifts that sustained the movement on a day-to-day basis. Assessing the everyday strategies to exert power and create space within culturally biased institutions is a way of understanding not only overlapping approaches of those blacks who vigorously articulated resistance but also the responses of those who imposed the various restrictions. Therefore the mustache saga bridges the gap between the social and cultural worlds of "everyday" political struggles of black students in Grand Rapids. The incident demonstrates how racial formation and the negotiation of rights for political gains played itself out through quotidian forms of black resistance that often blurred the line between civil rights and black power.[76]

In subsequent years, black student grievances would become more common and outspoken. For example, on Chicago's South Side, black students at Hirsh High School staged a walkout on April 2, 1968, to denounce "Operation Snatch." According to Dionne Danns's *Something Better for Our Children,* the plan was designed by Principal William J. Kelleher to curb student tardiness. Students found in the hall after the bell were subject to being snatched into a random classroom and held there until the end of class period. What would have been a tardy now became a class absence, and administrators punished students accordingly. Additionally, students decided to protest the postponement of an Afro-American Day. Unlike in Grand Rapids, the *Chicago Defender* reported, "The walk-out turned violent as rocks and a five-gallon gasoline can were thrown into the building. The gas can exploded at the entrance to the cafeteria." As a result, "classes were dismissed and the police were called in." Although the level of frequency, form of protest, types of demands, and outcomes varied, the one constant in Chicago, Brooklyn, and Grand Rapids was the desire for black student inclusion in decision-making affairs. The highly politicized student atmosphere often transcended school boundaries and proved impactful at the community level.[77]

As an example of the racial and cultural differences facing Grand Rapids and especially its public schools during the 1960s, the "Great Mustache Controversy" offers insight into political and social beliefs held by many whites and the development of racial identity and political strength, led by black youth, within the black community. By providing a clearer sense of how socially constructed meanings of race play out in everyday experience, the incident demonstrates how high school students engaged politically and how their actions came to include racial issues and provided the Grand Rapids black community with a rallying point for the black freedom struggle.[78]

If the authoritarianism imposed at South High had been an attempt to break the spirit and will of black students and impose the values and mores of the dominant Grand Rapids society, it had the opposite effect. The mustache ban became the rule that broke black patience. The incident helped infuse a new political consciousness and political assertiveness within the black community. Numerous editorials refused to believe that black students alone could orchestrate a walkout, newsletters, pamphlets, and petitions. Rather these editorials blamed a "few self-seeking adults in the Negro community"[79] and assumed that the "animal" element at South could not possibly operate so efficiently. The secondary students did organize efficiently, but it was done in an unfamiliar way to most residents in Grand Rapids. The actions of these students exceeded any local white expectations but mirrored the resourceful actions taken by black youth in numerous other communities. The naïve presumption of the editorials also failed to comprehend the larger issue: The student walkout signaled a new tactical shift in the Grand Rapids freedom struggle. The direct-action protest of the students set the tone for more assertive forms of collective self-expression. Their efforts caused many black activists to question the sole use of moral-persuasion tactics. Yet the students' willingness to negotiate once included in the dialogue demonstrated that direct action could serve as a means to a nonviolent, negotiated end.

The dialectic between assertiveness and moderation in the Grand Rapids black community required a new consideration. Certainly the mustache incident did not explode the managerial race system that governed the city. Neither did direct-action replace the politics of moderation within the black community. Rather it offered a new tactical alternative in the struggle for black equality that on occasion overlapped or intersected with other methods. Furthermore, the incident accentuates the consciousness of black youth. It offered high school students an opportunity to define the black freedom struggle and express their determination to retain their personal dignity after the implementation of disciplinary measures they regarded as restrictions on their individuality. Moreover, it served as the defining event for a new generation of black activists who from that moment constantly chipped away at the cornerstone of white authority in Grand Rapids because they dared to operate outside the conventional moderate approach to change. Thus, black student activism ushered in new strategies to convey continued frustration with America's racial policies.

To be sure, secondary students led this new movement; however, the literature on the civil rights movement has focused primarily on the role of college students. Although they were aware of the college protest movement, high school students did not simply imitate college activists. Rather, secondary students became increasingly politicized from defining moments in their own day-to-day experiences, and quite often these issues were decidedly manufactured at the local level. Thus, by attempting to compel school officials to recognize their rights, black high school students routinely challenged traditional social and cultural conventions. From demands for black history courses, black teachers, better facilities, and support for black students, youth rebellion at the secondary school level helped shape the course of the black freedom struggle as well as provided aesthetic solutions to contemporary problems. Aware of the limits placed on them by race, class, and age, these more self-consciously rebellious students redefined notions of respectability and privacy that aligned with their beliefs. Black youth emphasis on racial dignity, cultural heritage, and the power to determine black identity free from white authority in Grand Rapids affords a microhistory of the national trends within the black freedom fight.[80]

Less inclined to have access to "traditional" political power, secondary students relied heavily on nontraditional politics. The results of unorganized social-political movements like the mustache incident rarely surface in the legislative record and therefore remain veiled within a civil rights historiography that emphasizes normative values, highlights national leadership and national institutions, and presumes that policy changes are the most accurate measures of the civil rights movement. This top-down perspective conceals the complexity of the movement and suggests that the movement can be understood only through large-scale national events, while the social fabric that supported the day-to-day struggle at the local level remains obscure.[81] Instead, small-scale skirmishes or discursive conflicts often shifted into organized and collective movements. As James C. Scott and Robin D. G. Kelley have revealed, the effects of daily acts of resistance or the "hidden transcript" is visible in the creation of new cultural "subjects." That is, the movement creates a new collective identity by presenting participants with a view of themselves and their world that conflicts with the worldview and self-concepts offered by the established order.[82]

The mustache saga reveals how such factors as region, class, ideology, gender, and age shaped black resistance to oppression; the saga also helps identify why and how participants adapted throughout the struggle for black rights. Black activists routinely modifying their protest tactics and such complex arrangements reveal why it is necessary to move beyond the binary classification of the civil rights movement and black power movement: These two separate paradigms disengage the transformative nature of the black freedom struggle, black self-consciousness, and black culture.[83] Finally, the incident set the stage for increased protest activities that forced the GRSB to respond to the needs of the black community. Thus South High students forced the board to reassess the power and threat of youth activism. In doing so, the GRSB made a calculated move that subsequently created rumblings throughout the entire community and seemingly jeopardized the city's neighborly reputation.

5

A BLACK CHILD'S BURDEN

Busing to Achieve Racial Balance

Racial Balance

"Must we have our children standing before us all of the time?" This May 15, 1971, article in the local black newspaper asked readers to reassess why children were on the front line of the freedom struggle in Grand Rapids. The author warned, "If you as parents don't make up a plan of action your children will take action—either for better or worst [*sic*]." Indeed it was becoming quite apparent that black student direct-action protest had taken center stage since the South High walkout.[1]

The 1966 school walkout began to reflect national trends toward a more expressive form of black freedom activity, but it by no means marked an end to the pursuits of an older generation of black activists. Instead it began a shift whereby a younger generation of black protestors moved forward to carry the torch. The mustache saga heightened awareness of a rising youthful black population more open about expressing frustration over the prejudices that impacted their entire community. However that conflict only scratched the surface of black frustration. Discontent over segregated schools, deteriorating neighborhoods, housing discrimination, declining economic opportunity, and broken promises boiled to a new level by the mid-1960s, but did it represent enough to ignite citywide rebellion in Grand Rapids?

"Or Does It Explode?"

On Sunday, February 14, 1960, famed poet Langston Hughes came to Grand Rapids to lecture in a public forum held at Fountain Street Baptist Church. Known for his numerous short stories and plays, Hughes inspired generations of blacks with his ability to make visible the beauty, dignity, and frustration of the black community.[2] Two members of the Grand Rapids Study Club (GRSC), Ethel Coe and Louise Baldwin, served as cochairwomen for the GRSC-sponsored event.[3] The GRSC was responsible for bringing a wide range of notable black guests, such as the Fisk Jubilee Singers, Louis Lomax, and Etta Moten, to widen the scope of black cultural contributions.[4] Among the scores of renowned black visitors Coe had welcomed to the city, she held a special affinity for the self-proclaimed "literary sharecropper." In particular, Hughes's 1951 poem "Harlem" had direct relevance to the decade of educational, economic, and political indifference of the city's progressives and the rising transition in black resistance. In "Harlem," Hughes asks, "Does [a dream deferred] dry up like a raisin in the sun?"

Taking the title of her play from Hughes's poem "Harlem," Lorraine Hansberry wrote *A Raisin in the Sun,* which debuted on Broadway in 1959. Coe felt so strongly that the poetic message of "Harlem" revealed the black community's exasperation that she decided to audition for the Grand Rapids Civic Theater's run of the play.[5] According to the *Grand Rapids Press, A Raisin in the Sun* told the story of the "angers and frustrations of a young Negro in his fight for a decent job and decent housing in the world of prejudiced whites." Coe identified with the play's seriousness of purpose and hoped it would generate greater awareness of the shifting trends in the city. The play captured the city's imperfections and the growing discontent of a frustrated black community living the day-to-day heartache of a "dream deferred." "The 'message' cannot be ignored," Coe stated. The local production of the play, which featured all nonprofessionals, was sponsored by the GRSC and opened February 1, 1966.[6]

But by 1966, the play appeared as a mild protest on urban racial problems. By the mid-1960s, grievances over second-class conditions had exploded in inner cities across the country. During the summers of 1965, 1966, and 1967, racial uprisings broke out from Los Angeles to Detroit to Chicago. Although still relevant, the social impact of the play was giving way to a new resolve. In February 1966, Coe admitted she was "out of step with the young leaders of today." She recalled, "One Negro here called us old-timers." However, Coe correctly noted, "We were active long before these young ones came up and I feel we plowed the field so the progress that has been made would grow." In fact, Coe came to Grand Rapids when she was ten years old. In 1919, she "was refused service in an ice cream parlor," but her uncle, Stanley Barnett, decided to take the case to court. "We won," she recalled. Coe "was one of the first Negroes involved in a legal fight for civil rights," according to an article in the *Grand Rapids Press.*[7]

She later graduated from South High School and went on to complete nearly a year and a half of junior college.[8] Coe subsequently joined the GRSC, where she continued her education and support for black youth in the community. For example, in 1966, Jerry Whittington was one of a number of black South High School graduates to receive the Grand Rapids Study Club

Scholarship-Aid Award. The proceeds from such occasions as the production of *A Raisin in the Sun* allowed the GRSC to provide funds to South High students, such as Whittington, to help ease some of the financial cost associated with his premed course load at Calvin College.[9] Changes in the freedom struggle led Coe to state, "I don't consider myself a leader," but it was clear Coe and the members of the GRSC continued to help groom a younger generation of black leaders with their selections of venues and financial contributions.[10]

Perhaps the rise of youth activism should not have come as a surprise. Similar to Coe's commitment to challenge racial inequality throughout her lifetime, increasingly black youth in Grand Rapids began to protest against the modes of control that proved critical to the success of managerial racism. Never in the history of Grand Rapids had the system of managerial racism been opposed so openly. The strategy of direct-action protest was a clear rejection of the patron-client relationship that governed the city's race relations. However, the shift to a more direct assertion for racial justice left Coe searching for purpose and direction. Yet although some residents, such as Coe, felt increasingly disconnected from black-youth protest strategies, other South High parents, such as Lillian Gill, who served as the vice president of the GRNAACP under three different presidents, effectively communicated the need for black assertiveness. Although both women advocated for racial dignity and pride, Gill's message resonated with a rising tide of black youth determined to attack the cornerstone of managerial racism.

Gill was born on a farm near Tupelo, Mississippi, in 1917. "Things were segregated down south," she recalled, so to better their circumstances, Lillian and her husband, Robert Earl Gill, headed north in search of equality, independence, and mobility. They found Grand Rapids: "Along about June or July, my husband and another man hopped a freight train to Detroit. He had some people in Detroit. But they decided to come to Grand Rapids, because the man that was with him had relatives here." Robert found a job at the foundry: "When he would come home at night and [I would] kiss him I could smell the metal on his breath. But it was work and it paid more." That was 1944, when the promise of progressive-era politics made Grand Rapids a city of hope for optimistic newcomers like the Gills. In fact, during the war years, Lillian found work at the Hayes Manufacturing Company located on the Westside: "I was a repair girl for that company, repairing parachutes and then I was elevator girl to the harnesses department." Although Robert did not want his wife to work, Lillian realized that she had to draw an income for the family to purchase a home. "You couldn't get a home," she recalled, but eventually she "began to save up the money to pay down on the home at 131 Franklin. $300 was the down payment, and the payment was $25 per month. We got the house for $2,500."[11]

When her husband died suddenly at age twenty-nine, however, Lillian's life shifted: "I took on a major role. I did day work after Hayes Manufacturing. When the factory closed in 1946 after VJ Day, I converted my home into a rooming house." Fortunately, she noted, most of the boarders were family members, including her brother, a cousin who returned from the military, and her nephew, who also came back from the service. Additionally, she sent for her father, who was living in Mississippi, to come north to look after the children while she worked. Thus by charging boarders $7 a month and working multiple jobs, Gill managed to keep the house and provide for her three children.

Eventually, Gill went back to school to learn "all about life insurance and underwriting." She went on to sell life insurance for more than twenty-two years: "I was the first black woman to retire from life insurance in the city of Grand Rapids, and the first black lady to retire from life insurance anywhere in Michigan." In 1953, she decided to sell Nutralite Food supplement. "That helped my income as I traveled," she recalled. "They grew so fast and I happened to be the first black agent for Amway products. . . . I grasped every opportunity to help others and to earn a living." Her ambition put her in unique situations. For example, as the chosen representative from both the GRNAACP and the Grand Rapids Urban League (GRUL), she met President Harry S. Truman in 1951. Also, in 1960, she met George Wallace. That same year she spoke at the Sixteenth Street Baptist Church in Birmingham, Alabama, where she met Martin Luther King Jr. and John L. Lewis. "I came there all unaware," Gill remembered. "That was the first time I heard them sing 'We Shall Overcome. Before I be a slave, I be buried in my grave and go home and be free with my Lord.'" Three years later, white supremacists bombed the Sixteenth Street Baptist Church, killing four young girls. The murderous act shocked the nation and prompted many black residents, including Gill, to take to the streets of Grand Rapids in a silent protest.

On Sunday, September 22, 1963, more than three thousand Grand Rapids citizens marched in silence to protest the bombing in Birmingham, Alabama. Reverend Hugh Michael Beahan of the Grand Rapids Catholic Diocese captured the sentiment that unified black and white residents on this tragic occasion: "Four of our family were murdered last Sunday. . . . When a member of a family dies, it doesn't make any difference if we're 1,000 miles away. We mourn." With black and white marchers extending more than a mile on Division Avenue, it appeared residents had set aside their racial differences. Although local whites mobilized and protested against the horrific brutality of southern violence, some blacks wondered when white residents would unite against the local manifestations of managerial racism. Reverend W. L. Patterson urged white marchers to remain steadfast in their resolve to fight racial inequality and to turn their attention to the problems plaguing Grand Rapids. "White brothers," Reverend Patterson announced at the protest, "you have marched with us today, but please march with us tomorrow because we need jobs and places to live right here in Grand Rapids."[12]

Despite the strong showing of interracial solidarity, some blacks questioned whether these same white marchers really wanted substantive local racial change. Hezekiah Allen called the march "a disgrace." He correctly noted, "Even that march [was] segregated." Because "marchers were largely lined up according to organizations, most of which had either an all-white or all-Negro membership," the *Grand Rapids Press* observed, the procession appeared racially stratified. This angered some blacks, who "jeered and sang songs from the sidewalks." Ironically, delegations from local colleges, schools, churches, and fraternal organizations, which were predominantly segregated, had come together to condemn racial injustice. Thus the gathering illustrated the flawed racial system that had dominated the city's history for decades; yet, like the march, local whites had remained silent about it.[13]

With three children of her own, the bombing and the silent march in Grand Rapids reaffirmed for Gill that this was an ongoing fight for freedom and justice. More than anything, her children needed her to press on:[14] "I thank God for my three children. They all graduated from South High." On occasion, however, she recalled how white teachers at South tested her patience. Gill's son "Rob was told by his teachers in South High that he should not draw, because there was no place in art for colored people." Her daughter, Frances, "was told that she'd never become a secretary."[15] Black parents had good reason to question the motives of educators in Grand Rapids. In fact, the inner-city school director, Joseph McMillan, spoke his mind publicly about the problem when he said that "some teachers are just 'warm bodies' and that others do a poor job because they don't believe the children can learn very much." Although white teachers' expectations of black students remained a constant point of contention, what did endure since the forming of the GRSC was a conviction within the black community in the ability of their children to achieve. Gill cultivated this notion in her children and in other black students in the South High neighborhood: "Now Frances went on to teach school because she was told she could not be a secretary" and "Robert got his doctoral degree." Her younger son, Kenneth, "decided he didn't want to go to college. He saw what they had to go through. He got a job then at General Motors. He used to shake his check in their faces. 'You're educated, look what I've got. I'm making big money.'"[16]

Gill taught her children well: "You don't make a child do. You lead them into what they're doing and show an example by doing your share." Through her leadership training in the South, local NAACP and Urban League contributions, establishment of block committees in the South High neighborhood, and desegregation battles in the city, Gill exemplified the politics of struggle that fermented the seeds of change. Gill's determination and assertiveness exerted a greater influence on generations of the black youth in Grand Rapids than just her children. Frequently, South High students would visit her home: "There would be a lot of children in the house." Her message was, "Your mind controls your whole body. You become what you think about." Unwilling to accept the broken promise of equality, black students carried forward Gill's message that nothing was beyond their grasp. They were becoming politicized, and their experience as black students at South High was the force behind their rising tide of activity. Despite the questionable teacher-commitment level, black students understood the central role South High played in forming a nexus of shared relationships, memories, and ideals within the black community. Now, it appeared, black students were standing in front of their parents and fighting to preserve these fundamental principles. Their efforts would dramatically transform educational policy in Grand Rapids.[17]

Young black children became particularly notable agents in the black community's struggle for equality, because the politics of educational reform did not occur in isolation from the numerous race issues in Grand Rapids. Focusing solely on school integration distorts our understanding of the important factors that shaped the perceptions and ultimately informed the decisions of the students and the GRSB. Increasingly, secondary students in the city began to reflect the national trends toward a more open form of black resistance to white oppression. Following the mustache incident, Charles Davidson requested guard patrol for South High to quell any sporadic outburst by its students.[18] In a city that believed in the maintenance of the status quo, the rise of youth protest challenged the dialectic of managerial racism. Thus the ability of the GRSB to normalize or moderate black-youth activism became ever more important and in the best interest of the entire white community.

In a speech delivered to members of the Chamber of Commerce in 1963, Human Relations Commission (HRC) Executive Director Alfred Cowles informed the business community that "the local minority situation in housing, employment, and public accommodations was generally good, but some problems still existed in the field of education." He would later inform the city manager "that the local climate was healthy and the existing tensions were not the type which produced race riots."[19] In fact, Cowles felt his observations concerning the city's race relations were justified when nearly 2,200 white and black citizens marched again in conjunction with the right-to-vote demonstrators in Selma, Alabama. Serving as master of ceremonies, Cowles declared, "When people turn out in such numbers in weather like this, you know they're concerned." Echoing Cowles's sentiments, one marcher considered the 1965 Selma demonstration "much more impressive" than the silent march of 1963. After a mile-and-a-half march through the city, the crowd filled the steps of the Civic Auditorium to listen to civic and religious leaders admonish the continued presence of southern violence. It seemed Cowles interpreted the public fixation regarding the significance of brutal assaults in the South with a more general concern for the institutional and structural racism that governed the city's black-white relations. However the righteous indignation of many whites in Grand Rapids prevented them from understanding the detrimental impact inherent in both systems as mechanisms of social control.[20]

Juxtaposed with the vicious episodes of violence reoccurring in the South, the environment in Grand Rapids appeared tolerant, enlightened, and ostensibly progressive. These were the images of community living that business and political leaders used to obscure the social and economic realities of black life in the city. Indeed, progressive discourse fulfilled a crucial function of managerial racism by ensuring that racism would never become a point of conflict as it did in Selma, Alabama. But similar to Greensboro, North Carolina, where the use of the progressive mystique effectively forestalled substantive change, Grand Rapids never faced the brutality associated with Mississippi or Alabama; yet behind the mask of civility lay a harsh system of oppression designed to allow white business leaders and politicians to preserve their dominance even while making modest concessions. The effectiveness of this camouflaged arrangement of race relations caused Cowles to miscalculate just how deep the level of black frustration ran in Grand Rapids. Chamber of Commerce affiliates had built up the district in and around the city except the black community. Moreover, his inability to gauge the uniform dissatisfaction of the black community regarding the policy of disinvestment typified the complete disconnect with the one city agency designated to check the pulse of the black community.[21]

Following the Los Angeles uprising of 1965, WOOD-TV produced a documentary on the city's racial conditions. In interviews with WOOD-TV reporter Alex Barton, black residents expressed tremendous concern over the high level of discrimination within city life. They "believed that conditions similar to those existing in Los Angeles did exist in Grand Rapids but that the white population was not aware that these conditions were present." From education, housing, employment, and police brutality, blacks provided a litany of areas of concern. These were not new issues. Disconnect between black leadership, white conservatives, and changes in the black community seemed ever more apparent in the wake of the mustache incident.[22]

In response to the documentary, Cowles conceded that rampant unemployment did exist, but he pinned these circumstances on the arrival of allegedly unqualified black southern migrants. He posited the amount of "unfair employment practices in the local labor market [were] negligible." Furthermore, Cowles "denied that the alleged police brutality could be substantiated in a thorough and impartial investigation." Although he recognized positive elements of the documentary, Cowles remained steadfast in his earlier position regarding the implausibility of rebellion in Grand Rapids. Although philosophical differences established a discernable gap between the HRC and residents of the "black belt," the influence of city officials limited the effectiveness of the HRC.[23] The HRC, ironically, proved better suited to fit the needs of the business community than the black community.

During the mustache incident, Clingman notes, "the role of the HRC throughout this entire sequence was generally negative," despite the fact that "a few members of the Commission became actively and personally involved in most aspects from start to finish [and] in general these individuals were not in agreement with Mr. Davidson or the actions of the school officials." According to Clingman, however, these members were muted by the official stance of the HRC, which supported the "maintenance of discipline [as] the major issue and could not accept the reality of facial hair as a part of personal rights."[24] Similarly, during a City Commission meeting in 1966, Mayor Christian Sonneveldt chided the HRC for "misdirecting its activities by attacking the propaganda of the local John Birch Society." The John Birch Society maintained a strong presence in the community. The organization had "two reading rooms in the city, distributed free a considerable amount of printed materials, and frequently supplied speakers to service organizations and to Church and P.T.A. groups." The groups' representatives regularly "condemned the Civil Rights program as part of the Communist plot to overthrow the American Government and, at least by implication, stigmatized all civil rights proponents, national or local, as being suspect as fellow travelers." The mayor disagreed with members of the HRC who contended that "agitators of the extreme political right were as potentially dangerous to the city's tranquility as was the scheduled visit of Mr. Carmichael." The mayor complained that instead the HRC needed to prepare for "the scheduled visit of Mr. Stokely Carmichael," which he considered to be a "potentially more dangerous threat to the city's tranquility."[25] Carmichael did visit Grand Rapids in May 1967 without incident.[26] However, while in the city he urged more blacks to register to vote and encouraged high school students to become more politicized through such groups as the Student Nonviolent Coordinating Committee (SNCC).[27]

The work of the HRC did not indicate a lack of concern of the entire group; rather, it represented the strength of managerial racism, which controlled by business leaders rendered the HRC ineffective. The level of inactivity routinely practiced by the HRC raised concern within the black community. The bureaucratic foot-dragging of the HRC seemed unsurprising given the fact that the mayor and City Commission controlled the city agency. Neither demonstrated a sense of urgency to respond to concerns of the black community. Instead, behind the scenes, the mayor and City Commission bogged down the HRC's effectiveness by failing to fill vacancies in a timely manner. When they did act, the city commissioners often appointed unqualified residents to serve on the HRC. Mayoral appointees routinely missed meetings because of their own private business interests and as a result successfully mired down the HRC. The unresponsive nature of the HRC reflected the separation between city officials and residents of the "black belt." Moreover the distrust in progressive reform-minded politics escalated daily within the black community, particularly among black youth.

One HRC member was "shocked by the obvious tense hostility she experienced when addressing a group of young Negroes."[28] The one agency appointed to manage criticism within the black community failed to connect on any meaningful level. Blacks began to view the HRC as part of the larger establishment, and its practices of inactivity and gradualism actually fanned racial flames. Thus, the last agency to recognize that the black community was ripe for rebellion was the HRC, which meant city officials and the business community were completely unprepared for what occurred in July 1967. "There was a prevailing feeling at the time," recalled former Captain Victor Gillis of the Grand Rapids Police Department (GRPD), that a riot could happen "anywhere else, but not Grand Rapids." Indeed city officials believed that Grand Rapids would be spared. For example, at the City Commission meeting July 12, 1967, Mayor Sonneveldt articulated his "optimism relative to the progress made in the city's racial climate and denied positively that riots were possible in the city." City Manager Henry Nabers seconded the mayor's confident statement, but the coming weeks would prove the mayor, the city manager, and the HRC wrong.[29]

On the evening of July 24, 1967, a day after the Detroit rebellion, Grand Rapids experienced its own racial uprising, which lasted nearly four days. That evening, police received reports that a group of black juveniles was throwing rocks at storefront windows along South Division Avenue. Although police defused the early incidents, as the night progressed the calls became more frequent. Scattered pockets of disturbances surfaced throughout the night. The activity appeared to be unorganized, but each episode became more severe. Rumors spread that carloads of black residents from Detroit were headed to Grand Rapids to stir up trouble. The speculation and relative quiet the following morning triggered anxiety among local police and white residents that more unrest would take place. As darkness approached, police pulled over a carload of young blacks, which sparked another outburst. This time, black youth ages fourteen to twenty-four banded together in total rebellion.[30]

Police managed to squelch several scenes of unrest, but the number of fires and disturbances overwhelmed officers and fire crews. City officials contacted Governor George Romney to declare a state of emergency for Grand Rapids. In response to the request from the mayor and City Commission, Romney issued a proclamation that outlawed the sale of firearms and intoxicating liquors. He also restricted the sale of gas after 6:00 P.M. Finally, Romney implemented a citywide curfew from 10:00 P.M. to 5:30 A.M. The crisis-prevention tactics were also enforced in the adjacent suburban communities of East Grand Rapids, Wyoming, Kentwood, and Grand Rapids and Plainfield townships. After two days of unrest, the police finally managed to gain control of the streets. Almost 350 people were arrested and 44 injured, and an estimated $175,000 in property damage resulted from the racial uprising.[31]

Residents believed that police efforts and the citywide curfew provided minimal relief. The one group that received substantial praise from the black and white communities for its ability to prevent an ongoing rebellion was the Sheldon Complex "Task Force." The group of fifteen included twelve black adolescents and three white youth members who went into the streets to limit racial conflict. In a Great Society program initiative, federally funded by the

United Community Services youth program, the Task Force members spent the six weeks preceding the unrest covering inner-city neighborhoods "on foot, visiting homes, churches, barber shops, pool rooms, parks and gyms to keep in touch with what was happening in the community." They also "enrolled several hundred youngsters in various summer projects." In some instances these interracial teams formed lasting bonds.[32]

Richard Donley and William Pritchett, two Task Force members, "stoned out a relationship that still lasts, that time ain't gonna take away," Donley proclaimed. Donley, who was white, was known as "The Saint," and Pritchett, who was black, was "The Cowboy." Both were "supposed to try to be the cooler heads that were to prevail in different situations," recalled Pritchett. Both sensed something was going to happen that summer. In the week leading up to the racial upheaval, Donley remembered that "it'd been really tense. We were all together probably 80 hours that week, and it look like things had cooled down. . . . Then it rings: 'Oh, no!' I think everybody, to a man, *knew* when the phone rang. It didn't let up after that." It did not take long for them to understand the gravity of the situation. "People were getting hurt all over," Donley remembered. "Cowboy saved me from getting hurt in front of Hooker Paint. Some guy pulled a knife on me. I'll never forget that night. People were ready to do damage. That's all there was to it." In a separate incident, the two were confined to the floor of the Franklin-Hall Complex as bullets blasted through the windows.[33]

"Over the weeks I learned a lot," Donley admitted. "I had prejudices that were washed away from me, and they weren't washed away from me [by] any miracle. It was from getting next to some people that I hadn't had an opportunity to get next to." After the riot, he added, people in his neighborhoods began referring to him as "a nigger-lover."[34] The comments were reminders that, despite their forged friendship, others did not attempt to cross the chasm that ran deep that summer. The young activists prevented "splinter groups from being organized into a single force" and "aided tremendously in keeping the actual damage to a minimum," as Clingman notes.[35] Ironically, two of the Task Force members, Fred Brown and Harold Morris, were shot by state police officers who "did not recognize the pair as Task Force members." Brown and Morris responded to a call to prevent looting on Jefferson Avenue, and as they sat in their car, they were both shot. Without a white companion, Task Force members looked just like "rioters" to law enforcement.[36]

Following the racial uprising, the mayor and HRC members met with some of the "self-appointed leaders" of the rebellion at the House of Styles Barber Shop located in the heart of the "black belt." From that meeting, the Black Unity Council (BUC) was born. The BUC brought together "members of the older, established leaders of the Negro community as well as some of the young militants," according to Clingman. Although led by young people, Clingman states, "The majority of [the] black population believed the disturbances served a definite and dramatic purpose insofar as they drew the attention of the white population to the conditions existing within the ghetto." Equally important, Mayor Sonneveldt extended a verbal promise that he would listen to the "total Black community rather than the few, 'white-selected' leaders of the ghetto." He subsequently lifted the curfew on Thursday night.[37]

In the wake of the Grand Rapids riots, the School Board realized it had to act on the recommendations of the Racial Imbalance Committee (a citizens' committee that had been established by the Board of Education to investigate all aspects of de facto school segregation). The School Board had a new awareness of the gravity concerning public education and the rising urban crisis. Equally important, the GRSB understood the political capability of black secondary students. The walkout at South High and high level of youth participation in the racial uprising of 1967 demonstrated the collective power of black youths concentrated in the same environment. Thus the resolution the GRSB offered recognized the rising strength of youth protest. The GRSB contemplated whether the dangers of integrated schools seemed less ominous than the current unpredictable reality of concentrated black youth.

A Master Plan or Master Disaster?

On May 6, 1968, the school administration responded to the impending crisis with the presentation of a school master plan designed to satisfy the recommendations of the Racial Imbalance Committee. The master plan was unveiled in front of an unprecedented crowd of more than 2,300 at Northeast Junior High School. As Racial Imbalance Committee member Vernis Schad explained, it introduced "several bold steps toward integration, a change in school building plans and a reevaluation of how children should be taught." School administrators determined, she continued, that the changes marked a shift in the "education philosophy of the school administration, one that [took] into consideration the Kerner Report and other recent racial studies."[38] According to the *Grand Rapids Press,* the GRSB finally ventured to act on the recommendations of the Racial Imbalance Committee, which "urged the board to redraw elementary school boundaries to promote integration, allow students to enroll in schools outside their neighborhoods and reassign some black teachers to predominately white schools." As the paper noted, "reception in the community was less than enthusiastic."[39]

For nearly four years, the Board of Education claimed it had worked "toward solutions to the education problems for the City of Grand Rapids." During that time, the School Board held numerous sessions and provided many alternative school programs for debate. The high concentration of "culturally disadvantaged families" within the center city created an academic concern within the school administration. When studies revealed that a large percentage of the black families lived in the inner city, the GRSB claimed "it ha[d] a responsibility, not only for the academic achievement of the students, but also a broad responsibility to society and, in particular, to the economic and social well-being of the community of Grand Rapids."[40] In an effort to diminish these concerns, the Board of Education submitted its school master plan.

The unveiling of the school antibias plan generated rumors and speculation throughout the community. The secret nature of the strategic development process kept many citizens in the dark until the moment the School Board disclosed the final master plan. Board members requested that the few "people knowledgeable of the basic plans . . . refrain from public discussion until the May meeting."[41] Anticipation brimmed within the community, and the night of the meeting one thousand people quickly filled the all-purpose room at Northeast Junior High School to capacity. White and black citizens, concerned parents, and group members from such organizations as the Racial Imbalance Committee, the Sheldon Complex, the GRUL, and the BUC waited patiently, only to forfeit their strategic seating positions when the board announced a room change and rerouted the meeting to the school's gymnasium.

The decision proved wise, as more than 1,300 additional people poured into the gym. One newspaper reporter wrote that the patience of the spectators wore thin as they "sat quietly through the tightened business agenda waiting to hear the plan." After the GRSB completed the business agenda, the audience suffered through "an hour-and-a-half reading" of the master plan "that was difficult to understand without a copy to follow." The board did not provide copies for the listeners until the intermission and then distributed only one thousand reproductions. As assistant superintendents C. Robert Muth and Raymond L. Boozer read the formal document and recited the rationale for each proposed move, Elmer Vruggink, the third assistant superintendent "pointed to boundary changes on a map that was indefinable 40 feet away."[42] This only added to the frustration of viewers, as everything done by the school officials seemed to ignore their needs.

According to school officials, the grand scheme of the master plan guided the Grand Rapids Public Schools "toward an organization of Early Elementary Centers (PK–3), Elementary Centers (K–5 or 3–5), Middle Schools (6–8), High Schools (9–12), and Junior College education." In addition, the board announced its plan to continue designated programs, such as the special educational programs, functionally handicapped programs, vocational training programs, and the Educational Park for enrichment program, as well as expand the programs' capacity. The design of the proposal required that the school organization move "from the present five high schools to three great high schools and the Educational Park."[43] Furthermore, the GRSB recommended the establishment of only nine middle schools instead of the suggested eleven junior high schools, as proposed in 1966.

The plan, school officials contended, "was based on the idea that children in early elementary grades [would] continue in neighborhood schools."[44]

According to the School Board, psychological and physiological research demonstrated that a child age zero to nine was "dependent upon adults—his parents, his teachers, and other adults in life." Therefore, the board determined that the educational system must work hand-in-hand with parents to nurture the child. To achieve this end, GRSB members determined that "elementary schools must become neighborhood centers involving parents as well as students." This way, the board contended, both children and parents could access the educational centers, and parents could better partake in the academic development of their children. In addition, the School Board agreed that it was incumbent on the educational system to develop these centers to satisfy the outdoor recreational needs of the children. According to the board, "It would be a sociological tragedy to eliminate all neighborhood school facilities within the inner-city. This, in essence, would be a physical abandonment of the inner-city."[45]

The GRSB suggested that the elementary centers (K–5 or 3–5) "provide opportunities for developing innovative and diversified programs" for youngsters. As "peer group influence begins to replace adult influence at about age 8 and continues to have increasing effect on the child's behavior as he becomes older," the elementary centers would provide integration across economic, ethnic, and racial lines. According to the board, the placement of "Negro adults on the outer city school staffs [was] essential" for integration to work, "whether they be principals, teachers, secretaries, or custodians." The GRSB believed that the "child must be made ready to communicate with the children and adults in the new environment," but in its estimation, this was not a direct concern, as the board believed that inevitably "outer city neighborhoods will become integrated so that all youngsters will have an opportunity to work and play together before they reach school age."[46]

For middle schools, grades six through eight, the School Board appeared mainly concerned with maintaining homogenous age groupings. The board adopted its newest philosophy for middle schools in October 1966 after the GRSB experienced what it described as high "grade retention and failure, especially among the children of the inner cities." The board admitted that the use of the old standard achievement plan "piled up failures in the middle school grades so that our age distribution in grades 6 through 8 in some cases reache[d] the extreme of 11 years of age to 17 years of age." The wide age range added to the social and physiological strain of the overall school environment and placed difficulty on the proper maturation of preadolescent children. To alleviate these concerns, the GRSB agreed to hold age as a relative constant and adapt the educational program to youngsters as they moved through the first eight years of their school life.[47]

The final proposal addressed the changes in the high school structure from five to three facilities and the development of a central Education Park. The School Board offered a new "school within in a school" concept as the design format for the new high school building program. According to the board, this model meant "that the schools [were] divided into sub-units of administration, counseling, and student organization." As it explained:

> The present sub-organization by grades is a less formal approach to providing opportunities for student leadership and service. The "school within a school" concept actually creates sub-schools for student relationships within the context of a larger academic organization. It combines the inter-personal advantages of small schools with the academic advantages of a larger school program.[48]

The board considered the larger school units as a more appropriate way to provide more occasions for a comprehensive and diversified curriculum. To satisfy this recommendation, the board advised the crowd that "South High School would be eliminated as a high school and used in the interim years as a middle school. Central High School would be phased out as a high school and become part of the Educational Park-Junior College Complex."[49] To attain integration in the remaining schools located west, north, and south, the board adjusted the attendance areas to include parts of the inner city.

Several audience members exited the meeting after the board announced the final secondary school plans. According to the *Grand Rapids Press,* "Admittedly some of the white community came just to find out whether their youngster would be bused to the inner-city, and 'safe' from that," many elected to leave.[50] Protected from the ominous reality of entering the inner city on a daily basis, white parents and their children no longer had to ponder that unsightly scene. Although the Racial Imbalance Committee "had deliberately avoided the word 'busing,' that unspoken word hung in the air," noted a local newspaper account.[51] As Schad pointed out, the reality handed down by the School Board required that "inner-city pupils [be] bussed into school in the outlying areas" and that "students from the predominately black high school [be] bussed out of their neighborhood."[52] Therefore, the board successfully achieved its objective by addressing the primary concern of white residents. Once the chief stimulus of anxiety was resolved for these suburbanites, the meeting became anticlimactic, although angst still lingered regarding just where the GRSB intended to bus black students.

The first mission of the School Board endeavored to quell any unsettling feelings among the white suburban community. The School Board issued a statement that declared, "In this plan, it would not be proposed that cross busing be effected, but rather, that busing would be one way from the inner-city to the periphery educational centers."[53] As reported in the *Grand Rapids Press,* the need to provide boundary shifts necessitated busing elementary, junior high, and high school students, but "at no time [did] the plan call for cross-busing— moving pupils into inner-city schools." One of the master plan's "major principles [was] moving children in progressive steps toward large periphery schools." From the start, the board feared that "busing could cause white flight to the suburbs." Thus, its solution was to bus only black students. Integration, as foreseen by the board, meant that black children would pilot an experimental plan and travel to suburban schools and neighborhoods.[54]

While the stream of contented observers headed for the exits, John Bracey, a concerned South High student, asked a simple question that the board had surely anticipated but hoped it would not hear: "Can't you achieve quality education and integration by busing white students into the inner-city instead of busing black students to the outer city?"[55] From a logical standpoint, Bracey's inquiry made sense, as Central was the oldest high school among the bunch, and, as Bracey pointed out, "South's facilities [were] better than Central's."[56] As if rehearsed a hundred times, Assistant Superintendent Muth quickly retorted, "Central and South are in the same age group. Central High School [was] being used in the plan as an Educational Park because it is centrally located and easily accessible from all sections of the city." He continued, "South High School will be used as a middle school and eventually will be phased out as a school facility."[57]

Was South High the "first to be eliminated as a high school because it [was] predominately black," asked Evan McCullough, another concerned student from South. "Eliminating South High School," he continued, "[would] destroy the black power structure; they will be sprinkled in the other high schools and will have nothing to say about curriculum." The GRSB informed McCullough that "the main purpose of the plan was not to achieve integration but to alleviate overcrowding."[58]

School Superintendent Dr. Jay Pylman responded to the charge of racial steering by explaining, "The objective is to move from five high schools to three great high schools and an Educational Park. The second objective of integration could only be met by starting with the school where the greatest imbalance exists, which is South High School."[59] Pylman viewed integration as a secondary issue. Moreover, he felt that imbalance pertained only to majority black populations and not to the majority white student populaces elsewhere. The parochial vision of integration as a means of reducing the concentration of blacks left South High students with minimal options and maximum apprehension.

Many black South High students viewed their dispersal into other communities with trepidation. Before tears consumed her, Marsha Caruthers, a soft-spoken honor-roll student from South High, asked, "What prevents us from becoming numbers in another school?" She worried that black students would "have no say in government or activities in another school." She was also terrified that in predominately white schools, "the faculty would be prejudiced."[60] Her anxiety was real, similar to the other students who stood before the board knowing that integration would become a black child's burden and articulated their feelings, but perhaps Caruthers's honor-roll status captured the attention of Pylman, who immediately stated that it "must not, it cannot happen."[61]

Eleanor Burgess, a white female employee with the Grand Rapids Public Library, concurred with Pylman. She highlighted the possible advantages "for white children of Grand Rapids with this new plan as for children from ghetto areas. She felt that youngsters like Marsha, who, though they have done a great deal for South, have a great contribution to make in the schools that do not know youngsters like her."[62] Despite this reassurance from the superintendent and the placating optimism of Burgess, scores of minority parents and students still retained their own personal doubts.

Mixed feelings and intense emotions circulated within the gymnasium. One mother claimed that she "paid good money to have [her] child attend school where I wanted to live." To which another mother from the Northside responded, "This may be the best bargain in education you ever had." Another exchange was sparked when Wilbur Hawkins approached the microphone to say the "majority who have been up to this mike are colored. They are not interested in education but in integration." This provoked an immediate response from a black woman who responded, "We don't want to live next door to you and marry your son or daughter. We want an adequate education for our children."[63] She added, "[If] we had an adequate system we would stay right there in the inner-city school. But I want my daughter to get a decent education. If it's next door to you or in your living room that's where I'll go."[64] Historically, black and white schools in Grand Rapids did not receive equal treatment. Too often, whites misconstrued the demand for desegregated schools as a desire to intermingle with whites. The objective of desegregation within the black community pivoted on an incessant desire to obtain educational equality. Although blacks did not always agree on the bureaucratic scheme to accomplish educational democracy, the aim remained consistent.

The rhetorical discussion continued well into the night as the School Board periodically dismissed the concerns of the black parents and students. Dispirited board members communicated their disappointment that most of the initial comments concerning the proposed master plan were negative. In support of his colleagues, Paul Phillips addressed what was left of the audience, stating that "the program [was] a good one" and that "the community would support it."[65]

His sentiments combined optimism that the master plan would enhance the educational position of students as well as unite people from diverse backgrounds. The fact that none of the black organizations supported the master plan did not minimize his confidence. Instead, according to Phillips, the fact that black associations "didn't speak against it [was] an indication that they favor[ed] the program." As the executive director of the GRUL and the only black School Board member, Phillips publicly declared that the GRUL favored the program and that he expected to "receive full cooperation of 98% of this community, both black and white"[66] to pass the plan.

The deliberation process began after the meeting's conclusion. Perhaps Phillips's desperate plea to get other black organizations to speak publicly in favor of the master plan prompted the GRNAACP to step forward to voice its opinion. GRNAACP President Jerome Sorrells did so at a special community meeting held by the Board of Education. He indicated that "the plan presented at the May 6 Board of Education meeting represent[ed] a significant and constructive step toward a better education system for all." Sorrells made no objections toward the proposed busing design, nor did he voice opposition to the closing of South High School. Instead, his concerns stemmed from the fear that "the South Middle School would perpetuate racial isolation at that school for a lengthy period of time."[67]

Similar to Phillips and the GRUL members, Sorrells and the GRNAACP felt that integration provided the best avenue for progress, even if that meant a loss of community control. Moreover, the historical nature of the educational reform battle over public schools and the inequitable position of inner-city schools persuaded these two organizations to view triumph in simply getting black children into white schools. The integrationist beliefs of these associations determined that black children in the same school with white children would not only receive a high-quality education but also help change the negative perceptions for a new generation of whites. Well aware of the history in Grand Rapids that chronicled the misfortunes of educational equity within a "separate but equal" format, these leaders elected to secure equal resources by placing black children on a white playing field.

The perception among black community members varied, as some chose to openly support the plan, others candidly denounced the antibias plan, and some remained undecided. Carl Smith, the chairman of the Inner-City Organizing Committee, advocated leveling the burden. He wanted school officials to revisit the drawing board to provide an alternative plan. Smith felt the board ignored curriculum issues within the current proposal and believed that as outlined in the master plan, blacks would "never ha[ve] any say in what affects the education of their children." His outspoken remarks placed him diametrically opposite the GRUL and the GRNAACP. In the current design of the master plan, Smith asserted, the "Board [was] trying to force white middle class values on black people."[68] His militant tone was not the only distinguishable difference between the Inner-City Organizing Committee, the GRNAACP, and the GRUL.

Smith highlighted the complexity of integration. As the black community struggled, along with the community at large, to find a unified meaning of integration, Smith added crucial insights into the various ideological strands within the black community. He affirmed that "if white liberals want their children around black kids, let them be bused into the inner-city." Racial control molded social order, and the current school design ostensibly ensured that blacks would be inundated with white values, cultural orientations, and traditions. This was not the educational environment he wanted for his children, and this sentiment registered with many other blacks in the community. Smith claimed that the school design proposed a "perpetuation of institutional racism."[69]

The disappointment within the black community over the one-sided nature of the integration plan was overshadowed by Phillips's support for the plan. He used his position as a School Board member and leading black spokesperson to push the plan through. His views and opinions were trusted by a generation of blacks who watched him work wonders within the bureaucracy and obtain gains for blacks where none seemed possible. He urged the black community and city at large to be flexible and give the plan a try. He reminded them that "this plan [was] a first step" and that the "plan will be analyzed every year."[70]

But since the mustache boycott and recent racial uprising, it was apparent that more and more blacks began to challenge the moral persuasion tactics of the past. Smith questioned how could it be "implied that 20% black students at a school will create a racial balance," and why should black parents defer to whites to receive what should already be allocated equally? Surely "integration [meant] inter-action between two people, people exchanging views, and out of this comes mutual respect,"[71] but the present arrangement fell extremely short of being a shared enterprise, and certainly the present design would hinder the notion of mutual respect.

Once again the school administration did as little as possible to remedy the ills of racial imbalance or to consider the opposing viewpoints within the black community. According to a local newspaper article, after nearly one month of consideration, the board adopted almost entirely the same proposal. A change in the boundary attendance area involving students from Shawmut Hills and Westwood Hills Elementary constituted the only adjustment made by the School Board. The numerous suggestions and proposals offered "from the community were rejected," especially those geared toward the preservation of South High. Instead, the board decided to convert "South High School . . . to a segregated interim middle school to be phased out in six to eight years."[72]

The plan also required black children to shoulder the burden of integration as the board committed itself to a program "based on overbuilding in the outer city and underbuilding in the inner-city."[73] This time, however, school officials toed the fire line too closely, and, in a most prophetic declaration, Smith proclaimed that if "the Board of Education carries out this plan, in the next three to five years there will be such racial chaos in this city that 'you will regret the day you came here.'"[74] It did not take five years for his prediction to come to fruition. The fall school year ushered in a host of racial difficulties that the school department was unprepared to address.

White Resistance

Nowhere in the master plan was there a line suggesting that the use of mace or tear gas would be employed to achieve integration. Perhaps the GRSB should have inserted that precursor before sending kids into a hostile environment with little preparation. Or the board could have simply paid closer attention to the information presented to them by community members who detested the idea of change within the current structure. The board failed to recognize that the sentiments voiced by black secondary students and Smith were also harbored by the receiving communities occupied by whites directly affected by the resolution of the school administration.

Perhaps Lawrence Pojeski, a Westside community resident, voiced the concerns of many whites when he declared at a School Board meeting that the "voters of Grand Rapids clearly and emphatically rejected the master plan, yet the Board refuse[d] to accept the judgment of the voters; it has ignored the mandate."[75] The board's unwillingness to view outside perspectives and its business-as-usual approach underestimated the forces of racial animosity within the community and ultimately put black children at great risk. Yet school officials were well aware of the warning signs. At a heated public hearing, prior to the approval of the master plan, white community members vehemently voiced their displeasure. The *Grand Rapids Press* observed that an exclusively Westside crowd cringed at the thought that the design of the master plan denied would-be Westside ninth graders an opportunity to "go to the new multimillion dollar high-school and that its now almost nonexistent black enrollment would jump to 17 percent."[76]

A well-entrenched working-class Polish neighborhood existed on the Westside of Grand Rapids, dating back to the late nineteenth century. A tight-knit and almost secluded area within Grand Rapids, the Westside was home to Union High School, which the year prior to the decision to integrate by means of busing housed only two black students—the lowest number of any high school in Grand Rapids. Parents of Union High students publicly voiced their objection to the master plan. The Westside residents shared a feeling of resentment that the board seemingly took for granted. Westside residents, Schad commented, "finally had their new school," and now "they were being asked to share it with students from another section of the city, many of whom resented being bused there as a result of 'their' school being closed."[77]

The animosity and sense of betrayal cut deep among residents on the Westside. "We put every one of you in office," a Westside resident shouted at the board. "I don't know of any of you I didn't vote for, but we'll sure put you out."[78] The master plan presented Union High parents and students with a double negative. They not only had to share their high school but now were presented with possibly their most perplexing blow—they had to interact with blacks on a daily basis.

Former Racial Imbalance Committee member Schad recalled that "students in grades 10–12 were to be bused to three high schools in other parts of the district. Central High School had always had a small percentage of black students, Creston had just a handful of black students, but Union had probably never had a black student attend there."[79] The strategy employed by the GRSB appeared flawed in its decision to bus black kids out to the Westside. According to a local newspaper account, "Union High School opened, and you can't imagine how those people (on the Westside) felt. Here they had this new high school, and they had to share it with black students."[80] The variables leading to a volatile situation were quickly locking into position, but the school officials did not heed the many warning signs.

At public hearings held by the school department, Westside residents jeered school officials. Union parents and Westside residents shouted in a chorus, "Why don't you shut up?" as a board member attempted to explain their collective decision to bus. "How can you handle the kids with four high schools when previously you said you needed five?" asked another audience member. The Westside crowd booed a white woman as she tried to offer support for the School Board. One Union High parent even went so far as to proclaim that the "whole proposal of the board is to break up South so they don't have a colored majority."[81] Although the Westside residents were completely oblivious to the academic standards of the incoming students, GRSB members attempted to ease their racial fears by promising to send only "topnotch" students to Union. But when the audience was asked to respond to an ad hoc vote, more than three quarters still opposed busing.

By 1968, despite this criticism and frustration, few board members doubted that busing was the key to solving overcrowding issues and a resolution for racial imbalance. Led by Phillips, who did not hesitate to voice his stance on the need for integration and the use of busing to solve the dilemma, other board members began to realize that busing had to occur. Integration and busing fit like a hand in glove for Phillips. "I am committed to integrated education," Phillips would announce and follow up with "I am committed to busing, to total busing." Phillip's desire for equality was genuine, and his statements captured the depth of his passion. At a meeting for Concerned Citizens, Phillips fully endorsed the position of busing when he said:

> Every school in Grand Rapids, in the suburbs and the private schools if possible, ought to have in its student body children of all races, colors and creeds. In that way, the parent who says he wants his child to go to school only with children of his own kind will have no place to run.[82]

Other GRSB members remained a bit more reluctant to embrace busing to the degree endorsed by Phillips. Board member John P. Milanowski affirmed that "if we are going to get to know each other, some compulsory busing is necessary. The Board and the city are going to have to face a decision that busing . . . is inevitable."[83]

The record was clear that the majority of black children attended, one local newspaper article observed, "crummy inner-city elementary schools" and "crowded middle schools and ninth grade"[84] Charles F. Porter, a board member, contextualized the imbalance issue when he commented that there "are empty classrooms and others are overcrowded, and when the community is saying be careful about your spending, I see no way but to move the children from the overcrowded to the empty."[85] The parochial perspective of the Grand Rapids school administrators, however, failed to allow them to view their own complicity within the construction of a segregated school system.

Within the busing debate, school officials viewed busing to achieve racial integration as "only a by-product of its student transportation policy." The main function of the busing policy, GRSB members declared, was "relief from overcrowding and more economical use of schools relatively unpressured by space problems in outlying areas of the city."[86] Although busing students to "achieve integration [was] not Grand Rapids Board of Education policy,"[87] it was this notion that made "many whites object to busing for this purpose," according to the *Grand Rapids Press*.[88] Yet school officials ordered the transportation of more than five thousand students, primarily from the central city each school day, which happened to be the area that contained the majority of black children and contained the highest rates of overcrowding.

An alternative to busing meant building new schools where old overcrowded schools existed. The schools in the inner city time and again registered as inadequate and unsafe, and with the GRSB policy of building schools where children lived, it made complete sense to consider this option. Yet a local newspaper article claimed that school officials understood all too well that "an end to busing would cost the schools more money not less." According to Porter, a School Board member, if "you believe in neighborhood schools and lower teacher-ratios . . . the only answer is a fantastic building program in the inner-city and elsewhere."[89] The GRSB initially invested in a building program that developed schools disproportionately on the periphery despite the continued rise in population growth in the black community within the central city. Neglect and a preference for building schools on the foundation of race ultimately returned to haunt school officials, as numerous vacancies in new pristine suburban schools stood in stark contrast to the congested classroom settings of deteriorated inner-city school facilities.

The GRSB's futile building process mirrored the "separate but unequal" trends occurring in the de jure system of segregation in the South. If the business of building schools was as simple as counting the noses of the children, as posited by School Superintendent Pylman, then the black students within the inner city certainly should have been the beneficiaries of numerous new facilities, but this was not the case. Rather, the inner-city state of school affairs and subsequent overdevelopment of outlying area schools evolved part and parcel from the decisions made and executed by city school officials. Schools did not magically change themselves or provide self-upkeep. The constant neglect of inner-city minority complaints and a penchant toward overzealous responses and a desire to tend to white suburban needs ultimately created a pathway for disaster. This same shortsightedness convinced school officials that if busing had to occur, then it was imperative to conduct one-way busing or else whites might flee.

Prior to the one-way busing decision authored by the GRSB, busing in Grand Rapids had been employed since the early 1960s. Busing served as a means to allow "students to take at other schools courses their own schools did not provide," stated school officials.[90] In 1965, busing in Grand Rapids actually hit a high point with the "decision of the board to transfer the seventh and eighth grades at Ottawa Junior High School to Harrison Park Junior High School." Also, the *Grand Rapids Press* noted, "lower grade youngsters in the Central area were bused to West Middle School and the upper grades at South—and the students in them—were moved to new Union High School." Thus busing was not a new wrinkle in the educational system of Grand Rapids, as suggested by Assistant Superintendent Muth. Moreover, the use of busing during that time period solicited "few specific complaints."[91]

Not until busing was considered a feature in achieving racial balance did the issue turn political. The advent of black children in lily-white schools, particularly in neighborhoods designed to protect white residents from interactions with blacks, sparked extreme controversy. With the racial demographics of the receiving schools transformed dramatically overnight because of busing, schools that once contained virtually nonexistent black populations prior to busing experienced a startling increase that required parents and children alike to stand up and take notice. Although many white parents despised busing because it brought unwanted visitors into their racially manufactured world, many black parents, a local newspaper article claimed, equally resented the fact that "it is their children who are being bused out of their neighborhood, while white children for the most part continue to attend school close to home."[92]

The *Grand Rapids Press* reported that of the nearly 5,500 youngsters bused every school day, nearly a fourth, or 1,608, "attend special programs because they are mentally ill or handicapped." In addition, the article read, a sizeable portion of the 2,441 white students that were "bused live[d] in areas beyond walking distance of their schools."[93] Board policy affirmed two miles away from school as the radius for bus riders. Roughly 1,400 black students were bused daily between ten schools. Perhaps surprisingly, the School Board sent the greatest number of black students (270) to Union High School, which prior to busing had included only 2 black students. Central High School, situated in the central city, received only 80 black students.

As a tool used to relieve overcrowding, busing South High students to Union High School became the strategy of choice for the GRSB. Yet Union High, located on the Westside of Grand Rapids, existed as the most geographically distant school to travel to for former South High students. Although it stood as the newest high school in the city, traveling to Union required the busing of South students beyond high schools near their immediate neighborhoods. Furthermore, Union High, with the lowest minority enrollment, presented the most volatile atmosphere in which to bus black students. Inadequate preparation on the part of the school administration only heightened the force of an eventual collision between the two foreign groups (working-class blacks and working-class Polish whites), living in separate worlds, forced to interact for the first time within a nonneutral environment.

The "Proposed School Organization and Construction Plan," or master plan, according to a school report by Robert Gill, "did not address itself to the question of preparing the school body for receiving transfer students; nor was it concerned with the assignment of black teachers in schools where Negro students would be bused."[94] With overcrowding as the primary issue, the looming racial strife existent within the current framework barely registered with school officials. The disregard for racial dissent and outright turmoil by the school administration should not be pardoned as simple ignorance. Rather the mishandling of school segregation epitomized the twenty-plus years of disregard and general insolence for the educational future of black children located within the central city confines. As school officials continued to deposit more time, money, and effort in building up suburban schools, inner-city schools experienced a gradual decline and eventual bankruptcy by the late 1960s. For decades, the black community of Grand Rapids paid an expensive price under a regime of segregated schools. The concept of "separate but equal" never panned out, even masked by the notion of de facto segregation. Although school officials decided to utilize busing as the means to desegregate schools, the process continued the taxation on the black community, as the weight of the busing program rested squarely on the shoulders of black students.

Integration

Thursday, September 5, 1968, marked a new day in Grand Rapids community history: It was the first day of busing within the Grand Rapids Public School system.[95] The bulk of the busing plan applied to students in grades nine through twelve. It also called for the busing of South students to Central, Creston, and Union high schools. With the implementation of the master plan, the Board of Education hoped the monumental day would be a sign of the bright future ahead within integration.[96]

The 7:34 A.M. bus pickup of ten former South High students at the corner of Sheldon Avenue and Delaware Street was the first of their 182 trips scheduled for the 1968–1969 academic year. Forty-two students and one mother embarked on bus number 315 as it stopped seven times en route to its final destination, Union High School, which was located on the Westside. On that historical day, the *Grand Rapids Press* noted that the youngsters "were nervous in their first-day-of-school clothes . . . but at the bus stops it was still just 'kids' and the first day of school."[97] The tremendous impact of busing on the consciousness of these kids made the first day of the 1968 school year produce anything but common first-day jitters.

In addition to the seemingly ancillary attention given to the students involved in such a monumental and life-changing process, the article devoted significant space to the method and cost of busing. "For better or worse we are now in the transportation business," proclaimed Assistant School Superintendent Muth. The new industry was slated to "cost $356,935 to transport more than 3,000 students to and from school in the 1968–69 school year."[98] Although the assistant superintendent provided a few brief quotations that addressed the price tag and mechanics associated with busing, he offered no words regarding the extraordinary threshold crossed. Instead, the school representative viewed the school day as business as usual. Within a week's time, however, the hatred that school officials disguised with business-as-usual rhetoric surfaced to produce several clashes.

On Friday, September 13, 1968, Union High School closed unexpectedly at noon. "Everybody's emotions were running high. All it took to trigger things was one little something,"[99] proclaimed Assistant Superintendent Boozer. Apparently, emotions ran high all week, but neither the Board of Education nor the local newspaper publicized the simmering tension within the school environment. Buried deep underneath the surface portrayal of normalcy, "black students complained of racist remarks made by students in referring to their mode of dress, hair-styles and speech mannerisms."[100] The dismissal of black complaints represented a societal pattern of neglect by the larger white community, but on this occasion, the consequence of negligence reared its ugly head, as "racial trouble ignited a brawl in the school's cafeteria and a quarter mile of corridors," according to the *Grand Rapids Press*.[101]

According to Police Inspector Walter A. Gilbert, the spark was an incident in which a black female student allegedly pulled a knife on a hall monitor who questioned why the girl was not in class. That "afternoon a group of white students reportedly congregated in the school parking lot to discuss the incident. Webb Marris, a school discipline officer, said he saw 'white kids carrying chains outside the building.'" None of the information became public knowledge until the next day, when the violence erupted.[102]

School officials managed to assemble nearly two hundred black students in the auditorium. In a make-shift "beef" session, black students voiced their concerns in concrete terms. The black students at the assembly argued that there was a "need for more Negro students, need for more black teachers and demand[ed] that racially tinted innuendos from white classmates stop." As Robert Stark, the secondary school director, stated, the "kids were emotional but they were expressing what the real problems were."[103]

As the situation seemed to settle, Smith, accompanied by a local TV station crew, arrived. They attempted to join the black student assembly, but officials refused to let Smith or his entourage in the building. The black students became alarmed and started chanting, "We want Carl, we want Carl!" The *Grand Rapids Press* described a scene whereby students "stormed out of the auditorium and gathered around a television camera placed just outside the auditorium entrance."[104] As they attempted to tell their story, Principal Emery T. Freeman promptly "decided to dismiss school and called for buses to pick up the black students"[105] and return them home. Yet again, white school officials attempted to mute the concerns of black students and prevent them from publicly articulating their distress.

Violence erupted again in the time it took for the buses to amass at school. According to an article, "Negroes moved toward and threatened a group of white students leaving the building and when police attempted to get the students back to the bus pickup area, a small fight broke out."[106] Police used mace or tear gas to break up the fracas. By the end of the day, police reportedly had arrested six people, five boys and one girl. The events of the day left school officials with a better understanding that the grand task of integration was anything but business as usual.

A panoramic view of the events at Union High reveals a scene reminiscent of the attempts at school integration throughout the North. The all-too-familiar process was one that routinely required black communities to shoulder the task of school integration. White school officials in Grand Rapids attempted to remedy the complex matter of racial imbalance by amassing black students from inner-city schools and sprinkling them throughout "outlying all-white neighborhood schools."[107] Opposition from whites and blacks alike met this woeful decision. Although the verbal clamor of students often fell on deaf ears of school officials, the violent opposition exhibited by students forced school officials to reassess the depth of the issue.

In addition, the recent activity by secondary school students caused school officials to reevaluate the persistent and more-moderate efforts of black activists within the community. Many of these organizations openly berated the school administrations' consistent neglect of the academic needs of minority students. The efforts of black activists unanimously demanded that school officials level the academic playing field, but minorities initially varied on the appropriate course of action. Many within the GRNAACP and the GRUL committed themselves to the notion that academic equality could be achieved only through integration. Although such organizations as the Concerned Parents of the Inner-City backed school integration, the leadership did not agree with the method selected to accomplish incorporation. A solution that consisted of one-way busing simply represented an extension of racist policies designed to deplete the black community of its communal resources and force its members to shoulder the weight of integration. Although sections of the black community shared this sentiment, the voices of the GRNAACP and the GRUL often received the lion's share of attention within the larger community. These two long-established organizations initially placed emphasis on integration, even if it meant sacrificing the communal institutions within black neighborhoods.

Despite the variation in approach, the consensus among black community members centered on the reality that educational equality did not exist in the present school format. As the fifties gave way to the sixties, Schad noted, "civil rights groups were becoming more vocal in the community."[108] School officials could no longer mute their displeasure with the academic structure with promises of future solutions. A list of racial studies combined with countless complaints by black community members that followed the *Brown v. Board of Education* decision only delayed progress. As the black community witnessed dropout rates rise and inner-city school maintenance and performance drop, it became necessary to raise the stakes to force the School Board to remedy the inner-city school dilemma before another generation of black children was lost. The snail pace of advancement ostensibly put blacks two steps behind white progress, and this situation was no longer acceptable, as the promises of yesterday and tomorrow needed to be realized today.

Unsurprisingly, the blatant dismissal of minority concerns resulted in racial unrest at Union High School in 1968. It forced students, teachers, community groups, and most importantly the school administration to grapple with the racial tension tightly sealed in a segregated school system. In several meetings with Union staff, parents, and students, it became apparent that critical differences persisted at Union High. Gill's findings revealed that "a lack of understanding of cultural differences" existed. In addition, there was a "general nonacceptance of the integration caused by the school Master Plan . . . and . . . alienation toward the school administrators."[109]

Similarly, the meetings unveiled a series of complications as experienced by the staff at Union High. Faculty at Union complained of low "staff morale." The absence of self-confidence among staff members stemmed from a "lack of preparedness for bused students" and "an unclear definition of teacher's role in the integration plan," according to Gill.[110] The teacher complaints begin to address the larger haste with which the GRSB executed its master plan. Even viewed as a plan to relieve overcrowding, the GRSB needed to provide adequate support and guidance in the implementation of a preparation program for staff members, parents, and students alike. The GRSB did not attempt to forestall chaos, and, with an attitude of business as usual, it charted the course for a racial disaster.

Amid the community search for answers, and just two days after the racial unrest at Union High, Superintendent Pylman resigned. According to Schad, his post was filled by a new "Superintendent who had been employed by an all-white smaller school district in another part of the state." The new superintendent recommended and executed the hiring of a full-time public-relations person to create a more open line of communication between the school administration and the community. Unfortunately, Schad stated, the new director hailed from a "suburban school district out of the state and had not had much experience in the field of public relations." From the outset, she contended, the public-relations hire had "difficulty relating to the black community and did not feel that the Board was able to give him specific enough directions for a workable plan."[111]

Gill noticed that little changed under the new administration and the "lack of an adequate code of conduct for students and enforcement by administration," saddled with the "lack of communication among teachers and between administrators and teachers,"[112] continued to cultivate an atmosphere of resolute chaos as Union High became the scene of yet another racial uproar on December 18, 1968. The disruption and violence forced school officials to shut down the school until January 6, 1969, well after the holidays. In January, the principal of Union High resigned, leaving an unstable environment in further disarray. Moreover, the community vowed to demonstrate its stance on busing by running a three person antibusing bloc for School Board openings during the April 7, 1969, election.

Even the GRNAACP voiced its displeasure with the master plan. In a change from its initial position, the GRNAACP "requested that the Board give top priority to a cross-busing plan."[113] The GRNAACP firmly believed that a building program designed to furnish the inner city with new schools would delay the goal of integration. Yet, according to Schad, the new position contended that "the burden of integrating the schools" should not "continue to fall solely on the shoulders of black students being bused to formerly all-white schools."[114] The one-way busing design proved to be a burden that only black children had to endure. Mary Edmond, former assistant principal at South Middle School, recalled, "It was just like Little Rock. . . . We put our children out there, and they had to suffer the consequences—abusive stares and all sorts of subtle messages that they were not wanted. These children were facing hostility."[115]

As the assistant principal at South Middle School, the former home of South High School, Edmond remembered how black students unwelcome at Union High returned from their daily bus ride disheartened and demoralized. "You guys just want to come up here and rub the bricks?" she would ask as the students stepped off the buses and ostensibly "hung around the old South High, as if reluctant to leave."[116] Stories of similar deflation coupled with the violent episodes caused many blacks in such organizations as the GRNAACP to question the fruitfulness of a plan predicated on one-way busing. The sentiment began to catch fire within the larger black community, and on July 8, 1969, Smith managed to secure a petition on behalf of the black community that was signed by 1,406 people opposed to a one-way busing model and the loss of neighborhood control.

The hostility regarding busing boiled over in the city of Grand Rapids. One white Grand Rapids citizen recalled, "You would have thought you were in Alabama or Mississippi" while attending a School Board meeting. "People were just yelling racial epithets. 'We don't want no n— here.' It was just vicious,"[117] she recalled. The antibusing voices of blacks and whites began to rise within the community, and the displeasure among the children in the school continued to be acted out in violence. Although Union High received the lion's share of attention, it was not the only school afflicted with racial hostility. The decision to close the majority black high school, undeniably, had a lasting impact on the entire student body and the South High neighborhood.

"It was like a gap in time," recalled former South High School student William Kilgore, who, as a member of South's last graduating class, lived through the controversial episode. According to his classmate, Janice Noel, "He didn't always have a lot to say," but with his few words, Kilgore aptly described the historical moment. As a longtime educator and executive director of activities and services for the Grand Rapids Public Schools (GRPS), Melvin Atkins remembered how closing South "really affected the community." According to Atkins, who graduated from South in 1968, "It really took years for kids who live[d] in that neighborhood to regain their self-esteem."[118] Atkins recalled the students "who attended the seventh through 11th grades at South High, then suddenly got bused for their senior year to Union, that was difficult for them. They didn't really identify with Union. They identified with South." Atkins expressed the despair of his fellow South High students who were members of South's "lost classes" (1969–1971). Monique Marie Ciofu, for example, purchased her South High class ring as a junior, prior to the board's announcement of the school's closing. "So there I was, with my most prized and expensive possession: a memento from a school that didn't exist anymore," Ciofu said regrettably. Even though she was unable to afford a second class ring, Ciofu declared, after recalling her senior year at Union, "that such a token would hardly be cherished as much as her ring from South." She added, "My senior year was a disaster. It was difficult trying to make friends and participate in school events when you lived clear on the other side of town."[119]

Dr. Paul King echoed the sentiment of his classmate when he remembered, "It was mob violence at Union High School, and I was basically in the middle of that." King went on to graduate from Fisk University, and he later attended medical school at Michigan State University. Despite his accomplishments, during an interview conducted thirty years after South's closing, King's distress seemed obvious: "Certainly, it made you distrust people, made you wonder about people's political agendas particularly at an early age. People don't necessarily have your best interest in mind, just their own political agendas." As he reminisced about Union, King noted, "I realized there wasn't anything wrong with me and my friends at South High School. It was other people who wouldn't accept us."[120]

Kathy A. Bracey, a member of South's "lost classes," described her time at Union as "horrible." It took Bracey nearly twenty years before she "could step inside Union after graduation."[121] Bracey worked for the GRSB for nearly thirty years after graduation, but she found it difficult to overcome the memory of inequality. Another black student recalled the tough adjustment: "It was hard, because we thought about South all the time. When we first got there, there were some signs as we got off the bus, saying 'N—— go home.' I don't think I left there feeling like it was my school."[122] Former South student Terri T. Mileski, who graduated from Union in 1970, put the entire situation into context from a completely different perspective. She recalled, "My first year at Union was the first time in my life that I had ever been ashamed of being white." She continued, "African-American kids I had known since kindergarten were all of a sudden being treated as if they were monsters from another planet. The hatred expressed by many of the white students and adults was reprehensible."[123]

A review of the school-planning program conducted by the Equal Educational Opportunity Department of the Michigan Department of Education revealed that a number of concerns from both black and white parents stemmed from an absence of clarity in the goals of the school administration. Marvin Tableman, from the Equal Educational Opportunity Department, provided a report on the existing problems as uncovered in a number of meetings conducted with parents and other citizens of the community to decipher the effectiveness of the program. Along with the Michigan Civil Rights Commission and the U.S. Office of Education, Tableman and a team of experts reviewed the present school-planning program. The report concluded "that there [was] not complete understanding of the educational goal sought by reduction and elimination of racial isolation."[124] Furthermore, the report emphasized the fact that the educational necessity of eliminating racial isolation within the current school system was not "made clear to all the citizens of the district."[125]

Although board members, such as Phillips and even Porter, warned citizens in the *Grand Rapids Press* that immediate steps needed to be taken to integrate or Grand Rapids might "wind up like Washington, D.C., a segregated city surrounded by another segregated city,"[126] there was a clear disregard that Grand Rapids had long been "another segregated city" within a city. The urgency to desegregate surfaced alongside the Kerner Report, which in 1968 asserted that America was quickly becoming two distinct societies, one black and one white. The GRSB wanted to avoid walking blindly down the road of increased segregation or, worse yet, having a judge decide its fate. Yet for more than two decades, the efforts and policies of Grand Rapids school officials, like those of the nation at large, allowed whites to move freely with little worry that the inner-city woes would ever reach their newly built suburban doorsteps. As Porter said, "When we talk about integration, solutions aren't easy. The people in the surrounding countryside, East Grand Rapids, Forest Hills and others, have a stake in Grand Rapids too."[127] The number of violent racial disturbances continued to rise, and white suburbanites feared that inner-city strife might spread.

The racial unrest simply introduced whites to a reality that blacks lived with every day. It centered on a clear dissatisfaction with the present condition of the central city, in particular the undemocratic design of educational opportunity. Black progress was severely retarded not by hours or days lost but by decades of inequality following the post–World War II housing boom. The ability of whites to move freely in neighboring communities, such as Wyoming, Walker, East Grand Rapids, Plainfield, and Kentwood, and within the immediate suburban ring allowed the problems of inner-city neglect and underdevelopment to remain buried underneath the soil of suburban development. But the displeasure with current conditions of inner-city schools and the high rates of overcrowding brought the community to a crossroad at which it could either deal with the issue of inequality or allow it to go untreated.

Busing represented a means of not having to finance new institutions within the central city, but it also meant the inevitable interaction of resistant whites with a population of unwanted blacks. McMillan, the director of inner-city schools and the highest-ranking black school administrator, called the decision to close South High "the most racist thing that has occurred here."[128] Perhaps the alternative, two-way busing, would have been even more explosive; however, it would have evenly distributed the burden of integration. But the school administration selected a one-way busing program that it believed would sufficiently settle the fears of white parents worried about sending their children into the inner city. Eager to achieve the promise of educational equality, many blacks supported busing on unequal terms. In retrospect, Racial Imbalance Committee member Schad proclaimed, "I'm not sure it was a good idea to bus only black kids to white schools."[129] Even though a large portion of the black population shared this sentiment, the lure of integrated schools initially appeared worth the risk, but the daily abuse incurred by black youngsters quickly made many organizations and persons in the black community rethink this line. In retrospect, a "lost class" member said the decision to close South High "gutted the community," adding, "All the mothers, parents, and grandparents went to South. They took an institution out of a neighborhood and didn't replace it with anything. They never looked at the long run, at the big picture. They didn't think about what closing South would do to the community."[130]

In 1968, however, the undeveloped variable that the school administration in its effort to appease whites with a one-way busing program failed to recognize or anticipate was the level of racial animosity harbored by the white receiving communities. From racial epithets to racial violence, whites in the receiving communities openly displayed their objection to integration. Black students absorbed the brunt of white insults and physical violence on a day-to-day basis to an extent beyond measurement. With extreme fervor, whites defended their suburban turf. The GRSB failed to calculate how this factor would harm black children. With more than two decades of consistent neglect of inner-city facilities, even the most well-meaning school officials believed they had no choice but to send blacks into hostile environments and hope for the best. But the decades of disregard and the lack of preparation produced a number of explosive situations at suburban schools inside the city limits that the school administration and city at large were not prepared to deal with. It also presented integrationists, such as Phillips, with the stark reality that educational equality could not result from school reform constructed on unequal terms.

To be certain, board officials decided to close South High because they perceived the school and its black majority population as unmanageable. David Post, president of the board, asserted at a public meeting in September 1968, "South High School could no longer exist the way it was operating. The situation got pretty far out of hand there. No reflection on the teachers, but from action there I would question what those kids were learning or—more to the point— what they were not learning."[131] Political discourse and student direct action had chipped away at the cornerstone of managerial racism. School officials believed South High was the source of the new dissident culture. In response, the board put forward a "progressive" response that appeared concerned with achieving racial balance. It was a familiar response that sought to shape the pattern of racial dialogue. But black students had given rise to new possibilities, and the old response proved ineffectual even within conventional channels of black authority. Moreover, the School Board's decision to close South High and bus black students to white schools led to a political backlash from white neighborhood residents within Grand Rapids. With the congenial politics of moderation coming undone at the seams by the late 1960s, predictably the business community attempted to intervene to preserve harmony. Instead of committing to decisive action earlier, the Chamber of Commerce sat idle for decades until the racial troubles hit a fever pitch and a number of businesses as well as metropolitan growth plans came under attack. Thus it is necessary to understand how the business community sought to recede the wave of protest and build "a more livable community" through the promise of progress.

6

WHERE DO WE GO FROM HERE?

Setting the Course for Racial Reconciliation

Sowing Seeds

"It was the years," Ella Sims recalled, "that white groups and white organizations, who'd never thought of a black board member, were looking for one, and it seemed that I got stuck on every board throughout the city." Sims was exactly the type of black "indigenous leader" the business community needed to know to preserve the city's integrity in the wake of the 1967 racial uprising. In the coming years, black residents in Grand Rapids would continue to struggle with attaining racial equality. New actors would move center stage, while once prominent characters drew the curtain and retreated from public life. Although her behind-the-scenes efforts were already well known in the black community, Sims's contributions became more perceptible to the white community following the rebellion.[1]

"I'm really from Mississippi by way of Arkansas," Sims reminisced. "Remember Emmett Till? Where they found his body, that river just right up the hill is the house I was born in." Although she left Mississippi prior to the murder of Emmett Till, Sims recalled that while growing up in the South, she was surrounded by violence: "It was just plenty beatings and lot of, lot of violence, lot of violence." In one instance, Sims recalled a body was discovered a half mile from her house. The savage attacks worried her even as a child: "There was so many times we thought that my dad would be killed because my dad was . . . there was a good term they used for it . . . he never knew his place. He never knew his place." Outspoken, Sims's father was protective of his children and especially Sims's mother, who was "very crippled." One incident that arose between her father and a new plantation owner, who desired to have the whole family work, required the family to move at night to avoid physical harm. "He said, 'That's my wife, no man on earth says anything to her. No man goes to the house and tell her to go to work, as a matter of fact she does not work, she's handicapped and she does not work.'" The plantation owner responded, according to Sims, "Nigger, as fast you can you get off my farm, you'd better be gone tomorrow. And we moved, I remember that. . . . So, I missed a lot of the stuff that people went with white people because my dad just didn't allow it." But, Sims recalled, it was incidents like this that caused everybody to believe "he would be killed, but, thank God he never was."[2]

Sims attended "a one room school house with a potbellied stove and one teacher, teaching us all" before her parents sent her to stay with relatives to attend high school in Helen, Arkansas. "I certainly looked up to the teachers," she affirmed. "Black kids in the South then, those were the only professionals they knew, was a teacher and a preacher." Sims discovered relief from the racial strains of southern society inside the classroom and gained inspiration from her teachers. However, during eleventh grade, Sims left school. "I met a young man and got married, when I was seventeen." Three years later she gave birth to their first child in 1944. Sadly, Sims remembered, her son became seriously ill at ten months: "And so my baby was so sick and I took him to the doctor that Monday and the doctor took great pains in telling me . . . how dehydrated the baby was. He said, 'If you'd have stayed away until tomorrow your baby would have died.'" Tragically, that same night, Sims recollected, "my husband and I both heard a funny noise and we woke up and my baby died right there in his arms." Adding to her heartbreak, Sims's husband died the following year.[3]

"I just couldn't even, you know, I was . . . twenty-one years old—I couldn't even grasp how ill he was. . . . He died five days after Thanksgiving, of course, by the end it was over into December, and by March I was still in such a bad way, until my doctor said to me, 'Why don't you take a trip?'" Sims reached out to the relatives she had lived with during her high school days in Helen, Arkansas. They had moved to Grand Rapids, so Sims traveled to Michigan for a short stay. She acquired a job at the Pantlind Hotel. "You could easily do that. You could go down one day and start working the same day. Jobs were not that hard to find then, jobs like that," she mentioned. After three months, Sims started work for C&O Railroad. "I went out there and they hired me. You would clean coaches, trains that people went back and forth in. . . . I can't even remember what I made—money—but it was more money than I'd ever heard of in my life." It was more money, she observed, than her former husband made while working as a lumber truck driver while living in the South. Thus, nearly six months later, she recalled, "my cousin said to me, 'Why don't you stay?' And it took me another six months to think, well maybe I'll stay."[4]

Still overcome with grief, Sims reluctantly tried to put the pieces together again: "All I could think of when my first husband died was that life was over, my life was over. And all that year I felt the same thing. I was just existing for my baby. I never thought another man would come into my life, but just when I'd been here a year I met my future husband, Clyde." Sims sold her home in

Arkansas and immersed herself in the Grand Rapids community: "As my kids grew up I was right in school all the time." Sims started her work in the Sheldon School PTA in 1950. Later she served as vice president and president of Campau Park PTA, and eventually Sims made important contributions on the South High School PTA and South High School Action Council: "I can never emphasize enough . . . how I raised the whole neighborhood. My kids could never be away from home as much as the other fellas, but I always said, 'You can't go there, but they can come here.'" The Simses' house became the center of activity. "Kids just used to stay over at my house, sleep all over the floor," and Sims would not have it any other way. It allowed her the ability to "keep my boys on the straight and narrow. When I knew anything I was just mama-ing the whole neighborhood, and so many young people now give me credit for helping them." Like those influential people in her life back in Mississippi and Arkansas, Sims was investing in not only the growth of her ten children (nine boys and one girl) but also the future of the entire black community.[5]

That sense of shared responsibility pulled Sims in the direction of the Office of Equal Opportunity (OEO) as a volunteer in 1964. According to Sims, she joined forces with Ray and Melvin Tardy, "who had a self-help program, but what happened was once OEO came into being—it was created for the very thing they were trying to do in the community, help people help themselves, give [black] people a say in their own destiny, let them be involved with what was happening to them." The emphasis on community involvement lured "indigenous leaders" like Sims deeper into the OEO.[6] As part of President Lyndon B. Johnson's War on Poverty, new local community agencies were established to fight inner-city poverty. These agencies, federal officials believed, should provide for "maximum feasible participation of the residents" to promote a greater sense of communal responsibility and pride among residents living in poverty-stricken neighborhoods. Although the barrage of antipoverty programs never fully received sufficient resources to achieve their goals, the emphasis on increased participation among the poor provided "indigenous leaders," such as Sims, with a platform to effect change.[7]

Designed to "provide local citizen participation and responsibility," the OEO poverty initiative combined the notion of equal opportunity with community action. It was a strategy intrinsic in Sims's life. A high school dropout and mother of ten, Sims understood the struggle more intimately than most. She became one of the first urban agents of the Community Action Program (CAP), which was intended to help fight poverty by empowering poor people as part of the War on Poverty. CAP programs, such as On-Job Training (OJT), provided hiring and training for unemployed persons. In a ten-month period, OJT placed fifty-eight people in new employment opportunities, including "four bank tellers, a real estate agent, two news photographers, three electronic technicians, a draftsman, and a maintenance supervisor as well as cooks, secretaries, mechanics, clerks and other employees."[8] Although War on Poverty programs had varied results in San Francisco and Philadelphia, Sargent Shriver, the first national director of the OEO, cited Grand Rapids as "one of three national models of the type of federal and local collaboration the program was intended to foster" during Senate testimony.[9]

Neighborhood improvement centers, such as the Sheldon Complex, afforded a greater number of blacks an opportunity to have increased participation and control over issues in the black community in the mid-1960s. It offered poor blacks a critical voice in a community that often listened to only middle-class leadership. Through the Sheldon Complex, Sims was able to provide her neighbors with services in health, education, and welfare. From adult literacy programs, day care service, latch key, and family development classes, to social functions, newsletter publication, and senior citizens' services, neighborhood improvement centers attempted to centralize the needs of black urban poor residents. Many of these programs, such as Head Start, Neighborhood Youth Corps, and Job Corps, were geared toward young people, and neighborhood centers, such as the Sheldon Complex, became a central meeting place for black youth. However, in the minds of many black Grand Rapidians, Sheldon Complex staffers often heightened communal tension by exceeding their OEO province in their relationships with black youth.

For example, during the mustache controversy, Sims's organization served as a refuge for South High students. The Sheldon Complex offered an open environment for young students to discuss issues germane to their lives. High school students from South felt comfortable consulting Sims and the Tardy brothers. Theresa B. Crawford, however, worried that the community center was sending the wrong message to the city's black youth. "Many of us would like to know if the Sheldon Complex is still under the OEO," she wrote in a letter to then-Congressman Gerald R. Ford. If so, she questioned what gave the staff "the right to start a controversy like this." Crawford voiced the concerns held by a group of like-minded black residents who believed that black youth "should not be taught" by Tardy, Sims, or anybody else "to be defiant." Crawford concluded, "We sincerely hope this matter can be resolved peacefully as it is also antagonizing our white friends."[10] As a result of inquiries like this one that linked the Sheldon Complex to a rise in youth violence, Sims's organization fell under negative scrutiny.

After the mustache incident, Congressman Ford issued a letter to Shriver regarding the "dispute" at South High. Ford requested a copy of OEO's report marked "Administrative Confidential." He informed Shriver that the report "concerns a situation in my own Congressional District over which many people are very deeply concerned." In defiance, Shriver denied Ford access to the "Administrative Confidential" report.[11] Shriver defended his OEO employees at the Sheldon Complex. "Ray Tardy, the highly capable Negro director of the Sheldon Complex, did not call for either the walkout or the picketing," Shriver wrote to Ford. He also noted that "Ella Mary Sims, an anti-poverty worker with the Sheldon Complex, did not participate in either the . . . picketing or in the . . . walkout." Shriver determined that aside from the "questionable use of a Sheldon Complex mimeograph machine," used to print pamphlets and statements by the students, "there was no such unjustifiable activity on the part of the Sheldon Complex or CAA personnel." In a final thought, Shriver called Congressman Ford's attention to the fact that the ruling made by the committee to investigate the entire affair recommended "that the mustache rule at South High be dropped," and, according to Shriver, that seemed to prove "that this action should remove any doubt as to the legitimacy of the interest held by Sheldon Complex staff in communicating target-area discontent with the moustache regulation."[12]

Despite some criticism from within the black community and voices of discontent within the business community, Sims ardently believed the Sheldon Complex was a valuable resource in the black community: "I can't even emphasize to people how helpful, how helpful" it was; "I think it did just what it was created to do." Sims recognized that OEO programs "throughout the nation as a whole they were not that, you know, they were not that successful," but she added that Grand Rapids had a "very good program. . . . There would be many who will tell you that was just really a waste of money, but I'll tell you it was a good example of what could be done." Sims acknowledged that the War on Poverty programs were worthwhile ideas that should have been improved not discarded: "If you stop and think about it . . . since those years our nation has gone backward, backward, in the field of civil rights."[13]

Sims readily admitted, "There are those who will say that Ella Sims is a product of the OEO program, of the Poverty Program . . . and part of that is true, because it was a vehicle for me to emerge from." However, she added, "I was already emerging." Her time, effort, and influence had helped mold a generation of black youth activists who, like Sims's father, "didn't know their place" in Grand Rapids managerial system. She was central to the history of South High through her PTA activity and her support of its student population. Also, through the Sheldon Complex, Sims was forever linked to the mustache incident at South High. Although her efforts as an "indigenous leader" resulted in Sims's being named coordinator of urban agents at first Sheldon and then Franklin-Hall complexes, the Michigan State Committee on Adult Education, the President's Council on Adult Basic Education, and the Michigan Welfare League Planning Committee, the one position that eluded Ella Sims was a seat on the Board of Education.[14]

Surprisingly, jobs ranked second in a list of concerns enumerated by Michigan citizens in 1971, and social services were even farther down the list. According to a newspaper survey that extended over a region covering 1,200 miles of territory, "School pupil busing to achieve racial integration [was] the hottest public issue." Few could gage the pulse of the black youth community better than Sims. Perhaps Sims's connection with the mustache incident hindered her chances to win a seat on the School Board. Despite her clear capabilities, whites viewed Sims as standing outside the mainstream black leadership. Her position on busing further isolated her and placed her in the minority. When asked whether integration should be a goal of the School Board, and busing a means to achieve it, Sims responded, "Segregation has been called a disease of society and should be corrected by society. We cannot deny that our schools play a great part in continuing the traditions of our society. So integration should be the board's goal. If busing can help this goal, and it can, then busing and cross-busing should be used to this end."[15] Sims was the only candidate of the twelve running for the School Board in 1971 who favored cross-busing and the preservation of inner-city schools.

Given the rising animosity toward busing in black and white communities alike, progressive Republicans looked to Paul Phillips to chart a moderate course on educational reform. However the decision to close South High and bus black students to white schools generated a level of white backlash that exceeded managerial containment and arguably pushed Phillips to abandon hope for racial change. Thus, the busing controversy pushed the managerial culture of the city beyond its limits.

"Good Faith" No More

The fight to desegregate schools took a discernible toll on Phillips. He sought to win favor in two disparate camps and seemingly found little support in either one. According to the *Grand Rapids Press,* he faced insults from the black community as he stood on the stage of South High School and asked black parents to "trust him and allow 'their' high school to be closed and their youngsters to be bused to all-white schools."[16] Despite hearing chants of "Uncle Tom," Phillips always maneuvered in good faith, and he genuinely believed that equality could be achieved through integration. He hoped that more blacks would demonstrate confidence in the School Board's desire to achieve educational equality, even if the process proved slow. Phillips believed that his moral-persuasion tactics, which had once helped many blacks obtain employment in predominantly all-white industries, would produce similar results in obtaining educational equality through integration. "Sometimes when I get weary and wonder if it's worth it all," Phillips mused, "I turn out the lights and rock a little while, reflect a little while . . . then I get back up thinking it is worth it all and keep on going."[17] His commitment hinged on the integration ideal, yet Phillips's optimism became jaded during his stint as a GRSB member. Perhaps the empty promises of school administrators, subsequent violent episodes, and the rising tide of black displeasure with old educational reform methods caused Phillips to recognize that managerial racism was at work in educational-reform policies. He declared, "There has been an improvement from the standpoint of the number of high school and college graduates," but "the biggest problem is the segregated school system."[18] For all his success in securing jobs, Phillips failed to achieve parallel results with integrating the schools. In 1971, he stated, "the Grand Rapids school system is more segregated now than it was in 1947, because the percentage of nonwhites was smaller then and everyone went to school together."[19]

As the only black School Board member, Phillips understood the difficulties of negotiating racism and educational progress. After six consecutive years of service, he again challenged the general public and his fellow GRSB members in 1968 to increase their efforts toward racial equality. In his appeal, Phillips advocated for change in five areas he determined as critical concerns: (1) Employ more quality teachers in the inner-city school, (2) refrain from hiring teachers that harbor prejudice, (3) create a special vocational training program for expelled children, (4) hire additional counselors to work with hard-to-reach students of the inner city, and (5) implement a courageous policy whereby children of all races, creeds, and colors can converge for the educational experience of learning.[20] These issues did not represent new concerns but represented a shift in his tone and word choice.

"We talk about telling the Negro to pull himself up by his own bootstraps and then we take away his boots," Phillips declared. "We've done a good job in America of making the road very difficult for the Negro. . . . [W]e have given him hopelessness," he continued.[21] That sense of despair, which began to set in with the larger black community in the mid-1960s, finally gripped the unflappable integration apostle. According to Phillips, Grand Rapids "started on a higher level of potentiality for good race relations . . . but I have been disturbed and disappointed that we are not farther ahead. We have always had the tools, but the community has been reluctant to get involved in solving the problems."[22] As a result of the inactivity among the business community in particular, Phillips believed that a firm polarization began to set in Grand Rapids during the late 1960s that stemmed from the "Negro Revolution" of demands for minority improvements and resulted in greater resistance on the part of whites to acquiesce to these growing demands.

Phillips claimed that throughout the 1950s "the black man's hand was open, but the white man wouldn't grasp it." The 1960s ushered in a different sentiment among blacks, and Phillips warned that the "outstretched hand changed to the clenched fist."[23] The black community could no longer demonstrate "good faith." Rather, the trials and tribulations that Phillips attempted to put to sleep at night still awakened him with each new dawn. Surprisingly—or perhaps not—when Phillips emerged from his rocking chair on August 15, 1969, he did so to announce his retirement from the GRSB after deep reflection about the failure of school integration. He simply cited his "frustration over the city's lack of speed in integrating the schools."[24]

Members of the black community shared in Phillips's distress. In 1970, the parents of black students in the Grand Rapids Public School system initiated a class-action school-desegregation lawsuit against the GRSB. In an attempt to eliminate the dual educational school system in Grand Rapids, the local NAACP attempted to remove each school's racial identity by seeking a two-way busing judgment. Numerous white parents denied the relationship between busing and race. Instead, they framed the controversy over busing as a dilemma centering on the safety of their children. The importance of neighborhood schools became the rallying cry of parents from the prevailing white suburban school communities. Their membership in the exclusive predominantly white suburban club granted generational access for their children, and white parents set out to ensure that the elite membership criteria remained intact.

According to a local newspaper article, whites most often invoked the phrase "you pick your neighborhood, you have a right to send your children to school there."[25] Yet inner-city black families understood all too well that the marriage between neighborhoods and schools constituted an intricate web of racial opposition that denied black children equal educational justice and that, more often than not, their neighborhoods were selected for them. Phillips warned that there are "dangers in the trend of the movement to the suburbs by white families" and that "unless the whites stop running to the suburbs, we're going to face pockets of resegregation." Ultimately, he acknowledged, "we will never integrate our schools until we integrate our neighborhoods."[26] Therefore spatial composition and neighborhood schools seemed inextricably bound. The nexus between the two produced a portrait of metropolitan Grand Rapids painted in the stark contrasting colors of black and white.

After a nearly fifty-year struggle for educational equality, the GRNAACP filed suit on behalf of members of the black community against the Grand Rapids school system. Its efforts met with staunch resistance from not only the School Board but also members of the white community. The GRNAACP pushed forward with the suit, which followed a larger national trend by black citizens seeking to win court favor in the pursuit of educational equality. With Phillips no longer holding a seat of influence on the GRSB, blacks had little maneuvering power to affect change from inside the local bureaucracy. They instead took their complaints to a higher court of appeals. However, a strong antibusing tide was rising in the city. This reactionary movement would challenge not only the issue of busing but also the limits of the city's progressive mystique.

The Antibusing Movement

The arrival of black students to Union High School in September 1968 confirmed that the GRSB voluntary one-way busing initiative was underway. Determined to end busing, white school parents on the Westside, home to Union High School—the newest suburban high school in Grand Rapids—and a deeply rooted Polish working-class community, led the charge against mandatory metropolitan busing. In January 1969, Vernis Schad stated, "A political group was formed in the Union High area for the purpose of recruiting and electing to the board candidates who opposed the Master Plan."[27] Everett Van Slyke, a forty-two-year-old codirector of the Union High Parents Association (UHPA); Jack L. Boonstra, a forty-year-old former General Motor Corporation employee; and Lawrence F. Pojeski, a forty-four-year-old codirector of the UHPA, emerged from the Westside community to unite forces as the three-man parent contingent that ran for open seats on the GRSB on an antibusing ticket.

With "3 Is the Key" as one of their political advertisements, these men had done the most to establish a uniform antibusing movement in the suburbs. Van Slyke, Boonstra, and Pojeski resolved, "Our children shall have the finest public school system that we can provide, a system in which the talents of ALL can be channeled into productive, meaningful and enriched lives." In addition, the anti-busing nominees promised "to maintain local control over the education of our children." Furthermore, they vowed "to have order and discipline fairly administered in every school." These election promises, however, did not cause them to stand apart from the assurances made by other School Board candidates. Nevertheless, the Grand Rapids voting public gravitated toward the "ticket of three" because of their views against the transference of students outside their neighborhood boundaries. Their message, "3 Is the Key," let voters know metaphorically that if voted in together, all three men would serve as the instrument that could lock out black children from the door of suburban schools.[28]

The antibusing bloc trooped door to door, canvassing all neighborhoods with their campaign pledges, which, according to their advertisement, promised, "Except for transportation as a temporary device to relieve crowding, busing and/or cross busing [will] be eliminated." Furthermore, the three candidates considered busing a "discriminatory and demeaning experience for students bused, an economic extravagance utterly without merit or justification." They promised voters that they intended "to support and implement the 'neighborhood school' concept at every stage of public education" and "to subject the so-called MASTER PLAN to review and substantial revision." Firmly situated alongside the notion that "schools should be built where children live," the antibusing alliance proclaimed that a vote for it would ensure kids remained in their own neighborhoods and that "any other vote is a vote for busing!"[29]

The "Three Star Extra" pamphlet, which contained a cartoon illustrating tax dollars burning out of a bus exhaust pipe, helped bring widespread attention to the issue of integration throughout the community. Busing surfaced as the most contested topic of several School Board meetings and at various campaign appearances. Large audiences tracked the issue on a regular basis, and on occasion, similar to the circumstance of a January 1969 board meeting, meetings were adjourned before members of the audience were allowed to speak. Throughout the primary election of 1969, several political meetings ended in shouting matches. "School integration cannot be avoided," GRSB President David E. Post announced at an election gathering of the potential School Board contestants. Evidently Post underestimated the rising strength of the antibusing movement present at the gathering and throughout the community at large. Van Slyke, in his reply, complained that "busing is discriminatory." By appearing in numbers at these gatherings, the antibusing coalition used School Board meetings and election gatherings to corral more followers. Its message resonated positively with suburbanites, not only because it expressed fear and loathing toward blacks but also because that fear and dislike remained masked behind a veil of sentimental dispossession. "It is a fair request to want your children to go to school near where you bought your home," antibusing supporter George Bowman proclaimed. He added, "I am not against integration, I am against forced integration. . . . [T]he master plan should be reviewed from cover to cover, then 'start, all over.'" Similar comments invigorated white audiences while steering clear of espousing openly racist ideologies.[30]

Other School Board candidates, such as J. Warren Eardley, a forty-five-year-old former labor-relations supervisor at General Motors, and Schad, a forty-three-year-old member of the Persons against Racism group, voiced different opinions. Eardley favored the current one-way busing plan. He believed that the "Supreme Court, Congress and the Civil Rights Act 'all say it is the business of the Board of Education to integrate . . . and the sooner the better.'" Schad agreed that "board members are 'legally obligated' under the Supreme Court ruling to move toward full integration" but added, "busing might not be the solution." Rather she suggested "open enrollment, redistricting of school attendance areas, good planning on new facilities and the shared experiences of an educational park as other possibilities."[31] But the audience members and white suburbanites among the general public did not want to hear about ideas; instead they simply wanted an end to busing as well as a return to normalcy. And hard declarative statements, the *Grand Rapids Press* noted, which spoke out "against busing in any way" on the part of antibusing candidates received audience favor as well as the meetings' loudest applause.[32]

The three Union High School parents headed off charges that they held racist beliefs by spinning the issue of race. Despite the fact that the antibusing bloc based its entire campaign on a direct assault against busing, the master plan, and opposition to integration except via the means of open housing, it proclaimed that sentiments against busing did not equate to racism. Rather, Van Slyke argued that the present School Board members lacked "sensitivity to the black community because the plan was sold to whites on the basis of 'Breathe easy; we are only going to bus black children.'"[33] Mockingly, the antibusing bloc noted the obvious racial bias of the one-way busing plan and utilized that angle as a rallying cry to stop the racism caused by busing. Its rhetoric received overwhelming approval from Grand Rapids citizens.

It soon became clear that white citizens overwhelmingly opposed busing. Donald D. Cooper, a white citizen, stated firmly, "We oppose busing because it is racist." He added, "Whether children are bused to achieve integration, as in the North, or to destroy segregation, as in the South, the selection of those to be bused is based on the color of the skin. That is racism." But in underlining the ostensible claim for blind racial justice, Cooper also harbored a racialized sentimental dispossession that appeared to blame blacks for the current urban decline. Cooper claimed:

> We oppose busing our kids to scholastically inferior schools. We oppose putting our kids into the terroristic atmosphere of many of those schools. We oppose putting our kids into schools where bathroom doors are removed for 'safety,' where children are cautioned not to go to the bathroom alone, where teachers' functions are largely order-keeping, where kids sometimes urinate on the walls, where obscenity is not unusual.

Cooper concluded, "You can use all the euphemisms you want, these things are happening and most people know it."[34]

The support for the antibusing bloc came from voters who had similar concerns. Not until the advent of the antibusing contingent could voters openly express these concerns. But Van Slyke, Boonstra, and Pojeski developed a channel of communication for disgruntled white suburbanites. According to Cooper, suburbanites moved "to the suburbs, most of us, because we wanted to, and could afford more room, trees, space, fresher air, newer and modern schools, and for many of us because we wanted to live in a small community." He explained:

> If, in leaving, we left the core city's problems, or even if our leaving created some of those problems, it was coincidental. (I almost felt the need to say we didn't want to create those problems!) We left to go TO something, and go AWAY from the inherent crowding problems of the city.[35]

Yet the dilemma over busing students represented a widening gap between city and suburb. The balkanization of metropolitan landscapes intensified impoverishment within the inner city. As droves of urban residents, such as Cooper, moved to suburban neighborhoods, the School Board sought to meet their needs. The construction of schools, steering and placement of teachers, and overall inner-city school neglect produced an uneven educational playing field. And as black inner-city families pursued educational rights denied to them, white suburbanites attempted to preserve their suburban liberties via the ballot box.

According to the *Grand Rapids Press,* "In its first voting opportunity, Grand Rapids rejected the school system's integrating master plan."[36] Although adopted in 1968, the master plan received no citywide vote—only public hearings. But the GRSB victory of the antibusing bloc, the only candidates who opposed the master plan, clearly demonstrated that registered voters rejected racially balanced schools and busing of high school students. Of six candidates vying for three-year terms, Boonstra received the most votes (10,341), and Van Slyke obtained the second most (9,952). Similarly, for the one-year term, Pojeski topped all contenders, as the bloc of Union High School parents swept the election and sought to carry out the public's mandate.

The three-man contingent credited their victory to their platform described in a local newspaper as "junk the integrating master plan and busing."[37] Yet the way the antibusing bloc achieved victory is equally revealing. The *Grand Rapids Press* observed that "about 80 per cent of the city's voters did stay home on a warm, clear spring day." This represented a startling number indeed, considering the gravity of the election. Yet as one GRSB member noted, in "progressive" city fashion, "staying home was a conscience-soothing 'No' vote." Unsurprisingly, a community unwilling to overtly grapple with its racial feelings or engage in the rising racial backlash, as Phillips noted, decided to make silence their weapon and allow the chips on educational policy matters to fall as they might, even if that meant denying educational rights and turning their collective back on black residents. The efforts of the antivoting bloc made this possible. As the *Grand Rapids Press* explained, the "Three Star Extra" pamphlet and its overall campaign "got people to start questioning. . . . [I]t got them to change their votes or to stay home because they didn't know what to do." For those citizens on the fence, or who "couldn't feel right voting 'No,'" they simply "just didn't vote."[38]

Ironically, the occasion marked the one-year anniversary of the walk of hope that united black and white residents in a tribute march for the slain civil rights leader Martin Luther King Jr. With more than four thousand participants, the protest was supposed to represent "the beginning of a resurrection movement in Grand Rapids." At the demonstration, Marshall Purnell, a black high school student, read a poem he wrote entitled "The King." The first stanza of the poem reads:

> He died today, yes he died today,
> Yes, for you and me he died.
> Now I have a dream, as glorious as his,
> That America has at last opened its eyes.
> Oh God, let us believe in this dream
> More important, let us make it come about,
> For in this dream I visioned the sands of time,
> And time has just about run out.
> The King is dead
> Long live the King.[39]

Unfortunately, the "Dream" in Grand Rapids now faced the obstacle of overcoming the rise of a vocal antibusing contingent that ostensibly had the support of the majority of the white community. Indeed, school committee member William Steenland observed, "The board has got to take a look at what the public means. The voters are trying to tell us something. Maybe it is time we listened." The antibusing bloc agreed with this sentiment. Boonstra claimed that "we didn't get much support from the press. As a matter of fact, the press worked against us and that made the campaign tougher . . . but I feel the people came up with the answer, and that's [to] review the master plan."[40]

Similarly, new board member Van Slyke pronounced that this "was the vote of the people on the master plan." On the other hand, some board members, such as Phillips, expressed disappointment yet remained cautiously open to any alternative plans that the new GRSB members could author. On the extreme opposite side, board member Mary Ann Keeler stated, "I'm not even going to congratulate them. . . . I think the whole thing is disgusting."[41] Yet with the voting returns in, it remained apparent that a change also existed on the horizon, and the absence of voter participation ensured that a segregated Grand Rapids would once again thrive.

Four months later, Phillips ultimately decided that the recent turn of events meant he could not remain on the board. He retired from the GRSB during an unexpired term, citing utter disappointment over the city's apathy and unwillingness to integrate the schools. Circumstances prior to the appearance of the Westside clique seemed desperate, but the arrival of a united antibusing front made the situation appear all the more abysmal for Phillips. The sentiment that the antibusing bloc had its newly constructed high school and that it represented a small faction of biased people did not quite capture the more widespread appeal of its anti-integration message. Moreover, if the School Board election of 1969 had not made this point clear, the committee elections one year later would solidify this fact.

In addition to Phillips's retirement, long-time board members Steenland and Joseph Van Blooys announced that they, too, would not seek reelection. This meant that three additional seats opened up, and the antibusing bloc sought to seize the window of opportunity. Pojeski, who had sought a one-year term during the prior election, now wanted to secure a three-year term along with his running mate, Bowman; in addition, Carl H. Johnson, also a Westside candidate, attempted to secure a one-year appointment.

All three men ran in opposition to the master plan. In particular, they opposed the section that called for desegregating outlying schools by the busing of inner-city students.[42] As two new antibusing bloc members stood poised to capture additional School Board seats, their anti-integration coalition members already on the board began chipping away at the establishment. Their efforts to gridlock the "busing" process sparked the sudden departure of Nina Sleet from the School Board in February 1970.

Sleet, who in September 1969 replaced Phillips after his retirement, served on the board for roughly six months before making a decision to "quit her seat Monday night after accusing her colleagues of 'completely ignoring the black community,'" one newspaper account noted. Sleet commenced a ten-minute speech at the beginning of the monthly board meeting, which berated GRSB members who she claimed "disregarded appeals from black groups, recommendations on integration from the State Board of Education and a resolution to give 'leverage' to equal hiring practices on board projects." Before walking out, Sleet concluded, "When it is felt that we are able to take actions that will not only provide an improved atmosphere of learning for our middle class children but also our poor white, black, and Spanish-speaking children, you have my address and phone number, gentlemen. Please call me."[43]

The reaction among GRSB members remained mixed. Westside board representative Pojeski said that "he was shocked," and he insisted that the committee "met at least three times each with the NAACP and Urban League." But School Board member Rosemary Alland stated, "We haven't been able to cover the amount of material we should be covering and we aren't scheduling enough work sessions." The Black Unity Council (BUC), a local citizens' council, also supported Sleet's decision to walk away. In a public statement, the BUC stated that "we are deeply concerned about the members of the board of education who do not and will not address themselves to the feelings and concerns of the inner-city community."[44] The concerns of the black community stemmed from the ongoing disturbances at the high school level.

On Wednesday, May 27, 1970, approximately seventy black students, or nearly half the school's black population at Creston High School, located in the interior suburbs of Grand Rapids, faced arrest for disorderly conduct following a walkout precipitated by a morning hallway fracas. The incident began just before 8:20 A.M. The police report indicated that "the first fight broke out in the north doorway of the school and spread to the parking lot in front of the building." Black and white boys as well as girls fought intermittently until police cruisers arrived around 9:30 A.M.

The cops pronounced that the predominantly black youth gathered outside the schools "were a 'disorderly group' and ordered them to board buses" to return to their respective neighborhoods. Nearly all the students did so peacefully. The fight left one sixteen-year-old black student with cuts to his chin, arm, and wrist after he 'fell' into a glass door pane in a scuffle with a white student. Yet when the dust settled, only one black student—also age sixteen—remained detained at police headquarters. The police arrested the boy on assault charges and held him at the police station until his parents could pick him up.[45]

Yet another day of school came to a screeching halt because of racial animosity. Russell Waters, the principal of Creston High School, met with a predominantly black group of roughly ninety parents and additional faculty members later that same evening. Despite the conspicuous absence of white parents at the meeting, Waters, his staff, and the parents in attendance decided that "it would be 'good judgment' to close the school for a day."[46] Reportedly, racial tension at Creston High School had heightened daily since the arrival of inner-city black students, and a few recent minor altercations had helped fan the flames of an already existing fire.

Initially, School Superintendent Norman P. Weinheimer and School Board President Steenland opposed the idea of canceling classes. But after hearing the report from Waters, both agreed to "a one day cooling off period."[47] With the extra day off for Memorial Day, the students received four days of cool-down time, yet ninety-six hours would not provide enough time to find an adequate solution to the interracial bugbear that stood as an insurmountable obstacle for members in the Grand Rapids community.

The white residents of Grand Rapids did not want to deal with the supposed "race problem" present in their community. Many whites in Grand Rapids did not even acknowledge black people, except as viewing them as the "other" members of their city. Referencing white citizens of the community, Phillips declared that in Grand Rapids, prejudiced attitudes existed "on the level of not wanting to recognize the problem or to get involved in solving it."[48] The current one-way busing program supported Phillips's statement, and the recent incident at Creston High School simply magnified the great racial divide existing within the city. School officials and white community members alike placed great emphasis on the fact that nearly seventy black students "walked out" of school. Yet the reasons why these random individual black students transformed into a "disorderly group" remained of less importance.

In actuality, notes signed by the "Creston Ku Klux Klan" served as the impetus for Creston's racial controversy. Whether a real or fictional organization, the signature of a "Creston Ku Klux Klan" appeared at the bottom of several documents distributed to black students, which were later turned over to the principal. Although the *Grand Rapids Press* noted that school officials initially claimed that they "did not know what caused the fight," black students claimed from the outset that "racial tensions were high because of threatening notes."[49]

In addition, antiblack slogans found on the lavatory walls corroborated the accounts given by minority students. The effort to catch the perpetrators responsible for the racist scrawling on the bathroom walls and the notes circulated within the school received minimal attention. Perhaps that is because many of the white parents did not view their own children as "the problem"— rather, that label belonged to the black students who routinely "invaded" white space. White parents of Creston High School students deemed their children's behavior as acceptable, because it simply represented the extension and implementation of deep philosophical beliefs on race held by the parents. Every indication from a 1971 *Press* survey, which polled black and white high school seniors on their racial attitudes, sustained this notion.

As one student said, "When the Negroes and the whites want to get together, they will do it on their own. People don't like to be pushed into things and therefore they'll rebel just to show you can't make someone do something they don't want to do."[50] Unsurprisingly, comments from the youth in Grand Rapids like the one above often reflected the racial views of their parents. Of those questioned, roughly 73 percent of the seniors from the suburbs and 71 percent surveyed in the city claimed that their outlook regarding the integration of schools mirrored that of their parents.

Another student commented, "Our parents pay taxes for the building of public schools in the neighborhoods and then you bus kids out to schools where their parents did not pay taxes on. . . . Garbage, complete garbage."[51] The responses reflected clear support for neighborhood schools, but the reasons why varied tremendously. Regardless of the rationale behind supporting neighborhood schools, the reality held that white students still enjoyed the benefits of neighborhood schools, because board officials reserved busing duties for blacks only.

"In this plan, it would not be proposed that cross busing be effected, but rather, that busing would be one way from the inner-city to the periphery educational centers." This edict, authored in bold by the School Board in its 1968 master plan, ensured that suburban schools would remain intact as neighborhood schools. Inner-city schools, on the other hand, stood on an unsound foundation. With the 1968 decision to convert the only predominantly black high school into a middle school, the School Board set off a wave of controversy that rippled through the community. Black community members appeared far from certain that forfeiting their neighborhood schools would render educational equality, but the alternative plan to remain in a confined ghetto quadrant with inferior resources while the newest—and underenrolled—facilities went up along peripheral suburban lines seemed even more catastrophic.

Suburban parents and their children recognized that schools were the battlegrounds on which they could best defend neighborhood autonomy. The white community expressed its support for the suburban anti-integration movement again during the 1970 School Board race by electing Pojeski and Bowman to the board for a three-year term, as well as Johnson for a one-year stint. Ella Sims, the only black School Board candidate to survive the primary, failed in her attempt to secure a seat. The suburban voter movement against busing demonstrated the shift in metropolitan power as the antibusing forces secured a 5–4 advantage on the newly composed board. After achieving his victory, Bowman proclaimed, "The master plan is dead. . . . I think we can do now what the three candidates elected last year wanted to accomplish." He continued, "I don't think we will vote the same way on everything, but it is pretty clear which way a vote on neighborhood schools or busing will go." The prophetic statement by Bowman did not take long to come to fruition, as the antibusing-dominant School Board "scrapped the unpopular master plan" less then twelve months later, on March 22, 1971.[52]

The ensuing months produced even more unrest inside the schools that reflected the animosity existing within the larger community and seemingly validated the decision to rescind the master plan. A white student boycott on May 10, 1971, caused Union High School to close again for more than a week. The boycott turned violent, as the article noted, after "about 200 white students refused to attend classes to protest 'preferential treatment' of blacks and lack of disciplinary action against blacks."[53] The racial incidents did not remain confined to Union High School. Instead, the chaos spilled over to Ottawa Hills High School and subsequently forced that school to close the following day. The complaints voiced by white students accompanied their parents' sense of sentimental dispossession. Despite the fact that black students waited in inclement weather for late buses, witnessed the closing of their neighborhood high school, and found themselves transported to racially hostile environments, white students still believed that blacks somehow received "preferential treatment."

Similar to the altercations at Creston High School the year prior, blacks still received no consideration regarding their circumstances. Instead, transportation of black students continued to represent an "invasion" that required the white community to align forces to impede efforts toward integrated schools. The result of the mounting racial violence produced an increased police presence that met students on their return to school on May 19, 1971. Police enforcement represented the school administrations' new answer to solving the ongoing race problem.[54] The "school administrations' 'police state policy'" carried over into the 1971–1972 academic year. The new existence of police forces in school buildings underscored the GRSB's lack of preparedness and understanding regarding the integration process.[55]

Thus, the master plan died half-completed, but the *Grand Rapids Press* stated that the "plan's immediate effects riled certain quarters of the community and enabled many opponents to bump from the board incumbents who adopted it." At the end of the day, the GRSB that revoked the master plan consisted of none of the board members who had adopted it. The progressive educational reform movement had come to an end. As former School Board candidate Sims asserted, "Frankly, I think people got what they wanted. This is a very racist society and I think the . . . men who were elected represent the majority." She continued, "We have to face the facts about how that majority feels. To most people neighborhood schools mean lily-white schools."[56] In many ways, Sims stated the obvious on behalf of the black community. Historically, the educational experience, whether implemented by "progressive" reformers or the new antibusing candidates, placed a premium on white privilege. In a short span of two years, the long movement toward integration died in the Grand Rapids public court of opinion. But members of the black community sought to obtain a more favorable integration resolution through the judicial system. The antibusing bloc may have accomplished its immediate goal; however, the question remained open regarding whether the courts would uphold this emergent popular opinion.[57]

Victims of Happenstance

On August 20, 1970, the GRNAACP made good on its two-and-a-half-year promise to dispute the alleged segregationist practices of the city school system. The GRNAACP filed a class-action lawsuit that accused the Grand Rapids Board of Education of managing a segregated school system.[58] The suit registered the names of fifty-one school children as the chief complainants while listing the Grand Rapids Board of Education as well as the school superintendent as defendants. The grievance charged the School Board with "maintaining and perpetuating a bi-racial segregated public system" that violated due process of the law and ultimately denied children equal educational opportunity.[59] The lawsuit sought changes in school attendance boundaries, new schools in the black community, and a new integration plan.

The filing capped an adversarial history between the School Board and the GRNAACP. GRSB member Charles F. Porter viewed the suit as "not designed to bring the community closer together." Porter commented, "The Board has taken many steps to improve educational opportunities for all students despite the NAACP, which continues to take actions that promise little benefit for the city or its children." Somewhat more poised, in his first public reaction, Superintendent Weinheimer admitted, "We don't have fully integrated schools through the city," but "it's all due to present housing patterns." Weinheimer captured the common sentiment of his era, which viewed de facto housing patterns as the sole reason for racial imbalance in northern schools. Yet the GRNAACP contended that other factors, such as "segregated employment practices and budget appropriations and 'racist curriculum,'" also constituted evidence of a bi-racial school system. The filing also represented the second such suit against a Michigan school district in consecutive days, as the NAACP had also sued the Detroit school system a day prior, listing similar grievances.[60]

Former NAACP President Jerome Sorrells stated that the concession of one-way busing appeared as "the only way our children had a chance for significant learning."[61] Thus, when Phillips approved the closing of South High, the GRNAACP supported this undertaking, and even promoted it, because the Grand Rapids Urban League (GRUL) and the GRNAACP viewed this as the best way to achieve integrated schools. Without the local black high school, minority students would have to be bused to neighboring white schools, which would result in a less-segregated landscape. But the master plan and busing ignited an uproar throughout the community. Antibusing factions called Phillips "a communist" and considered his methods "radical."[62]

Whereas most whites in Grand Rapids opposed "Negro pupils attending their formerly all-white school," according to an account from the *Grand Rapids Press,* blacks also combated the idea of one-way busing and sought to achieve a two-way busing resolution instead. Dr. Joseph McMillan, former supervisor of inner-city schools, took exception to the fact that the plan "over a period of years would strip the black community of all its schools." Moreover, he contended that "integration should not be shouldered by one group."[63] Sims echoed this position in her candidacy for the School Board.

This sentiment became the focal point for the GRNAACP after the resignation of Phillips. With the loss of internal leverage, as one *Grand Rapids Press* article asserted, the "NAACP and other black community groups had 'second thoughts.'" Certainly the racial violence pervasive within the Grand Rapids high schools also weighed heavily in the decision to shift positions. Referencing racial violence at schools, Sorrells explained that "if this is the way integration is going to turn out, it won't do anyone any good." He continued, "We aren't against integration as a goal of the master plan . . . we are against one-way busing." Instead, the GRNAACP declared that the solution to the racial problems in the city had to include "total integration. . . . We still want schools in the black community but we want white children on the buses, too, going to them."[64]

Although few white community members embraced the new GRNAACP policy, Betty Tardy did. At a time when speaking out in favor of two-way busing resembled race treason, Tardy, a white activist, passionately voiced her concern about the apparent educational inequality in Grand Rapids. In a 1971 editorial, she proclaimed, "Just as no man is an island . . . certainly no city can afford to be one. Like it or not, we are dependent on each other and the problems of the minority have a great and everlasting effect on the majority." Tardy stated that whites needed to "start paying the price now for the years of containment of inner city children and start desegregating every classroom in every school of the city," because even whites "who care nothing for the future of black children cannot be so blind as not to realize their children's future in Grand Rapids is bound up with the futures of all children." Finally, she declared, "We have left this mess too long in the very core of our city, and it is time the Board of Education stopped trying to pacify the narrow-thinking, wall-building racists among us and do the job that needs to be done."[65]

Yet the controversy over busing produced a tug-of-war that backlash-provoking board members ultimately won. As the GRSB filled up with antibusing proponents, they managed to debunk the master plan and any notion of cross-busing as well. "I also cannot support cross-busing as it would only compound the situation we have now," newly elected School Board member Bowman proclaimed. He added, "Housing is the only answer to reach a complete and long-lasting integrated system."[66] Perhaps the resignation of Phillips and the walkout of Sleet should have raised red flags regarding the new tenor of the School Board, for at that point, the racial disunion of the board had certainly hit its apex. GRUL records acknowledged that a "master plan for gradual integration of Grand Rapids area schools was developed several years ago, when Phillips was a member of the Board of Education, but the plan was subsequently thrown out by a newly-elected Board" and the Grand Rapids school system now faced "the likelihood of court-ordered busing."[67]

"I assumed I would have to bus," recalled Judge Albert Engel, the presiding judge assigned to the federal lawsuit against the Grand Rapids school system. Yet Judge Engel also stated he understood that "the very specter of busing [was] going to drive whites out." He added, "If you're going to have white flight, the remedy's not going to work."[68] Judge Engel ostensibly bolstered the GRNAACP's case when he allowed the organization a motion to include eleven suburban adjoining school districts: Comstock Park, East Grand Rapids, Forest Hills, Godfrey Lee, Godwin Heights, Grandville, Kenowa Hills, Kentwood, Northview, Rockford, and Wyoming. In 1970, roughly 8,345 black children attended school inside the city limits, comprising 22.8 percent of the 36,480 total students. According to reports by the Kent Intermediate School Office, only 410 black students of the total 60,693 pupils enrolled attended a school in the aforementioned suburban school districts. Unsurprisingly, the number of black teachers resembled this low trend, as only 6 black teachers of the total 143 received employment within the eleven suburban school districts added to the trial.

The evidence seemed to decisively favor the GRNAACP complaints. Even the *Grand Rapids Press* published an article on April 13, 1972, entitled, "City Schools Are Preparing for Defeat in School Integration Suit." With some legal experts giving the school districts "only an outside chance of defeating the local NAACP," Grand Rapids school officials began to consider a contingency plan. The School Board counsel placed the odds at 50–50, but professionals, such as Elwood Hain, a professor of law, predicted that "the court [would] order Grand Rapids to integrate fully next fall." Although he seemed less confident that the order would include integration across district lines, he did believe that Judge Engel had "the gumption to do it."[69]

After a twenty-seven-day trial, Judge Engel retreated for four months before he returned with a decision determining (1) that the Grand Rapids school system had, at all times, managed a unitary school system, and trepidation over white flight "could not be rationally ignored by a school board charged with the Constitutional duty of maintaining such a system or by a committee that sought by its own preference to ease racial imbalance within its jurisdiction"; (2) that the GRSB developed a building program designed to construct schools "where children were" and that decisions regarding this strategy did not equal segregationist intent; (3) that, although not complete, the action the GRSB had taken to establish greater racial balance since 1965 was impressive; (4) that the South High School closing did not represent an improper tactic, because the racial balance remained similar to that of South Middle School; and (5) that the decision not to bus students from the outlying areas not only reduced white flight but also subsequently created lower student–teacher ratios in urban schools that afforded inner-city students the opportunity to attain a broader educational experience.[70]

Judge Engel stated, "I kept looking for reasons to do it [order busing], proof other than just assumption from the statistical data, which really didn't tell you much." The only discriminatory proof that Engel did find concerned the School Board assignment practices of black teachers and administrative personnel. Still, Judge Engel determined that discriminatory teacher assignments did not substantially contribute to a dual school system. On the basis of the facts considered, Judge Engel "declined to order busing, but directed the school board to reassign some black teachers to white schools." Thus, similar to the antibusing bloc, Judge Engel declared that "segregation was not the fault of the schools but a reflection of the city's segregated housing patterns."[71]

The GRNAACP attorney suggested that Judge Engel declined to bus because "he hoped to be appointed to the federal appeals court," which did subsequently occur seventeen days after the trial, when Engel received a nomination from Michigan Republican Senator Robert P. Griffin. Despite the fact that Judge Engel had four children enrolled in one of the suburban school districts named in the lawsuit, he stated that "I find my pleasure in being fair." But the black community viewed the decision as anything but fair. As the children of the judge who denied a busing order sat comfortably in a suburban school system, black schoolchildren still had to wait on the unfilled promises of educational equality. The fight for integrated schools had received no support in either the court of public opinion or in the judicial court.

The order by Judge Engel offered no relief for inner-city residents suffering from suburban expansion. According to the *Grand Rapids Press,* in 1974, "fewer than 1 per cent of all of the children enrolled in metropolitan area schools outside Grand Rapids are from minority groups—black, Latinos, American Indians and Orientals." The threat of continued polarization had become a reality. The verdict provided for the continual growth and prosperity of suburban school districts, while city taxpayers, on the other hand, geared up for increased tax contributions. Through locally levied taxes, the city covered nearly 57 percent of the Grand Rapids school budget, while the state provided almost 40 percent, with interest accounting for the remaining 3 percent. With the consistent exodus of white residents, the current funding formula put a tremendous strain on the city's school system and its remaining residents. Yet the arrival of whites to the suburbs ensured the increase of suburban state aid and strengthened the stronghold of segregation.[72]

Judge Engel's decree satisfied public opinion and validated the effectiveness of managerial racism. Engel stood as the lone federal judge to issue such a verdict in a Michigan integration school case. The *Grand Rapids Press* reported that "busing was ordered by federal courts for Pontiac and Kalamazoo after those systems were found guilty of operating segregated schools." The decision also further divided the Grand Rapids metropolis along a black and white axis. That Judge Engel accepted the board's voluntary program as an appropriate strategy, so as to not prompt white flight to the suburbs, fully illustrates the racial dilemma that plagued Grand Rapids. Clearly, historical analysis reveals that the process of white out-migration persisted as a steady factor dating back more than three decades. Moreover, Judge Engel's resolution seemingly condones the board's decision to secure white favor before moving forward with a plan that attempted to achieve racial equality. Thus, to accommodate the immediate concerns of white residents, the School Board chose to postpone educational equality for blacks.

Even after the decision, the GRSB still relied heavily on a good-faith policy of allowing race relations to change naturally. As a response to Judge Engel's request that the city school system demonstrate "continued progress," the board simply expanded the number of schools whose students could partake in its open enrollment plan. The policy, utilized by the board since 1968, allowed "a student whose race is in the majority at one school to transfer to one where his race is in the minority." Nearly "all the open enrollment volunteers have been blacks," yet the natural or voluntary form of integration hardly "produced enough widespread results to justify the lack of new efforts the last few years." As a matter of fact, in 1968 the number of racially imbalanced schools totaled nine, but in 1974 the number actually increased to eleven, with the possibility of two more schools "tipping" over. Thus, the GRNAACP's decision to appeal the verdict seemed promising.[73]

"Segregated conditions still exist," proclaimed Tardy, "[and] if there's been progress, it hasn't been in the right direction." But the U.S. Court of Appeals for the Sixth Circuit in Cincinnati "ruled unanimously that there was insufficient evidence to conclude that the Grand Rapids school board had violated the constitutional rights of black students." In a bad case of déjà vu, the black community came face to face with the seemingly preposterous claim that the "suburbs were innocent of intentional school segregation." Judge Engel had absolved the defendants of unlawful segregation on July 18, 1973, and little more than a year later, the appellate decision upheld the lower court ruling. Simply put, the three-judge panel declared that "Grand Rapids was not guilty of acts of intentional segregation, but that much progress has been made toward eliminating the de facto (it just happened) segregation resulting from housing patterns."[74] Although the NAACP pushed for an en banc hearing of the U.S. Court of Appeals for the Sixth Circuit in Cincinnati, the federal appeals court denied the request on February 6, 1975.

The efforts of the GRNAACP and other black organizations heightened the awareness of racial inequality existent within the metropolitan school system. Judge Engel, the Sixth Court of Appeals, and the Grand Rapids white community at large failed to grasp the severity of this problem, because they viewed the source of the trouble through a narrow lens. Ultimately, the problems of inner-city residents did not match up with the concerns of suburbanites. As the city school system sought white appeasement, blacks remained trapped within a community that effectively built around them yet at the same time managed to close down an institutional lifeline within the black community.

White suburbanites paid minimal attention to the growing reality of "the city within the city" because of the success of suburban maturity, which revised school districts had contributed to immensely. As the majority white periphery continued to bathe in prosperity, inner-city neighborhood residents suffered from the institutional fallout of suburban development. Absent vital resources, poverty began to mount, and problems snowballed throughout the inner city during the 1970s. Such nicknames as "Dodge City" and "Hell Hole" surfaced to describe depleted black inner-city neighborhoods, such as Madison Square. With the verdicts in from the court of public opinion and the federal court system, it seemed that little hope for change existed.

Although many of the black neighborhoods appeared to be down, the residents refused to be counted out. Black citizens—such as Alda Conley, who organized the first block club in Madison Square; Ezell Brown, former president of the Southeast Community Association; and William Pritchett, former executive director of the Southeast Community Association—continued to try to make their environment better despite the absence of generational benefits. Most of the residents of this community represented a cadre of forgotten citizens. They lived within a section of the Grand Rapids metropolis that suffered the most from a form of segregation that "inadvertently" happened to construct a city within a city.

In September 1978, the school superintendent created a Racial Balance Building Utilization Committee. Designed to assess the current status of racial balance in the city district school system, the superintendent called on central office personnel to carry out the study and to make recommendations. The committee turned its attention to South Middle School, formerly known as South High School. Although the building's capacity was set at approximately one thousand students, only half that many were present. The underutilization of the facility caused the committee to promote the closing of South Middle School and suggest the implementation of student reassignment for the 1979–1980 school year. The plan received a unanimous vote, and the closure of South Middle School marked the end of an era for minority students.

"A More Livable Community"

De facto segregation served as the obvious and easy response for white residents seeking to explain the residential color lines that divided Grand Rapids. Used to denote a far more genteel form of racial separation that was void of legal or official standing within the city, de facto segregation, white residents maintained, just happened to create a city within a city. Employed by the business community, the School Board, and city officials, the term "de facto" was used to conceal the obvious role of municipal policies in developing and maintaining racially stratified neighborhoods. Viewed through the lens of managerial racism, however, the municipal policies engineered by local politicians, city planners, and businessmen to develop and sustain a privileged racial geography in Grand Rapids become transparent. Fashioned to make Grand Rapids "a more livable community," these policies racially divided the community and left blacks isolated from the rest of the city. Thus, the racial geography of Grand Rapids extended beyond the happenstance often erroneously framed by the term "de facto segregation" and instead revealed the complex interconnectedness of housing, educational facilities, and municipal policies.

Phillips delivered an address in 1956 to encourage white citizens to proactively address racial concerns, arguing that "along with its plans to meet the problems of water, a new airport, parking facilities and a new civic center, [Grand Rapids] must also face realistically the mounting problem of avoiding and reducing racial tension and its accompanying effects" before they could reach "volcanic proportions."[75] A decade later, the city's racial problems exploded anyway, indicating the failure of progressive Republican reform politics. In the aftermath of the student walkout in 1966, the citywide racial uprising in 1967, and the closing of South High in 1968, an air of uncertainty surrounded Grand Rapids. The question remained to what extent these events would alter the long struggle for black equality and the structure of managerial racism that influenced black daily life. The 1967 upheaval in Grand Rapids was small compared to the fallout in Detroit, which had left forty-three people dead. The issues involved, however, were no less real. At the heart of both uprisings was a lack of opportunity, second-class citizenship, and poverty. Particularly in Grand Rapids, however, the turmoil posed a grave threat to the city's business interests and stability.

Historically, the Chamber of Commerce promoted the city as a quiet, conservative town. Grand Rapids was, the Chamber of Commerce advertised, "A Good Place to Live and to Work," but the racial disturbances were proving otherwise. Insofar as it pertained to race in Grand Rapids, the chamber never fulfilled its duty, for its businessmen remained silent on the racial problems that had long plagued the city. But following the public urban unrest, the Chamber of Commerce realized that the city would "face far greater problems if we and other employers fail to do what we can to help disadvantaged people overcome the barriers that keep them from sharing in the abundance of American economy." The chamber's 1968 declaration signaled a new tactical approach to the city's racial dilemma. "The first step became obvious," Chamber of Commerce President Van Blooys observed. "Find *meaningful* jobs for the unemployed—particularly the unemployed of minority races and those who for various reasons have become known as the 'unemployables.'"[76]

Following the racial unrest of 1967, the Grand Rapids Planning Division (GRPD) authored a summary report entitled "Anatomy of a Riot." According to the GRPD, "Young angry negro males were the main participants," and this younger generation of blacks "[believed] that action speaks louder than words and that he does not have anything to lose by being destructive."[77] Mindful of the GRPD's findings and aware of the tangible destruction caused by urban dissent, the Chamber of Commerce initiated Grand Rapids Project 1003. "It appeared to our Board of Directors that a catalyst was needed," Van Blooys stated, and that "it was also apparent that a crash program was needed if more riots were to be averted."[78] The Chamber of Commerce was following the recommendations of the GRPD, which decided, "Our collective plans and action must have the comprehensive objective of building a more livable community" and added that "riots do not occur where there is full employment." In consequence, the chamber resolved to provide one thousand jobs in three months. It marked the first time in the history of Grand Rapids that the chamber engaged in such a robust employment program.[79]

The reason for the chamber's sudden benevolence may not have been entirely altruistic in nature. Few blacks in the city would have disagreed with the words of Smith, who caustically observed, "Listen, if you can train a dumb white boy, you can train a dumb black one." Labeled by *Look* magazine as "the city's angry young man," Smith's views often raised controversy. He denounced the closure of South High at School Board meetings, and, like Sims, Smith promoted the idea of having white students bused to South instead. His role was gaining increased importance to a young black constituency who shared Smith's emphasis on black assertiveness instead of accommodating white expectations. He wanted to improve the black community from the inside. Black secondary students turned to Smith during crisis moments at Union High. Students at South High who shared the cultural awakening of the mustache incident now hoped to define a new political agenda. Smith was "committed to social revolution, black power." He believed that "society need[ed] a total change." Smith's defiant tone and criticism of "white middle class values" worried the business community. And if Smith were able to influence others to embrace his ideological beliefs, the chamber realized Grand Rapids would become a very different city. Providing jobs to young blacks would certainly undermine the need for a "social revolution."[80]

Employment constituted the largest proportion of complaints to the Michigan Civil Rights Commission (MCRC) statewide. According to the MCRC, "In 1968 there were 1,440 employment complaints filed, representing 70.6% of the total claims filed during that year." The pattern of discrimination was evident even in Grand Rapids. One black woman contended she was denied employment at a factory in the city because of her race. During the MCRC investigation, the personnel manager claimed that the factory's hiring policy required him to seek out individuals with "prior work experience, good attendance records, means of transportation, non-union feelings, good references, and 10th Grade education." Moreover, for assembly work, he looked for "someone 5'4" to 5'9" in height and 110 to 150 pounds in weight. He determined that the claimant was denied because of her height. She was 5'2"." Further investigation of the two-week period prior to the claimant's denial of work resulted in the discovery, by the MCRC, that "the factory hired 13 white people 5'2" or under and four white people with a 9th grade education or less." Also, in the six weeks after her denial, the MCRC found "that the factory hired 23 applicants, 22 white and one black. Four white applicants had no car, and two white applicants hired had no access to transportation." In this instance, the MCRC managed to secure employment for the claimant commensurate with her skill and ability. Furthermore, the factory agreed to eliminate height and weight standards, and it promised to adhere to Equal Employment Opportunity policy. Thus with the increasing voice of youth opposition and the threat of oversight, the Chamber of Commerce sought to coordinate a plan of action in Grand Rapids.[81]

"The essential goal," according to President Van Blooys, "became the provision of jobs for residents of the city's ghetto. And that goal required the fullest and fastest application of all the leadership resources in the metropolitan area." The chamber contacted several organizations and "arranged a luncheon meeting to which 160 of the city's principal employers and personnel officers came—and which they left in agreement on the value of the program." A "persuasive description of the plan and chart of organization" was sent out as a mailing to all chamber members. Through an elaborate information-sharing program, employers exchanged information about black applicants. Members met regularly to chart progress, set up interviews, and "follow up on behavior and attitudes of the people previously placed." But job placement was the key issue.[82]

To achieve this end, according to Van Blooys, business leaders were asked "to be more lenient in their employment practices, giving consideration to those previously excluded." Additionally, the Chamber of Commerce requested that employers provide on-site job training as well as prejob counseling and posthiring follow-up. Finally, employers were instructed to make "meaningful jobs available, not merely menial ones, and . . . salaries [should] be sufficient for the head of a household to adequately support his family." For decades prior, Phillips had pushed for equity in hiring. He had experienced the arduous task of getting local businessmen to mention race or acknowledge the influence of race in hiring practices. Now in a single stroke, President Van Blooys declared, "We submit that it is time that the businessman stands up and faces his responsibilities." The racial uprising had placed the "total economic well-being of the community . . . in danger," he observed.[83]

The Chamber of Commerce recognized the severity of the situation. After a chamber delegation presented judges with a compelling narrative of communal success that ultimately persuaded the National Municipal League competition committee to award Grand Rapids with the city's second "All-American City" award in 1961, the business community capitalized on the momentum by pushing their economic growth plan forward during the 1960s. Assured they were on the right track to solving the city's problems, despite the failure of the New City Plan, the chamber moved "decisively to create jobs and stimulate economic growth by attracting new companies."[84] According to Mayor Christian Sonneveldt and City Planner John Paul Jones, the plan was based on converting downtown "from the city's major retail area to a center of government, finance, entertainment and other services." As a result, the chamber "sent thousands of brochures to prospective industries, placed advertisements in national publications, and met directly with firms considering plant moves." For nearly a decade, the business community concentrated on building up the downtown central business district. Yet in one instant of rebellion, black youths in Grand Rapids had jeopardized the new structures, future business opportunities, and the city's progressive image.[85]

Bringing in new business was extremely competitive throughout the Midwest. Grand Rapids had to compete with such places as Flint, Ann Arbor, and Lansing as well as regional towns, such as Fort Wayne, Gary, Indianapolis, Toledo, and other locations that provided such inducements as reduced tax assessments and quality transportation. Making Grand Rapids a "Good Place To Live and To Work" was critical to the success of attracting new industrial tenants and sustaining existing ones. Although Grand Rapids made use of cutting-edge ideas, such as the 360-acre Kent Industrial Park, it also regularly brought in new businesses, such as the Sys-Con Company, which opened in 1966 and occupied the top floor of the Michigan Consolidated Gas Company Building.[86]

During the 1960s, business leaders persisted in arguing that "development of a strong central-core area [was] the key to continued growth of a vital and progressive metropolitan expansion plan."[87] Federal funding guaranteed expansion; it also ensured that private investment would soon follow. With urban-renewal commitments coming together, Old Kent Bank announced that it planned to build a new $7-million building in the renewal area. It would become the first major office structure built downtown since the mid-1920s. Patrick McNamara, U.S. senator from Michigan and chair of the Senate Public Works Committee, added to the hopeful news when he announced that the city would receive $6.2 million for a new federal building in the renewal area. Construction was set to begin in 1964. Furthermore, in late 1964, the Michigan Consolidated Gas Company disclosed its plan to build a new $3.5-million building set for completion in 1966, and Union Bank announced it would build a $4-million facility. According to Gordon Olson, "To no one's surprise, year-end figures for 1964 showed a record $60 million in new business and industrial construction, higher than any annual total of the previous boom in the mid-1950s."[88]

A series of celebrations followed. Former Chamber of Commerce President and Mayor Sonneveldt encouraged retail stores to "get on board and help develop a 'modern downtown shopping center' adjunct to the commercial district."[89] The downtown flowered with the Old Kent Bank opening in May 1966, followed by the *Grand Rapids Press* building in September 1966, and Union Bank and Michigan Consolidated Gas in 1967 and 1968, respectively. A Chamber of Commerce–sponsored contest to name the new civic center area produced the winning entry of Vandenberg Center, honoring Arthur H. Vandenberg, a well-known political figure who served as a U.S. senator from 1928 to 1951.[90]

The downtown development was so prosperous that the *Grand Rapids Press* declared:

> Frameworks of more new buildings reach for the sky. From downtown the expressways stretch from this new heart of a thriving city into the metropolitan area. Here it stands—Grand Rapids, the new entry into the ranks of the Great American cities. . . . Once described as a city built on wood because of the furniture industry, it is now a city also built on concrete and steel. Generations yet unborn will someday note the birth of the Metropolitan Man. He's a banker, industrialist, factory worker, homeowner, every resident of this throbbing city who now joins in the greater adventure of the new metropolis.[91]

Given this self-image, therefore, the desire of business leaders to secure peace and safety seemed a prerequisite given the amount of money poured into developing the downtown area during the 1960s. Clearly, the racial upheaval of 1967 threatened to destroy the progress that had been made, but it also served as a hazard for business owners, workers, and clients. Thus, the nature of political struggle, community development, and urban sustainability was recast in a way that forced the chamber to take "an active, dynamic role in providing 'Business Leadership for Human Rights.'" Reportedly, Project 1003 resulted in 1,053 employed workers, and approximately two-thirds were still on the job six months after the program began.[92]

The implementation of Project 1003 coincided with the election of the first black city commissioner, Rev. Lyman Sterling Parks. With inner-city problems and race relations at a fever pitch during the late 1960s, Parks made Grand Rapids his new home. Upon his arrival, Parks naively inquired, "Why was no one involved with the government?" In so doing, he failed to recognize that, dating back to the Progressive Voter League activity, other blacks had also tried to win control of the third ward, which contained more blacks than the other two wards combined. Not until 1968, however, when Parks's 5,976 votes topped the 4,942 received by a white real estate developer named Herbert Soodsma, had a black resident achieved such distinction.[93]

"To begin with, I was realistic, and recognized that this particular section of the state was conservative, Republican, and . . . I put myself in the position of being willing to assess people and their manner," maintained Parks. Unlike the coterie of mostly Democratic black politicians struggling for political representation during the late 1960s and early 1970s, Parks was a Republican who admired Richard Nixon, Martin Luther King Jr., and Whitney Young. His heroes included George Washington Carver and Booker T. Washington, not Malcolm X and W. E. B. DuBois. Therefore, even in a Republican city, Parks's views posed no threat, and, given the social unrest, Parks "recognized that the timing was right" for a black candidate to break through.[94]

"The theme of my campaign was unity," Parks recalled. "I went into many, many homes, many Dutch homes . . . and I just talked about my background, and where I had come from, and what I felt I could contribute toward making this a better place."[95] The self-promoted message of a "conventional public servant who was interested in good government and safe streets" found a home in a community hoping to "replace friction with understanding and cooperation." Alongside episodes of disorder, Parks claimed, "people began to see the need for black people being involved." Parks not only won in 1968; he was elected president of the City Commission three years later. Parks had reached a political level utterly inconceivable twenty years prior. And with the resignation of Mayor Robert Boelens, who had been elected in 1970, Parks emerged as the pro tem mayor of Grand Rapids. In the following election, Parks was elected outright.[96]

In 1972, at the National Black Political Convention, revolutionaries, black nationalists, and integrationists along with Baptists and Muslims assembled in Gary, Indiana, which was a majority black city. Welcomed by the city's black mayor, Richard Hatcher, this diverse group of organizations created a National Black Political Agenda. Among their stated goals were community control of schools, proportionate black representatives to Congress, and national health insurance. The publication included a note regarding the idealistic nature of the process: "At every critical moment of our struggle in America we have had to press relentlessly against the limits of the 'realistic' to create new realities for the life of our people. This is our challenge at Gary and beyond, for a new Black politics demands new vision, new hope and new definitions of the possible. Our time has come. These things are necessary. All things are possible."[97]

The "critical moment" of "struggle" in Grand Rapids pressed against the "limits of the 'realistic,'" proving that indeed all things were possible with the election of the city's first black mayor. However, the "new vision, new hope and new definitions of possible" looked strikingly familiar to black Grand Rapidians, even with Parks now in the mayoral seat. Unlike the delegates at the National Black Political Convention, Parks did not believe the American system was broken, nor did he feel that the system could not "be made to work without radical, fundamental changes." In fact, Parks expressed the thought, "Perhaps we'd reached the point where we need to sit down and assess where we had come, and evaluate it on the basis of what this meant for the future, rather than continue to push for 'freedom now.'" His stand on civil rights guided him to muse, "What do you do with the gains we've made, and how do we get people prepared to get into the mainstream to take advantage of the opportunities provided by those gains?" Although the newly appointed mayor seemed reticent about pushing a civil rights agenda, the *Grand Rapids Press* noted that Parks had "already acknowledged the conservative, essentially Republican habits of his city, thus leading you to believe that he would adopt . . . the easygoing approach of a conservative," moving forward with business as usual.[98]

In particular, following the urban renewal years, according to the *Grand Rapids Press*, Parks worked "with business leaders to continue redevelopment of downtown." Parks, in fact, played a central role in the development and completion of the Grand Center. Pitched as a "flexible guide to future downtown development, the plan and its $20 million price tag were endorsed by city commissioners and business leaders." Former City Commissioner Carl Eschels headed a nine-person steering committee overseeing public and private interest. The steering committee also had the responsibility of promoting the project and securing passage of the special millage necessary to make the project financially feasible. However in 1972, despite official support, residents opposed the millage funding, ultimately leaving the project on hold until Mayor Parks stepped in and obtained $2.3 million to get the project moving forward.[99]

In 1974, Mayor Parks assembled a high-powered committee to conduct a blue-ribbon study and compose a Study and Coordination Committee to supervise the project. Parks appointed Old Kent Bank President Richard Gillett and Amway cofounder Rich DeVos as cochairs.[100] "I remember walking across the street from City Hall to ask Dick Gillett of Old Kent Bank and Trust Co. to become chairman of the Downtown Development Authority. I knew I would take a lot of heat for it, but it had to be done," Parks reminisced.[101] Additional committee members included Arend Lubbers, president of Grand Valley State College; Edward Frey, president of Union Bank; Robert Pew, president of Steelcase; Frederik Meijer, retailer; Willard Schroeder, owner of WOOD-TV; John Bissell, manufacturer; Jack Roberts, owner of Pantlind Hotel; Robert Steketee, retailer; John Uhl, president of the Public Museum Board; and Mary Ann Keeler and Buck Matthews, arts activists. This committee was charged with setting community priorities and determining what Gillett called the "multiplier effect."[102] According to Gillett, the designation of a central facility, such as a convention center or concert hall, was the first priority to bring people downtown. The idea was that each subsequent decision would "multiply the need for and support of other projects that would completely revitalize the downtown area." Within a year the committee had a final report that Mayor Parks and the City Commission approved. The initiative sparked the type of city revitalization that "was just a dream until Parks."[103]

Former ambassador to Italy and local businessman Peter Secchia, who was urged by Gerald Ford to become Parks's mayoral campaign adviser, referred to Parks as "a Martin Luther King Jr. type of guy" who had a soothing presence. Quite simply, City Commissioner Eschels observed, "He was the right man at the right time in the right place. He helped this community move toward accepting more diversity in its people."[104] City historian Olson also believed that "Parks was what this city needed at that moment. He was a calming influence. He emerged as someone who could bring people together."[105] But bringing people together and moving them forward remained two very different realities.

Perhaps the election of Parks did, in fact, provide a degree of calm during what appeared to be an extraordinary time of social change; however, it also seemed apparent that his election buried the racism evident in other frames of reference within the city, if not eliminating it from the conversation entirely. Reviewing the urban landscape nearly twenty years after the 1967 riots offers a more complicated narrative. According to Grand Rapids attorney John Allen Johnson, "The prevailing attitude in this country is that . . . from the time Martin Luther King died to 1972 national attention was focused on Afro-Americans," and "the general opinion was, 'you should be able to solve the problem, and we don't have to deal with you anymore.'"[106] Rather than improving the situation, however, the School of Urban Studies at Michigan State University indicated blacks were worse off in 1987 than they were in 1967. Joseph Darden, dean of the School of Urban Studies at Michigan State University, observed that following the social unrest of the late 1960s, measures were taken at first to address problems, but "that action declined in the early 1970s and as it dropped off, conditions for the black population started to become worse again." He added "Blacks are in an area of decline while whites are in an area of growth, and the black underclass is increasing."[107]

The increased concentration of blacks in Grand Rapids left black residents, such as Lucille Taylor, wondering whether their lives had improved since 1967. "I can't say that my life is better now than it was 20 years ago. . . . [I]t's about the same or, maybe, it's worse," decided Taylor. The criteria remained available housing, quality education, jobs, and health services. In 1980, nearly 30 percent of the black families lived below the poverty level, unemployment for blacks was three times the unemployment for whites, and the median black family income was 61 percent of the median income for a white family. To make matters worse, many of the meaningful War on Poverty programs came under attack by the Reagan administration during the 1980s.[108]

According to Cedric Ward, director of program development for community education with Grand Rapids Junior College, "During the riot we had one (black) person on the school board and there are two today; we had one person on the city commission and we have one now. Things really haven't changed that much." Beverly Drake, executive director of the Grand Rapids Area

Employment and Training Council, added, "Manufacturing jobs are being cut back while service jobs are growing, but service jobs pay the least. So there are new jobs being created every day and jobs being lost every day, but look at the difference between jobs and what they pay. When you lose a $9-an-hour job and have to take one for $5 an hour, what happens? It makes people at the bottom go further down the ladder."[109]

The reality was that when compared to the poverty located in such cities as Detroit, Chicago, Newark, or Cincinnati, Grand Rapids seemed to offer hope at the outset of the process. NAACP Vice President Robert Hurd, observed, "Grand Rapids is a great city, by far the best city of its type in the Midwest. It's a beautiful place to take a look at these problems."[110] Indeed, Grand Rapids was a good place to examine William Chafe's important question: "Are civility and civil rights compatible?"[111] It would seem the answer in Grand Rapids, Michigan, as Chafe had also discovered in Greensboro, North Carolina, was no. Managerial racism in Grand Rapids was used to forestall substantive change throughout the long fight for freedom and equal rights. However often the architects of managerial racism promised that progress and racial reform would follow in a gradualist sense, it did not. Instead, the acrimonious disputes over school integration and busing ripped apart the city, much as they had in Detroit during the late 1960s and 1970s.

Under the Republican regime in Grand Rapids, it would appear that the resulting white backlash further complicated the situation of postwar racial politics. A number of historians have argued that the "Democratic party made a grievous political error in the 1960s by ignoring the needs of white, working-class and middle-class voters in favor of the demands of the civil rights movement, black militants, the counterculture, and the 'undeserving' poor."[112] It thereby followed that the "structural limitations of liberal reform"[113] produced a white backlash. However, the case of Grand Rapids offers a withering critique of this view, for Grand Rapids was a solidly Republican community that made no effort to favor racial politics in the postwar era. Instead, the guarded power structure used free enterprise as a veneer to mask similar forms of oppression. Business leaders committed to the New City Plan and downtown redevelopment shaped local politics in Grand Rapids by minimizing the importance of race in the city's political, social, and economic discourse. The politics of managerial racism so effectively downplayed the importance of race that it afforded the antibusing contingent the ability to fashion a language of discontent that received at least a tacit acceptance from a majority of the electorate. For many years, the business coalition had ignored the needs of the black community that the antibusing supporters refused to consent. Racial conservatism helped build segregated neighborhoods throughout the metropolitan region, and the antibusing movement reinforced the desire to defend these homogenous neighborhoods.

The business community held a distinct advantage in terms of political control throughout the postwar era; however, black protests persistently challenged business leaders to fulfill the promise of reform. The patience of moral persuasion gradually shifted in the direction of a more direct challenge by black youths. And although their efforts chipped away at the structure of managerial racism when it appeared the city's progressive image would take a hit, the city was able to strike back with the election of Parks. The first black mayor offered blacks a renewed incentive to acquiesce to the prevailing political and economic system. But had power really changed hands? Not so much—conservatives undertook only the minimal actions necessary to tamp down insurgency following the social unrest of 1967. Even during Parks's administration, the results were the same: The high-powered business coalition set the priorities of the community that once again reinforced the "city within a city" framework. Once again, the pernicious power of managerial racism was used to curb substantive change at a moment when the black youth of Grand Rapids had seemed to seize the initiative and had momentum on their side. To be sure, the battle for equality did not end in Grand Rapids. Rather "rowing, and not drifting" in present-day Grand Rapids means coping with a storied racial past to understand whether today's society has progressed or whether it simply reflects a more sophisticated form of managerial racism.

CONCLUSION

Secondary Cities and the Black Experience

According to the 2000 U.S. Census, Detroit, Saginaw, Flint, Benton Harbor, and Muskegon were listed among the top twenty-five most racially segregated metropolitan regions in America. With two more Michigan cities—Grand Rapids and Jackson—listed just on the outskirts of the top twenty-five, Michigan ranked as the most segregated state in the nation.[1] On the opposite side of the spectrum, according to research conducted by the Civil Rights Project at Harvard University, in 2002 *Time Magazine* listed Sacramento, California, as America's most integrated city.[2] Despite the prevalence of secondary cities on both sides of the racial spectrum, the issues that led to the racial geographies of these secondary cities are almost invisible to scholars. Aside from Detroit, what does the historical literature tell us about the storied racial pasts of the remaining seven metropolitan regions? How does the black urban experience offer similarities and distinctions between the freedom struggle in Saginaw, Flint, Benton Harbor, Muskegon, Jackson, and Sacramento and the freedom struggle in Detroit? Do the experiences of blacks living in secondary cities bear a greater resemblance to similar smaller cities or to bigger cities? Equally important, why is there a need to begin a comparative of a secondary city with a bigger city, such as Detroit, when nearly 150 midsize cities of the postwar era represent the majority experience? Answering these questions carefully means scholars must include a greater variety of black urban perspectives and paint a more inclusive portrait of the freedom struggle. As it stands, taken as a whole, scholarly histories of the black urban experience and the freedom fight have often privileged the narrative of blacks living in primary cities, and these studies suggests that the primary-city narrative is the normative experience.

Most notably, Arnold R. Hirsch's impressive book, *Making the Second Ghetto: Race and Housing in Chicago, 1940–1960*, is the first groundbreaking work to examine the African American urban experience in the post–World War II era. Shifting the focus from the formation of ghettos in early-twentieth-century northern cities, Hirsch's work confirms that discriminatory neighborhood patterns intensified into the making of a "second ghetto" in postwar Chicago. Building on a generation of scholarly work by Gilbert Osofsky, Allan H. Spear, David M. Katzman, and Kenneth L. Kusmer, among other scholars, whose work focused on the creation of first ghettos prior to 1930, Hirsch innovatively demonstrates how federal government programs contributed heavily to Chicago's emerging as the most-segregated big city in the nation by the 1960s. However, Hirsch mindfully understands that "the universality of segregation should not imply an identical process in every case." Instead, he argues, "there are variants of racism in the United States and a textured complexity to problems of race and ethnicity."[3]

The second ghetto thesis contains remarkable explanatory power, offering a historical context for understanding the governmental role in establishing and maintaining de facto segregation in urban northern communities. To be certain, although Thomas J. Sugrue's *The Origins of the Urban Crisis* grapples with variants of racism involved in establishing a geography of segregation in the postwar era, taken as a whole, the recent literature on African American urban history concentrates on cities with large black populations and focuses primarily on the creation of the second ghetto.[4] Studies of urban black life in rapidly industrializing cities in particular, such as Chicago and Detroit—by far the scholarly research emphasis of the post–World War II era—tend to mask the fact that smaller black communities in the Midwest, the West, and the North developed differently. *A City within a City* offers several variations on the black urban experience in the industrial heartland. For example, situated in the Rust Belt region, the primary center of manufacturing and industry, Grand Rapids did not include a notable industrial black working class like Chicago, Detroit, Pittsburgh, or Cleveland. The majority of black workers in Grand Rapids remained outside organized labor even after the 1940s. Despite the noticeable influx of black migrants during the Second Great Migration, the black population of Grand Rapids remained relatively small at a time when many midwestern and eastern cities experienced sizable increases. Although historical research by Hirsch and Raymond A. Mohl focuses exclusively on the making of the second ghetto in the post–World War II era, the absence of a clearly defined first black ghetto before 1960 distinguishes this study from previous histories of black urban life in the post-1940 era, when high levels of ghettoization already existed. Moreover, the racial crisis that beset Grand Rapids had less to do with the limits of the left-liberal alliance and more to do with the triumph of racial conservatism. Thus this book answers Kenneth L. Kusmer and Joe W. Trotter's call in *African American Urban History since World War II* for a greater emphasis on African American urban history during the postwar period by providing a distinct framework for understanding the dynamics of black urban development in smaller cities during the post-1940 era.[5]

Analyzing the past of these secondary cities will provide invaluable lessons for understanding the present and better structuring the future of metropolitan racial politics. The journey from the days of "No Negroes and Dogs" signs positioned in local businesses in Sacramento, California, during the 1930s to the city's 2002 ranking as America's most integrated metropolitan area contains a narrative of American race relations that can no longer be ignored. The racial geography of Sacramento, during the post–World War period, underwent a significant transformation as blacks flocked to the area after the development of two air bases, McClellan and Mather. A myriad of community agencies, including the Negro Women's Civic and Improvement Club, the NAACP, and the Black Panther Party for Self-Defense, became center pieces of the black urban experience in Sacramento. Plagued by segregated neighborhoods, racially separate schools, and widespread discrimination in employment and public spaces, black resistance gave shape and form to the freedom struggle in Sacramento.[6]

Although early black Sacramento was shrouded with racial conflict, Springfield, Massachusetts, began as a model city for racial innovation. *It Happened in Springfield* read the movie title in 1945, and it could happen in your town too. From newspapers, magazines, radio dramatizations, and a Warner Brothers film, Springfield was applauded for its efforts to democratize race relations in its city's public schools. One advocate, Norma Jensen, assistant field secretary with the NAACP, believed that the "Springfield Plan" was unique. "It permeates every division of the school," she said, "from the nursery grades through the senior high schools, and the administration itself, to the community." The pioneering "Program of Education for Democracy" as it was entitled, or "The Springfield Plan" as it was known nationally, was an attempt to eliminate "racial and religious prejudice in its schools under a warm, human and workable plan."[7] So lauded was this plan that such cities as Pittsburgh and New York announced their all-out endorsement. Yet the storied racial past of Springfield is a narrative of constant struggle. Unlike Sacramento, where, according to *Time Magazine,* in 2002 "people seem to live side by side more successfully,"[8] Springfield was recently, once again, divided by racial violence. At approximately 3:00 A.M. on Wednesday, November 5, 2008, as the world celebrated president-elect Barack Obama's historic victory, three white men defiantly engaged in the age-old tradition of resorting to racial violence to oppose racial progress by burning down a predominantly African American Pentecostal church in Springfield, Massachusetts. Reminiscent of the age of Jim Crow or the mid-twentieth-century civil rights struggles commonly witnessed in the South, the actions of three white arsonists were designed to send a message to the larger African American community. Their hostility was not solely directed toward the Macedonia Church of God in Christ; rather, their actions were designed to singe the communal fabric of the black community in Springfield. The fact that the new church was set to be the first predominantly black church located in a white suburban neighborhood adds another layer of complexity and speaks to the historical battles of racial geography in Springfield. The message they sent echoed a historical reminder that, perhaps the "Springfield Plan" failed and that even despite Obama's victory, a postracial society did not exist.[9]

Although *A City within a City* focuses on a fragment of the nation, it has broader implications illuminating the twentieth-century African American urban experience in secondary cities. As it stands, these smaller cities in the United States, such as Grand Rapids, Sacramento, and Springfield, to mention but a few, fall outside the historiographical lens of contemporary African American urban studies and civil rights movement literature. Much previous work has explored the black experience in large cities and rural settings, but black community life in midsize cities during the post–World War II era remains unexamined. Therefore some of the most significant questions facing American society, including the function of race and racism in fomenting many of the problems in American cities and the paradoxical roles of racial diversity and African American agency in forging much of the vitality of American cities, remain only partially explored.

Although the new African American urban history has increased our understanding of the black urban experience significantly, the post-1940 period has been defined by histories of the political economy of race in larger cities and has neglected to examine black agency, specifically in secondary cities. This is particularly surprising given the innovative outpouring of literature on the civil rights movement. Recent publications by Martha Biondi, Robert O. Self, Matthew J. Countryman, and Thomas J. Sugrue, to mention but a few, all point to a "long civil rights movement," which recognizes the temporal and ideological sweep of the twentieth-century freedom struggle that stretched beyond the Montgomery to Memphis framework. Although Biondi, Self, and Countryman examine individual communities, Sugrue's *Sweet Land of Liberty: The Forgotten Struggle for Civil Rights in the North* offers a sweeping account of civil rights activism in a number of big cities in the North and further proves that the region was a pivotal factor in the struggle for racial equality. However, although Sugrue's work is summative, it is also—necessarily—explorative. With the absence of secondary cities in the literature, there is still too much work to be done before anyone can truly write a definitive history of the freedom struggle in the North. Although this growing body of research contributes to a reinterpretation of the history of the freedom fight, my study speaks to the similar but often distinct ways smaller communities in the North engaged in the struggle for equality. Collectively, the theoretical innovations of these important works underline racism as a national problem, not one solely confined to the South. Similarly, *A City within a City* recasts black activism in the North by providing a systematic look at how blacks in Grand Rapids participated in and defined the freedom struggle. Despite the proliferation of civil rights movement literature, urban historians have devoted little attention to post–World War II African American urban life and agency. Instead, recent works depict blacks as victims, being acted on by economic forces and racism. Emphasis on the structural and political economy of race has rendered these studies incapable of telling the story of African American resistance and agency in a way that illuminates how blacks defined the urban experience.

By analyzing the construction of segregated space, *A City within a City* also challenges conventional notions of de facto metropolitan development and illustrates how housing stratification in secondary cities did not materialize as a natural result of migration patterns or market forces. Building on work by Kenneth T. Jackson, Hirsch, and Sugrue, secondary cities offer a layered perspective of a tri-level effort of resistance used to thwart housing desegregation between 1940s and 1960s. The Federal Housing Administration (FHA), racially motivated restrictive covenants, and white residential hostility combined to obstruct black migration to suburban Grand Rapids. Urban historians, including Jackson and Sugrue, and more recently Self, do a notable job of highlighting FHA Security Maps, surveys, and residential color-coded classification systems, but the federal government's role in developing segregated metropolitan space in the postwar era only scratches the surface of discriminatory housing practices. *A City within a City* examines how local builders, real estate brokers, bankers, and businessmen also ensured the development of separate housing at the municipal level. The inextricable relationship of these factors resulted in anything but a natural ordering of de facto neighborhood space. With 60 percent of the black population owning their own homes and on average paying 10 percent more than whites for comparable housing, according to the 1950 census, the majority of blacks in Grand Rapids had the means but minimal access to homes outside the inner city. In particular, the Grand Rapids Real Estate Board handled nearly 95 percent of all housing transactions, yet by 1950 only a handful of black families lived in suburban homes. *A City within a City* centers the northern black freedom struggle and helps elucidate the role of not only the state but also local organizations in perpetuating racial segregation beyond the South. Thus a secondary city vantage point suggests elaborations on the role of municipal policies and politicians in the construction and preservation of racialized landscapes in the postwar era.

The issue of black residential patterns sparked not only the explosive question of neighborhood control but also the larger problem of community power amid suburban expansion in such cities as Sacramento, Springfield, Lansing, Gary, and Flint. Although race relations on Grand Rapids did not conform to the strict pattern that developed in many twentieth-century urban centers defined by Democratic machine politics, labor unions, and their rank-and-file member race relations, the black community routinely faced declining economic opportunities, inadequate housing, and educational inequality in the post-1940 era. To outsiders looking in, these issues remained shrouded by the "progressive mystique" of civility that surrounded the city. Similar to the southern originated framework described in Greensboro, North Carolina, the white power structure in Grand Rapids also managed to deny equality to blacks yet maintain an image as a progressive city. Business leaders and city officials avoided conflict and even took pride in their efforts to study race relations, yet their benevolent paternalism denied the substance of black civil rights. Unwilling to endorse a public stance against racial discrimination, business leaders and city officials offered minor concessions to evade definitive institutional changes in racial policies. The prestigious "All-American City" award bestowed on Grand Rapids in 1949 and again in 1961 confirmed a naive communal sense of racial tolerance among white residents. Yet civility only concealed the antipathy whites felt toward blacks in conservative Grand Rapids, which in turn scrupulously masked the practice of "northern managerial racism" effectively used to suppress black equality in Grand Rapids. And it suggests that in the absence of southern Democrats in the North, it is necessary to further understand the emergence and strength of racial conservatism in the social, economic, and political formation of postwar northern communities.

Despite these circumstances and their relatively small size, black communities in secondary cities actively engaged in the campaign for metropolitan resources. Overcrowded, underfunded, poorly equipped majority black schools became crucial urban battlegrounds of the black freedom struggle. Although the industrial narrative so widely referenced in the literature may not have impacted secondary communities in the same ways it did in Chicago and Detroit, schools were omnipresent in every community, and they offer a way to understand racial transitions in neighborhoods that illustrate the contested nature of racial geography. Additionally, the school integration literature, urban studies, and civil rights movement histories have not paid adequate attention to the students involved in these daily struggles. *A City within a City* demonstrates that these students significantly contributed to and altered the black freedom struggle. Battles over personal hygiene, dress codes, and school resources intensified student involvement in local racial and cultural politics. Many of these high school students associated their identity with the racial communities beyond school grounds. Their effort to gain greater control of their lives reflected the struggle for autonomy, respect, and equality of Grand Rapids' black population. Certainly high school students found inspiration from the overall climate of protest of the 1960s, but my study demonstrates that often these students served as the impetus for dramatic shifts in the flow of local civil rights activities in smaller communities.

The *Brown v. Board of Education* decision placed high schools squarely at the center of the black freedom fight. This book's focus on secondary student participation and their use of "infrapolitical" opposition also builds on the recent civil rights movement studies to broaden the conception of resistance during the civil rights movement, including daily struggles, youth participation, and cultural shifts that often sustained the movement on a day-to-day basis. School integration studies often emphasize federal legal and legislative battles, yet quotidian acts of resistance sustained the movement. Instead of viewing civil rights solely through legislation and protest, *A City within a City* shifts to the world in which people lived, including schools, clubs, businesses, and neighborhoods. This vantage point allows scholars to examine the black urban experience on its own terms. In this study, school desegregation judicial decisions serve as a small component of a much larger and longer struggle to achieve educational equality that meant much more than black children sitting next to white children. Thus *A City within a City* tells the story of the black fight for equality in Grand Rapids at the community level in response to local conditions and concerns. These circumstances varied in each secondary community, and it is critical to develop a sampling of these trends.

In Grand Rapids, South High became the stimulus for black youth activism. The closure of South touched a number of lives deeply, and the social memory of that loss has not been erased. As a member of South's "lost classes," Dr. Paul King reminisced about the school desegregation plan during an interview in 1998. He said, "There's some bitterness. I think the Grand Rapids style of quasi-apartheid atmosphere was my biggest problem" and "there's still that base concept there."[10] Even though King, who was serving as a professor of Neurosurgery at Wayne State University at the time of his interview, was far removed from the mob violence at Union High, it was obvious the scars had not completely healed. King was not alone. "There was just this camaraderie that we had as students," Deborah Jones recalled, "that still remained in our adult lives." Indeed, Jones was in a laundromat in Atlanta, Georgia, in 1996 when she asked another customer, "Didn't you go to South High School?" The woman turned in disbelief and answered that she *had* attended South High.[11] The question was not "Are you from Grand Rapids?" Even though the two had graduated nearly six years apart and their only connection was through one of Jones's relatives, the point of contact was South High. Not only does the encounter between the former South High students suggest the importance of social memory and racial geography among black communities in secondary cities, it also informs scholars of how ordinary black people constructed notions of black politics. The dialogue and reflections from the "lost classes" provide context for understanding politics in ways that mattered in the lives of black Grand Rapidians, unraveling how they experienced life, and understanding how they perceived life during the fight for racial equality.

Finally, the black struggle for equality in Grand Rapids reveals that fundamental economic changes often associated with impersonal factors, such as the decline in manufacturing jobs, cannot account entirely for the rise of the urban crisis. The themes and issues raised by underclass theories, in particular the "spatial mismatch theory," place disproportionate emphasis on geography. However, the efforts of blacks in Grand Rapids precipitated a number of urban shifts in the postwar era. Their struggle indicates racism was central in the creation of urban decline and a growing urban underclass. The manufacturing trends evident in Detroit and Chicago are not equally apparent in other Rust Belt cities. It remains to be seen whether other secondary cities also follow such trends. However, as it stands, much of the scholarship on deindustrialization and the underclass suffers from narrow conceptualization. The story of Grand Rapids confirms that racism, not impersonal factors, had sustained significance in the postwar urban decline. The struggle for equality in Grand Rapids more closely resembles the hardships and gains experienced by blacks in the nearly 150 midsize cities spread across the country. Therefore, understanding African American urban life and history means broadening the scope to fill substantive gaps in the literature. *A City within a City,* then, is not solely about the geography of color: Rather, it examines the intersection of the black freedom movement and metropolitan reorganization in post–World War II society, through the lens of urban history. This lens must be expanded to include the black urban experience in secondary cities, because in many ways, the black struggle in secondary cities continues today.

NOTES

PREFACE

1. Karen L. Parker, "Diary, Letter, and Clippings, 1963–1966," Southern Historical Collection, Wilson Special Collection Library, University of North Carolina at Chapel Hill, Folder 1, July 1965.

2. Jeffrey D. Kleiman, *Strike: How the Furniture Workers Strike of 1911 Changed Grand Rapids* (Grand Rapids, MI: Grand Rapids Historical Commission, 2006), 15, 35.

3. Parker, "Diary, Letter, and Clippings, 1963–1966," July 1965.

4. Ibid.

5. Ibid., August 1965.

6. Ibid., January 1966.

7. Ibid., June 1966.

8. Ibid.

9. Ibid.

10. Ibid.

11. Ibid.

12. Ibid.

13. "Man in a Hurry Directs Chamber of Commerce," Grand Rapids Chamber of Commerce Records, Collection 46, Grand Rapids Public Library (GRPL), Grand Rapids, Michigan.

14. Thomas J. Sugrue, *The Origins of the Urban Crisis: Race and Inequality in Postwar Detroit* (Princeton, NJ: Princeton University Press, 1996), 268.

15. Anthony Chen, *The Fifth Freedom: Jobs, Politics, and Civil Rights in the United States, 1941–1972* (Princeton, NJ: Princeton University Press, 2009), 231.

16. William H. Chafe, *Civilities and Civil Rights: Greensboro, North Carolina, and the Black Struggle for Freedom* (New York: Oxford University Press, 1980), 7.

17. Randal Maurice Jelks, *African Americans in the Furniture City: The Struggle for Civil Rights in Grand Rapids* (Urbana: University of Illinois Press, 2006), xiii, xii.

18. Kevin K. Gaines, *Uplifting the Race: Black Leadership, Politics, and Culture in the Twentieth Century* (Chapel Hill: University of North Carolina Press, 1996), 4.

19. "Riot Legacy: 20 Years Later a Haunting Question: Have We Progressed?" *Grand Rapids Press,* July 26, 1987.

20. Jelks, *African Americans in the Furniture City,* 152.

21. The body of academic literature on urban histories of blacks in Michigan focuses on Detroit; see David M. Katzman, *Before the Ghetto: Black Detroit in the Nineteenth Century* (Urbana: University of Illinois Press, 1972); August Meier and Elliot Rudwick, *Black Detroit and the Rise of the UAW* (Ann Arbor: University of Michigan Press, 2007); Richard W. Thomas, *Life for Us Is What We Make It: Building Black Community in Detroit, 1915–1945* (Bloomington: Indiana University Press, 1992); Sugrue, *Origins of the Urban Crisis*; and Heather Ann Thompson, *Whose Detroit? Politics, Labor, and Race in a Modern American City* (Ithaca, NY: Cornell University Press, 2001). For Chicago, see Allan H. Spear, *Black Chicago: The Making of a Negro Ghetto, 1890–1920* (Chicago: University of Chicago Press, 1967); James R. Grossman, *Land of Hope: Chicago, Black Southerners, and the Great Migration* (Chicago: University of Chicago Press, 1989); Arnold R. Hirsch, *Making the Second Ghetto: Race and Housing in Chicago, 1940–1960* (Chicago: University of Chicago Press, 1998). Also, for a call to greater attention to African American urban history during the postwar period, see Kenneth L. Kusmer and Joe W. Trotter, eds., *African American Urban History since World War II* (Chicago: University of Chicago Press, 2009).

22. Hasan Kwame Jeffries, *Bloody Lowndes: Civil Rights and Black Power in Alabama's Black Belt* (New York: New York University Press, 2010), 4.

23. Although primarily a black urban history, this study examines the totality of metropolitan racial geography and improves upon groundbreaking urban studies of the first half century limited by the "ghetto synthesis model," including Gilbert Osofsky, *Harlem: The Making of a Ghetto; Negro New York, 1890–1930,* 2nd ed. (New York: Harper and Row, 1971); Spear, *Black Chicago*; Katzman, *Before the Ghetto*; and Kenneth L. Kusmer, *A Ghetto Takes Shape: Black Cleveland, 1870–1930* (Urbana: University of Illinois Press, 1976). Whereas these works concentrate primarily on black elites and their institutions, this study presents a more textured black community that includes diverse cultural, ideological, economic, and gender divisions, and—in part by tracing the evolving political consciousness through a variety of strategies used to create black autonomy—it moves beyond black victimization to uncover the powerful impact of black agency in the postwar era. See Robin D. G. Kelley, "'We Are Not What We Seem': Rethinking Black Working-Class Opposition in the Jim Crow South," *Journal of American History* 80 (June 1993): 75–112; Earl Lewis, "Connecting Memory, Self, and the Power of Place in African American Urban History," *Journal of Urban History* 21 (March 1995): 347–371; and Elsa Barkley Brown and Gregg Kimball, "Mapping the Terrain of Black Richmond," *Journal of Urban History* 21 (March 1995): 296–346.

24. A number of important studies note the construction of the "second ghetto," including Hirsch, *Making the Second Ghetto*; Charles F. Casey-Leinninger, "Making the Second Ghetto in Cincinnati: Avondale, 1925–1970," in *Race and the City: Work, Community, and Protest in Cincinnati, 1820–1970,* ed. Henry Louis Taylor Jr. (Urbana: University of Illinois Press, 1993); and Raymond A. Mohl, "Making the Second Ghetto in Metropolitan Miami, 1940–1960," in *The New African American Urban History,* ed. Kenneth W. Goings and Raymond A. Mohl (Thousand Oaks, CA: Sage Publications, 1996). Although the "second ghetto" thesis distinguishes the second wave of black migrants from the first, it is primarily helpful for examining larger cities with distinct pre-Depression migrations, such as Chicago, Detroit, Philadelphia, and New York. This thesis does not adequately account for Grand Rapids and numerous other smaller secondary cities in

America that had no established first ghetto until the postwar era, when Hirsch introduced the term "second ghetto."

25. A number of critical studies emphasize black agency during the pre-1945 era, including Earl Lewis, *In Their Own Interests: Race, Class, and Power in Twentieth-Century Norfolk, Virginia* (Berkeley: University of California Press, 1991); Tera W. Hunter, *To 'Joy My Freedom: Southern Black Women's Lives and Labors after the Civil War* (Cambridge, MA: Harvard University Press, 1997); and Leslie Brown, *Upbuilding Black Durham: Gender, Class, and Black Community Development in the Jim Crow South* (Chapel Hill: University of North Carolina Press, 2008).

26. Even the best historical accounts of urban history, such as Sugrue, *Origins of the Urban Crisis,* and William Julius Wilson, *The Truly Disadvantaged: The Inner City, the Underclass, and Public Policy,* 2nd ed. (Chicago: University of Chicago Press, 2012), do not assess the causes and consequences of school desegregation in their urban analyses. Of equal significance are the glaring omissions in educational literature, which fails to evaluate the various metropolitan issues that contributed to the spatial distribution of racial groups. Thus, this study bridges the two disciplines in an attempt to construct a metropolitan analysis that centers on the issues that engendered school segregation, evaluates the treatment and process of school desegregation, and analyzes the communal impact of school desegregation. For earlier accounts of the black community's struggles for educational equality, see Michael Homel, *Down from Equality: Black Chicagoans and the Public Schools, 1920–41* (Champaign: University of Illinois Press, 1984); Vincent P. Franklin, *The Education of Black Philadelphia: The Social and Educational History of a Minority Community, 1900–1950* (Philadelphia: University of Pennsylvania Press, 1979); and Judy Jolley Mohraz, *The Separate Problem: Case Studies of Black Education in the North, 1900–1930* (Westport, CT: Greenwood Press, 1979).

27. Northern school desegregation studies favor characterizing white working-class resistance to integration as a fight for community control and neighborhood schools. Although the role of class is important, the tendency to underline it has resulted in a loss of historical perspective regarding race privilege. This scholarship, best described by Ronald Formisano as "reactionary populism," relies disproportionately on a class-based analysis that situates antibusing protestors as well-intentioned victims. The result is a narrative almost exclusively about whites, not blacks, thus ignoring the importance of black institutions. For example, see George Metcalf, *From Little Rock to Boston* (Westport, CT: Greenwood Press, 1983); Ronald Formisano, *Boston against Busing: Race, Class, and Ethnicity in the 1960s and 1970s* (Chapel Hill: University of North Carolina Press, 1991); Anthony J. Lukas, *Common Ground: A Turbulent Decade in the Lives of Three American Families* (New York: Knopf, 1985); Alan Lupo, *Liberty's Chosen Home: The Politics of Violence in Boston* (New York: Little, Brown, 1977); and Michael Ross and William Berg, *"I Respectfully Disagree with the Judge's Order": The Boston School Desegregation Controversy* (Washington, DC: University Press of America, 1983). Several recent works on school desegregation in the South succeed in accounting for the importance of black schools and the impact of black school closings. See David S. Cecelski, *Along Freedom Road: Hyde County, North Carolina, and the Fate of Black Schools in the South* (Chapel Hill: University of North Carolina Press, 1994); and Vanessa Siddle Walker, *Their Highest Potential: An African American School Community in the Segregated South* (Chapel Hill: University of North Carolina Press, 1996). For important contributions on the subject of black high school activism, see also Dionne Danns, *Something Better for Our Children: Black Organizing in the Chicago Public Schools, 1963–1971* (New York: Routledge, 2003); and Gael

Graham, *Young Activists: American High School Students in the Age of Protest* (DeKalb, IL: Northern University Press, 2006).

28. For critiques of the "classical" narrative, see Peniel E. Joseph, "Black Liberation without Apology: Reconceptualizing the Black Power Movement," *Black Scholar* 31 (Fall–Winter 2001): 3–19; Jacqueline Dowd Hall, "The Long Civil Rights Movement and the Political Uses of the Past," *Journal of American History* 91 (March 2005): 1233–1263; and Van Gosse and Richard Moser, eds., *The World the 60s Made: Politics and Culture in Recent America* (Philadelphia: Temple University Press, 2003). For "March against Freedom," see Clayborn Carson, *In Struggle: SNCC and the Black Awakening of the 1960s* (Cambridge, MA: Harvard University Press, 1981), 191–211; John Dittmer, *Local People: The Struggle for Civil Rights in Mississippi* (Urbana: University of Illinois Press, 1995), 389–407; Adam Fairclough, *To Redeem the Soul of America: The Southern Christian Leadership Conference and Martin Luther King Jr.* (Athens: University of Georgia Press, 2001), 309–320; and Peniel E. Joseph, *Waiting 'til the Midnight Hour: A Narrative History of Black Power in America* (New York: Henry Holt, 2006). See also Martha Biondi, *"To Stand and Fight": The Struggle for Civil Rights in Postwar New York City* (Cambridge, MA: Harvard University Press, 2002); Robert O. Self, *American Babylon: Race and the Struggle for Postwar Oakland* (Princeton, NJ: Princeton University Press, 2003); and Matthew J. Countryman, *Up South: Civil Rights and Black Power in Philadelphia* (Philadelphia: University of Pennsylvania Press, 2006). Not only do these works challenge historians to rethink the periodization and geographical scope of the civil rights movement, they also collectively force scholars to reconsider the influence of the black power movement on the civil rights movement. Together, the theoretical innovations of these important works underline racism as a national problem, not one confined solely to the South.

29. The literature devoted to student participation in the civil rights movement deals mostly with college students, not secondary students. See, for example, August Meier and Elliott Rudwick, *CORE: A Study in the Civil Rights Movement, 1942–1968* (New York: Oxford University Press, 1973); Carson, *In Struggle*; Chafe, *Civilities and Civil Rights*; and Aldon Morris, *The Origins of the Civil Rights Movement: Black Communities Organizing for Change* (New York: Free Press, 1984). For works devoted to secondary students, see Richard Wormser, *The Rise and Fall of Jim Crow* (New York: St. Martin's Press, 2003); V. P. Franklin, "Black High School Student Activism in the 1960s: An Urban Phenomenon?" *Journal of Research in Education* 10 (Fall 2000): 3–8; Countryman, *Up South*, 223–257; Danns, *Something Better for Our Children*; and Graham, *Young Activists*. For a journalistic account, see Robert C. Smith, *They Closed Their Schools: Prince Edward County, Virginia, 1951–1964* (Chapel Hill: University of North Carolina Press, 1965).

CHAPTER 1

1. Darlene Clark Hine, "Black Migration to the Urban Midwest: The Gender Dimension, 1915–1945," in *The Great Migration in Historical Perspective: New Dimensions of Race, Class, and Gender,* ed. Joe William Trotter Jr. (Bloomington: Indiana University Press, 1991), 128; *Grand Rapids Press,* September 10, 1967.

2. Emmett J. Scott, *Negro Migration during the War* (1920; repr., New York: Arno Press, 1969), 106; Joe William Trotter Jr., "Introduction: Black Migration in Historical Perspective; A Review of the Literature," in *The Great Migration,* 16.

3. Cheryl Lynn Greenberg, *"Or Does It Explode?" Black Harlem in the Great Depression* (New York: Oxford University Press, 1991), 14; E. Franklin Frazier, *The Negro in the United States,* rev. ed. (New York: Macmillan, 1957), 263.

4. U.S. Bureau of the Census, table 23, "Michigan—Race and Hispanic Origin for Selected Large Cities and Other Places: Earliest Census to 1990."

5. The National Urban League, "The Negro Population of Grand Rapids, Michigan: 1940," National Urban League Papers, Library of Congress, Washington, DC, 11.

6. University of Michigan, Alumni Relations Office, "Oliver Meakins Green, Law Graduate and Member of the Alpha Phi Alpha Fraternity," *University of Michigan Annual 1923* (Ann Arbor: University of Michigan).

7. Randal Maurice Jelks, *African Americans in the Furniture City: The Struggle for Civil Rights in Grand Rapids* (Urbana: University of Illinois Press, 2006), 67.

8. "Ku Klux Klan to Stage Big Parade Here," *Grand Rapids Herald,* November 11, 1924.

9. See Robert Alan Goldberg, *Hooded Empire: The Ku Klux Klan in Colorado* (Urbana: University of Illinois Press, 1981); William D. Jenkins, *Steel Valley Klan: The Ku Klux Klan in Ohio's Mahoning Valley* (Kent, OH: Kent State University Press, 1990); Leonard J. Moore, *Citizen Klansmen: The Ku Klux Klan in Indiana, 1921–1928* (Chapel Hill: University of North Carolina Press, 1991); and Kathleen M. Blee, *Women of the Klan: Racism and Gender in the 1920s* (Berkeley: University of California Press, 1991).

10. Joel Carpenter, "Michigan's Klan in a Small Town: The Ku Klux Klan in Adrian, Michigan 1923–1925" (unpublished manuscript, Grand Rapids Public Library [GRPL], Grand Rapids, Michigan, 1974).

11. Robert S. Lynd and Helen Merrell Lynd, *Middletown: A Study of Modern American Culture* (New York: Harcourt Brace, 1929), 481–484; "South High Annual, 1919," Grand Rapids Public Library (GRPL), Grand Rapids, Michigan, 103–104.

12. "Ku Klux Klan to Stage Big Parade Here." See also Jack Swertferger, "Anti-Mask and Anti-Klan Laws," *Journal of Public Law* 1 (Spring 1952): 182–197; and David M. Chalmers, *Hooded Americanism: The History of the Ku Klux Klan,* 3rd ed. (Durham, NC: Duke University Press, 1987).

13. "Klan Breaks Camp after It Meets," *Grand Rapids Press,* July 6, 1925; Carol Tanis, "A Study in Self-Improvement," *Grand Rapids Magazine,* January 21, 1987, 41.

14. Neil Betten and Raymond A. Mohl, "The Evolution of Racism in an Industrial City, 1906–1940: A Case Study of Gary, Indiana," *Journal of Negro History* 59, no. 1 (January 1974): 53–54.

15. Anita N. Green, "The Grand Rapids Study Club: The Oldest Black Organization in Grand Rapids," *Info Magazine,* April–May 1989, 31.

16. "Colored Men Will Demand Their Rights," *Grand Rapids Press,* July 11, 1904.

17. "Cannot Buy Shoes," *Grand Rapids Press,* May 5, 1913.

18. Lewis B. Clingman, "The History of the Grand Rapids Human Relations Commission" (Ph.D. diss., Michigan State University, 1976), 21.

19. The National Urban League, "The Negro Population of Grand Rapids: 1940," 70.

20. Ibid. See also Hine, "Black Migration to the Urban Midwest."

21. Tanis, "A Study in Self-Improvement," 42.

22. The National Urban League, "The Negro Population of Grand Rapids: 1940," 24–25.

23. U.S. Bureau of the Census, Special Bulletin, no. 18; Department of Commerce and Labor, Census of Manufactures, 11, 13.

24. Jeffrey David Kleiman, "The Great Strike: Religion, Labor and Reform in Grand Rapids, Michigan, 1890–1916" (Ph.D. diss., Michigan State University, 1985), 3.

25. Duncan E. Littlefair, "Race Relations," November 17, 1946, Duncan E. Littlefair Manuscript Collection, Bentley Historical Library, Ann Arbor, Michigan, 7. See also Mary

Patrice Erdmans, "The Poles, the Dutch and the Grand Rapids Furniture Strike of 1911," *Polish American Studies* 62, no. 2 (Autumn 2005): 5–22.

26. U.S. Census of the Population, 1920, Population Vol. III, table 6.

27. Erdmans, "The Poles, the Dutch and the Grand Rapids Furniture Strike," 12.

28. *Reports of the Immigration Commission* (Washington, DC: U.S. Government Printing Office, 1911), table 11, 481.

29. James D. Bratt and Christopher H. Meehan, *Gathered at the River: Grand Rapids, Michigan and Its People of Faith* (Grand Rapids, MI: Eerdmans, 1993), 97–98.

30. Linda Samuelson, Andrew Schrier, and Grand Rapids Area Council for the Humanities, *Heart and Soul: The Story of Grand Rapids Neighborhoods* (Grand Rapids, MI: Eerdmans, 2003), 92.

31. The National Urban League, "The Negro Population of Grand Rapids: 1940," 29.

32. Ibid., 30.

33. Home Owners' Loan Corporation, "Confidential Report of a Survey in Grand Rapids, Michigan and Its Suburban Area," November 12, 1937, National Archives, Washington, DC, 2–3.

34. The National Urban League, "The Negro Population of Grand Rapids: 1940," 32.

35. Ibid., 13.

36. Tom LaBelle, "Black Powers," *Grand Rapids Press,* February 8, 1981.

37. For pre–World War II ghettoes, see Gilbert Osofsky, *Harlem: The Making of a Ghetto; Negro New York, 1890–1930,* 2nd ed. (New York: Harper and Row, 1971); Allan H. Spear, *Black Chicago: The Making of a Negro Ghetto, 1890–1920* (Chicago: University of Chicago Press, 1967); Kenneth L. Kusmer, *A Ghetto Takes Shape: Black Cleveland, 1870–1930* (Urbana: University of Illinois Press, 1976); and David M. Katzman, *Before the Ghetto: Black Detroit in the Nineteenth Century* (Urbana: University of Illinois Press, 1972). For black migration, see Peter Gottlieb, *Making Their Own Way: Southern Blacks' Migration to Pittsburgh, 1916–30* (Urbana: University of Illinois Press, 1987); Joe William Trotter Jr., *Black Milwaukee: The Making of an Industrial Proletariat, 1915–1945* (Urbana: University of Illinois Press, 1985); James R. Grossman, *Land of Hope: Chicago, Black Southerners, and the Great Migration* (Chicago: University of Chicago Press, 1989); Earl Lewis, *In Their Own Interests: Race, Class, and Power in Twentieth-Century Norfolk* (Berkeley: University of California Press, 1991); and Nicholas Lemann, *The Promised Land: The Great Black Migration and How It Changed America* (New York: Knopf, 1991).

38. Grand Rapids Urban League Papers, "Urban League History," Black History Manuscript Collection, GRPL.

39. Bettye Collier-Thomas, *Jesus, Jobs, and Justice: African American Women and Religion* (New York: Knopf, 2010), 268.

40. Tanis, "A Study in Self-Improvement," 42.

41. Anita N. Green, "The Oldest Black Organization in Grand Rapids," Grand Rapids Study Class/Grand Rapids Study Club Manuscript Collection, GRPL, 31.

42. Club, "Grand Rapids Study Club Scrapbook," Grand Rapids Study Class/Grand Rapids Study Club Manuscript Collection, GRPL.

43. Michigan State Association of Colored Women's Clubs, "Lifting as We Climb," Grand Rapids Study Club Manuscript Collection, GRPL, 6.

44. Hine, "Black Migration to the Urban Midwest," 129.

45. *Grand Rapids Magazine,* May 2004.

46. Lewis, *In Their Own Interests,* 91–92.

47. George Lipsitz, *A Life in the Struggle: Ivory Perry and the Culture of Opposition* (Philadelphia: Temple University Press, 1988); Elsa Barkley Brown, "Womanist Con-

sciousness: Maggie Lena Walker and the Independent Order of St. Luke," *Signs; Journal of Women in Culture and Society* 14 (Spring 1989): 610–633; Elsa Barkley Brown, "Uncle Ned's Children: Richmond, Virginia's Black Community, 1890–1930" (Ph.D. diss., Kent State University, 1994); Robin D. G. Kelley. *Race Rebels: Culture, Politics, and the Black Working Class* (New York: Free Press, 1994); and Tera W. Hunter, *To 'Joy My Freedom: Southern Black Women's Lives and Labors after the Civil War* (Cambridge, MA: Harvard University Press, 1997).

48. Florette Henri, *Black Migration: Movement North, 1900–1920* (Garden City, NY: Anchor Press, 1975); Trotter, *Black Milwaukee*; Gottlieb, *Making Their Own Way*; Grossman, *Land of Hope*; and Lewis, *In Their Own Interests*.

49. Tanis, "A Study in Self-Improvement," 43.

50. Kelley, *Race Rebels,* 52.

51. Green, "The Grand Rapids Study Club," 31–32.

52. Tanis, "A Study in Self-Improvement," 43.

53. Green, "The Oldest Black Organization in Grand Rapids," 31.

54. Tanis, "A Study in Self-Improvement," 43.

55. Ibid.

56. Esther Colston Hill, "History of the Grand Rapids Study Club," Grand Rapids Study Class/Grand Rapids Study Club Manuscript Collection, GRPL, 2, 31.

57. Kelley, *Race Rebels,* 50.

58. Green, "The Oldest Black Organization in Grand Rapids," 31.

59. Club, "Grand Rapids Study Club Scrapbook."

60. Green, "The Oldest Black Organization in Grand Rapids," 31.

61. Tanis, "A Study in Self-Improvement," 43.

62. Green, "The Oldest Black Organization in Grand Rapids," 31.

63. Bloom, "Sarah Glover: Fulfilling Her Dream to Help Others," Grand Rapids Study Class/Grand Rapids Study Club Manuscript Collection, GRPL.

64. Green, "The Oldest Black Organization in Grand Rapids," 31.

65. "Negro Educator to Give Address Here," *Grand Rapids Herald,* April 29, 1917.

66. "Sharing the White Man's Burden," *Grand Rapids Press,* May 4, 1917.

67. For an overview of the history of the NAACP, see August Meier and John H. Bracey Jr., "The NAACP as a Reform Movement, 1909–1965: 'To Reach the Conscience of America,'" *Journal of Southern History* 59 (1993): 3–30. See also Denton L. Watson, "Assessing the Role of the NAACP in the Civil Rights Movement," *Historian* 55, no. 3 (Spring 1993): 453–468.

68. Jelks, *African Americans in the Furniture City.* See also Arna Bontemps, ed., *The Harlem Renaissance Remembered: Essays* (New York: Dodd, Mead, 1972); and Nathan Irvin Huggins, *Harlem Renaissance* (New York: Oxford University Press, 1971).

69. "Grand Rapids, Michigan 1913–1926," NAACP Collection, Group I, Series G, Container 99, Library of Congress, Washington, DC.

70. Randal M. Jelks, "Making Opportunity: The Struggle against Jim Crow in Grand Rapids, Michigan, 1890–1927," *Michigan Historical Review* 19, no. 2 (Fall 1993): 33.

71. LaBelle, "Black Powers."

72. Ibid.

73. *Public Acts, 1885, No. 130* (Lansing: State of Michigan, 1885), 131–132; and *Public Acts, 1919, No. 375* (Lansing: State of Michigan, 1919), 657.

74. Gordon Olson, *A Grand Rapids Sampler* (Grand Rapids, MI: Grand Rapids Historical Commission, 1992), 153.

75. *Public Acts, 1885, No. 130.* See also *Public Acts, 1919, No. 375.*

76. "Grand Rapids Operating Corporation," 1925, Grand Rapids Superior Court Case No. 2986, Western Michigan Regional Archives, Western Michigan University, Kalamazoo, Michigan.

77. Brian Todd Anderson, "William M. Glenn 1903–1986: Black, White, Red, and Right," 1997, William M. Glenn Papers, GRPL, 5.

78. "Election at a Glance," *Grand Rapids Herald,* April 6, 1926.

79. Jelks, "Making Opportunity," 42.

80. Ibid., 43.

81. "Court Rules against Jim Crow Tactics: Reverses Decision in Theater Case," *Chicago Defender,* June 18, 1927.

82. Gerald Elliot, "With Us Today: Milo M. Brown Calm and Successful," Grand Rapids Study Class/Grand Rapids Study Club Manuscript Collection, GRPL.

83. Ibid.

84. Ibid.

85. Ibid.

86. LaBelle, "Black Powers."

87. Laura D. Walker, "A Constant Struggle: The Landmark Voting Rights Act, up for renewal next year, faces an uncertain future," Grand Rapids Study Club Manuscript Collection, GRPL.

88. Elliot, "With Us Today."

89. Ethel B. Burgess, "Committee Report," National Urban League Papers, Library of Congress, Washington, DC, July 21, 1927.

90. Correspondence, Ethel B. Burgess to Eugene Kinckle Jones, National Urban League Papers, Library of Congress, Washington, DC, July 26, 1927.

91. "Declares Negroes Need Social Work," *Grand Rapids Urban League,* September 23, 1927, 2.

92. "To Discuss Welfare of Colored Folk in City," *Grand Rapids Press,* September 30, 1927.

93. Jelks, *African Americans in the Furniture City,* 91.

94. Correspondence, Ida W. Wilson to W. E. B. DuBois, December 28, 1927, W. E. B. DuBois Papers, University of Massachusetts, Reel 22.

95. Correspondence, W. E. B. DuBois to Ida W. Wilson, December 30, 1927, W. E. B. DuBois Papers, University of Massachusetts, Reel 22.

96. R. Maurice Moss, "Preliminary Report to the Grand Rapids Inter Racial Council June 14, 1928," National Urban League Papers, Library of Congress, Washington, DC, Conclusion, 1.

97. Ibid., 2.

98. "Need for Greater Social Work among Negroes Is Cited," *Grand Rapids Herald,* January 22, 1929.

99. "A Gift the Negroes Do Not Want," *Grand Rapids Press,* May 21, 1930.

100. "Cab's Head Hasn't Swelled," *Grand Rapids Herald,* July 24, 1933.

101. Elliot, "With Us Today."

102. Thomas J. Sugrue, *Sweet Land of Liberty: The Forgotten Struggle for Civil Rights in the North* (New York: Random House, 2008), xiv. See also Martha Biondi, *"To Stand and Fight": The Struggle for Civil Rights in Postwar New York City* (Cambridge, MA: Harvard University Press, 2002); Self, *American Babylon: Race and the Struggle for Postwar Oakland* (Princeton, NJ: Princeton University Press, 2003); and Matthew J. Countryman, *Up South: Civil Rights and Black Power in Philadelphia* (Philadelphia: University of Pennsylvania Press, 2006).

CHAPTER 2

1. Jimmie Franklin, "Blacks and the Progressive Movement: Emergence of a New Synthesis," *OAH Magazine of History* 13, no. 3 (Spring 1999): 20–23.

2. Maureen A. Flanagan, *America Reformed: Progressives and Progressivisms 1890s–1920s* (New York: Oxford University Press, 2007), 26.

3. Sidney Fine, "'A Jewel in the Crown of All of Us': Michigan Enacts a Fair Employment Practices Act, 1941–1955," *Michigan Historical Review* 22, no. 1 (Spring 1996): 19.

4. Anthony Chen, *The Fifth Freedom: Jobs, Politics, and Civil Rights in the United States, 1941–1972* (Princeton, NJ: Princeton University Press, 2009), 20.

5. William H. Chafe, *Civilities and Civil Rights: Greensboro, North Carolina, and the Black Struggle for Freedom* (New York: Oxford University Press, 1980); Davison M. Douglas, *Reading, Writing and Race: The Desegregation of the Charlotte Schools* (Chapel Hill: University of North Carolina Press, 1995); and Tera W. Hunter, *To 'Joy My Freedom: Southern Black Women's Lives and Labors after the Civil War* (Cambridge, MA: Harvard University Press, 1997).

6. Samuel P. Hays, *The Response to Industrialism 1885–1914* (Chicago: University of Chicago Press, 1957); James Weinstein, "Organized Business and the City Commission and Manager Movement," *Journal of Southern History* 28 (1962): 166–182; Robert H. Wiebe, *The Search for Order, 1877–1920* (New York: Hill and Wang, 1967); and Matthew J. Schott, "The New Orleans Machine and Progressivism," *Louisiana History: The Journal of the Louisiana Historical Association* 24, no. 2 (Spring 1983): 141–153.

7. Carl Abbott, *How Cities Won the West: Four Centuries of Urban Change in Western North America* (Albuquerque: University of New Mexico Press, 2008); and Flanagan, *America Reformed.*

8. Stanton W. Todd, "History and Purpose of the Republican Home Front," Stanton W. Todd Papers, Bentley Historical Library, Ann Arbor, Michigan.

9. Stanton W. Todd, "A Synopsis of My Experience in Republican Politics, 1942–1947," Stanton W. Todd Papers, Bentley Historical Library, Ann Arbor, Michigan.

10. Correspondence, The Home Front to Citizens, "Republican Party 'Home Front,'" September 15, 1942, Stanton W. Todd Papers, Bentley Historical Library, Ann Arbor, Michigan.

11. "History and Purpose of 'The Home Front,'" *Grand Rapids Press,* August 4, 1942. [Located in Stanton W. Todd Papers, Bentley Historical Library, Ann Arbor, Michigan.]

12. Todd, "History and Purpose of the Republican Home Front."

13. Correspondence, Oscar E. Waer to Stanton W. Todd Jr., July 21, 1944, Stanton W. Todd Papers, Bentley Historical Library, Ann Arbor, Michigan.

14. *Grand Rapids Herald,* October 30, 1955.

15. Ibid.

16. "He Once Was the Life of the Grand Old Party," *Detroit Free Press,* November 17, 1963.

17. Dorothy Judd, "Grand Rapids Frees Itself from Boss Control after 20 Years" (report), n.d., Dorothy Leonard Judd Papers, Bentley Historical Library, Ann Arbor, Michigan, 1.

18. Ibid., 8.

19. Dorothy Judd, "Muddling through to Measurement: A Tale of One City," April 1945, Dorothy Leonard Judd Papers, Bentley Historical Library, Ann Arbor, Michigan, 2–4; Judd, "Grand Rapids Frees Itself from Boss Control after 20 Years," 3–4.

20. Msgr. Hugh Michael Beahan, "'The Gentleman Fighter,'" *Western Michigan Catholic,* January 7, 1977, Paul I. Phillips Manuscript Collection, Grand Rapids Public Library (GRPL), Grand Rapids, Michigan, 1.

21. Duncan E. Littlefair, "Race Relations," November 17, 1946, Duncan E. Littlefair Manuscript Collection, Bentley Historical Library, Ann Arbor, Michigan, 7.

22. LaBelle, "Black Powers," 1B.

23. Lillian Gill, interview, June 6, 1997, interview #014, Greater Grand Rapids Women's History Council Oral Interviews, Grand Rapids History and Special Collections, GRPL, 3.

24. Paul I. Phillips, "Brief Account of Our 25 Years of Stewardship," 1947, Paul I. Phillips Manuscript Collection, GRPL, 1–2.

25. O. A. Rogers Jr., "The Elaine Race Riots of 1919," *Arkansas Historical Quarterly* 19, no. 2 (Summer 1960): 142–150; Patricia Scott West, "Race Riot! Press Coverage of Urban Violence, 1903–1967" (Ph.D. diss., University of Southern Mississippi, 2003).

26. Mike Lloyd, "Paul Phillips Dies; Civil Rights Leader," *Grand Rapids Press,* January 1, 1977.

27. Ibid.

28. Beahan, "'The Gentleman Fighter.'"

29. Ibid.

30. LaBelle, "Black Powers," 1B.

31. Phillips, "Brief Account of Our 25 Years of Stewardship," 1.

32. LaBelle, "Black Powers," 2B.

33. Lloyd, "Paul Phillips Dies."

34. Beahan, "'The Gentleman Fighter.'"

35. "Brough Center Joins League," *Grand Rapids Press,* February 4, 1947.

36. "Grand Rapids Urban League and Brough Community Association," *Grand Rapids Press,* July 31, 1948.

37. "Brough Center Joins League."

38. LaBelle, "Black Powers," 2B.

39. Lloyd, "Paul Phillips Dies."

40. Phillips, "Brief Account of Our 25 Years of Stewardship," 2; "Mrs. Jones Wins Position in Personnel Department," *Grand Rapids Herald,* October 18, 1950.

41. Obituary: Hillary Bissell, *Greenville Daily,* March 3, 1975.

42. "Crusader in Rights Causes," *Grand Rapids Press,* March 3, 1975.

43. *Sioux City Journal,* June 26, 1943; July 12, 1943; April 22, 1949; April 28, 1950.

44. Hillary Bissell to Thurgood Marshall, 1949, NAACP Papers, Group II, Box 91, Folder 1945–1950, Library of Congress, Washington, DC.

45. Randal Maurice Jelks, *African Americans in the Furniture City: The Struggle for Civil Rights in Grand Rapids* (Urbana: University of Illinois Press, 2006), 139–140.

46. "Segregation of Students in Grand Rapids Protested," *Pittsburgh Courier* (Detroit Edition), June 16, 1951.

47. "NAACP Membership Drive—Grand Rapids; Hillary Bissell, Publicity Chairman," NAACP Papers, Group II, Box 91, Folder 1951, Library of Congress, Washington, DC; Gloster B. Current, Director of Branches, to Mrs. Wadsworth Bissell, June 18, 1951, NAACP Papers, Group II, Box 91, Library of Congress, Washington, DC; emphasis original.

48. Hillary Bissell to Gloster B. Current, June 15, 1951, NAACP Papers, Group II, Box 91, Library of Congress, Washington, DC; emphasis original.

49. Ibid.

50. Hillary Bissell to Gloster B. Current, June 9, 1951, NAACP Papers, Group II, Box 91, Folder 1952, Library of Congress, Washington, DC; emphasis original.

51. Hillary Bissell to Roy Wilkins, n.d., NAACP Papers, Group II, Box 91, Folder 1952, Library of Congress, Washington, DC.

52. Grand Rapids Chamber of Commerce, "Legislative Action!" March 12, 1953, Grand Rapids Chamber of Commerce Records, GRPL.

53. Grand Rapids Chamber of Commerce, "State Affairs," Grand Rapids Chamber of Commerce Records, GRPL.

54. Grand Rapids Chamber of Commerce, "Manufacturers Department," Grand Rapids Chamber of Commerce Records, 1950–1953, GRPL.

55. Review Committee of the Grand Rapids Urban League, "Grand Rapids Balance Sheet on Race Relations, 1950–1953," Grand Rapids Chamber of Commerce Records, GRPL, 1.

56. Ibid.

57. Thomas J. Sugrue, *The Origins of the Urban Crisis: Race and Inequality in Postwar Detroit* (Princeton, NJ: Princeton University Press, 1996), 173.

58. Fair Employment Practices Commission, File 34, Grand Rapids Chamber of Commerce Records, GRPL.

59. Hillary Bissell to Roy Wilkins, n.d., NAACP Papers; emphasis original.

60. Ibid.; emphasis original.

61. Helen Jackson Wilkins Claytor, interview, March 2, 1990, interview #010, Greater Grand Rapids Women's History Council Oral Interviews, Grand Rapids History and Special Collections, GRPL, 7.

62. Ibid., 1, 3.

63. Ibid., 4–5; Roy Wilkins and Tom Mathews, *Standing Fast: The Autobiography of Roy Wilkins* (New York: Da Capo Press, 1994), 177.

64. Helen Claytor, interview, 7.

65. Ibid., 9–10.

66. Ibid., 10.

67. Ibid.

68. Jelks, *African Americans in the Furniture City,* 144.

69. Lewis B. Clingman, "The History of the Grand Rapids Human Relations Commission" (Ph.D. diss., Michigan State University, 1976), 2.

70. Ibid., 6.

71. Ibid., 25–26.

72. Jelks, *African Americans in the Furniture City,* 145–146.

73. Clingman, "History of the Grand Rapids Human Relations Commission," 25.

74. Ibid., 26–27.

75. Helen Claytor, interview, 13.

76. Ibid.

77. Clingman, "History of the Grand Rapids Human Relations Commission," 30.

78. Sugrue, *Origins of the Urban Crisis,* 173–174.

79. Ibid., 175.

80. Carter G. Woodson, *The Mis-education of the Negro* (Trenton, NJ: Africa World Press, 2006).

81. *Grand Rapids Herald,* December 20, 1908.

82. Hillary Bissell, "A Report to the Grand Rapids Human Relations Commission: Current Statistics on Non-White Enrollment in the Grand Rapids Schools," Helen Claytor Papers, Michigan Historical Collection, Bentley Historical Library, Ann Arbor, Michigan, 2.

83. Donald H. Bouma and James Hoffman, *The Dynamics of School Integration: Problems and Approaches in a Northern City* (Grand Rapids, MI: Eerdmans, 1968), 49.

84. Campau School Committee, "Integration: A School Problem in the Campau Area," Helen Claytor Papers, Michigan Historical Collection, Bentley Historical Library, Ann Arbor, Michigan, 1.

85. Ibid., 5.

86. Ibid., 1.

87. Ibid., 4.

88. "Clash on Educational, Social Ideas Marks Campau School Site Hearing," August 2009, Special Collections and Archives, Collection #003, Loretta Ort Manuscript Collection, GRPL.

89. Clingman, "History of the Grand Rapids Human Relations Commission," 66–67.

90. Hillary Bissell, "Selected Information on the Negro Population in Grand Rapids Schools," Helen Claytor Papers, Michigan Historical Collection, Bentley Historical Library, Ann Arbor, Michigan, 3.

91. National Association for the Advancement of Colored People, "Noncurrent Records and Photographs of the NAACP," Part IV, v. 1096, National Association for the Advancement of Colored People Manuscript Collection, Library of Congress, Washington, DC.

92. Bouma and Hoffman, *Dynamics of School Integration,* 28–29.

93. Irving R. Kaufman, "The New Rochelle Decision: The Facts," *Journal of Educational Sociology* 36, no. 6 (February 1963): 263–269.

94. Hillary Bissell to Gloster B. Current, June 9, 1951, NAACP Papers.

95. "Our Schools and Others," Loretta Ort Manuscript Collection, GRPL.

96. Jeffrey Mirel, *The Rise and Fall of an Urban School System: Detroit, 1907–81,* 2nd ed. (Ann Arbor: University of Michigan Press, 1999), 217, 218.

97. *Grand Rapids Herald,* February 20, 1949.

98. "Six Seek Seats on Board of Education," *Grand Rapids Press,* February 16, 1955.

99. Hillary Bissell, "The Effects of White and Non-White Population Changes in the Central City," 1961, Black History Manuscript Collection, GRPL, 8.

100. Campau School Committee, "Integration: A School Problem in the Campau Area," 5.

101. "Clash on Educational, Social Ideas Marks Campau School Site Hearing," Loretta Ort Manuscript Collection, GRPL.

102. Clingman, "History of the Grand Rapids Human Relations Commission," 65.

103. "School Board Winner Credits 'Organization,'" *Grand Rapids Press,* February 25, 1962.

104. "Phillips to Ask Negro Pupil Counselors, Technical High School Revival," *Grand Rapids Press,* May 24, 1962.

105. Ibid.

106. "School Board OK's Race Relations Inventory," *Grand Rapids Press,* July 3, 1963.

107. "Paul Phillips and the Impatience of Patience," *Grand Rapids Press,* March 25, 1973.

108. Bouma and Hoffman, *Dynamics of School Integration,* 31.

109. Vernis Schad, "Revisiting Racial Segregation in the Mid-1960s: Grand Rapids Public Schools" (unpublished lecture, 2003, GRPL), 4.

110. Ibid.

111. Chafe, *Civilities and Civil Rights,* 22.

CHAPTER 3

1. Arnold R. Hirsch, *Making the Second Ghetto: Race and Housing in Chicago, 1940–1960* (Chicago: University of Chicago Press, 1998); Charles F. Casey-Leinniger, "Making the Second Ghetto in Cincinnati: Avondale, 1925–1970," in *Race and the City: Work, Community, and Protest in Cincinnati, 1820–1970*, ed. Henry Louis Taylor Jr. (Urbana: University of Illinois Press, 1993); Carolyn Adams, David Bartelt, David Elesh, Ira Goldstein, Nancy Kleniewski, and William Yancey, *Philadelphia: Neighborhoods, Division, and Conflict in a Post-industrial City* (Philadelphia: Temple University Press, 1991); and Nicholas Lemann, *The Promised Land: The Great Black Migration and How It Changed America* (New York: Knopf, 1991).

2. For studies on the development of pre–World War II ghettoes, see John H. Bracey, August Meier, and Elliott Rudwick, eds., *The Rise of the Ghetto* (Belmont, CA: Wadsworth, 1972); Gilbert Osofsky, *Harlem: The Making of a Ghetto; Negro New York, 1890–1930*, 2nd ed. (New York: Harper and Row, 1971); Allan H. Spear, *Black Chicago: The Making of a Negro Ghetto, 1890–1920* (Chicago: University of Chicago Press, 1967); Kenneth L. Kusmer, *A Ghetto Takes Shape: Black Cleveland, 1870–1930* (Urbana: University of Illinois Press, 1976); Joe William Trotter Jr., *Black Milwaukee: The Making of an Industrial Proletariat, 1915–1945* (Urbana: University of Illinois Press, 1985); and James R. Grossman, *Land of Hope: Chicago, Black Southerners, and the Great Migration* (Chicago: University of Chicago Press, 1989). For studies on the second ghetto during the postwar period, see Hirsch, *Making the Second Ghetto*; Casey-Leinniger, "Making the Second Ghetto in Cincinnati: Avondale"; and Raymond A. Mohl, "Making the Second Ghetto in Metropolitan Miami, 1940–1960," in *The New African American Urban History*, ed. Kenneth W. Goings and Raymond A. Mohl (Thousand Oaks, CA: Sage, 1996).

3. Robert O. Self, *American Babylon: Race and the Struggle for Postwar Oakland* (Princeton, NJ: Princeton University Press, 2003), 13. The best historical accounts of this period, most notably Arnold R. Hirsch's impressive book *Making the Second Ghetto: Race and Housing in Chicago, 1940–1960*, Thomas J. Sugrue's splendid study *The Origins of the Urban Crisis: Race and Inequality in Postwar Detroit* (Princeton, NJ: Princeton University Press, 1996), and Raymond A. Mohl's "Making the Second Ghetto in Metropolitan Miami, 1940–1960," offer a spatial analysis of inequality that does not consider how civil rights activists shaped the process of postwar metropolitan development.

4. Roger W. Wilkins, *A Man's Life: An Autobiography* (New York: Simon and Schuster, 1982), 39. For more on pivotal racial encounters or "racial baptisms," see Leon F. Litwack, *Trouble in Mind: Black Southerners in the Age of Jim Crow* (New York: Knopf, 1998); Thomas Holt, "Marking: Race, Race-Making, and the Writing of History," *American Historical Review* 100, no. 1 (February 1995): 1–20; and W. E. B. DuBois, *The Souls of Black Folk* (New York: Bantam Classic, 1989).

5. Wilkins, *A Man's Life*, 40. For black suburbanization, see Mary Pattillo-McCoy, *Black Picket Fences: Privilege and Peril among the Black Middle Class* (Chicago: University of Chicago Press, 1999); Bruce D. Haynes, *Red Lines, Black Spaces: The Politics of Race and Space in a Black Middle-Class Suburb* (New Haven, CT: Yale University Press, 2001); and Andrew Wiese, *Places of Their Own: African American Suburbanization in the Twentieth Century* (Chicago: University of Chicago Press, 2004). For residential segregation, see Douglas S. Massey, Gretchen A. Condran, and Nancy A. Denton, "The Effect of Residential Segregation on Black Social and Economic Well-being," *Social Forces* 66, no. 1 (1987): 29–56; Benjamin Kleinberg, *Urban America in Transformation: Perspectives on*

Urban Policy and Development (Thousand Oaks, CA: Sage, 1995); Kenneth W. Goings and Raymond A. Mohl, eds., *The New African American Urban History* (Thousand Oaks, CA: Sage, 1996).

6. Wilkins, *A Man's Life*, 40.

7. Helen Jackson Wilkins Claytor, interview, March 2, 1990, interview #010, Greater Grand Rapids Women's History Council Oral Interviews, Grand Rapids History and Special Collections, Grand Rapids Public Library (GRPL), Grand Rapids, Michigan.

8. Linda Samuelson, Andrew Schrier, and Grand Rapids Area Council for the Humanities, *Heart and Soul: The Story of Grand Rapids Neighborhoods* (Grand Rapids, MI: Eerdmans, 2003), 146.

9. Helen Claytor, interview.

10. Ibid.

11. Ibid.

12. State Advisory Committee, *1961 Report to the Commission on Civil Rights*, 261. See also Douglas S. Massey, "Residential Segregation and Neighborhood Conditions in U.S. Metropolitan Areas," in *America Becoming: Racial Trends and Their Consequences*, Vol. 1, ed. Neil J. Smelser, William J. Wilson, and Faith Mitchell (Washington, DC: National Academy Press, 2001), 391–434; Douglas S. Massey and Nancy A. Denton, *American Apartheid: Segregation and the Making of the Underclass* (Cambridge, MA: Harvard University Press, 1993); and George Lipsitz, *The Possessive Investment in Whiteness: How White People Profit from Identity Politics* (Philadelphia: Temple University Press, 1998).

13. Wilkins, *A Man's Life*, 40.

14. Donald B. Bouma, "Challenges of Our Expanding Community," Lecture Series, No. 2, Donald B. Bouma Manuscript Collection, Hekman Library, Calvin College, 5.

15. Paul I. Phillips, "A Study of Ten Inter-Cultural Areas in Grand Rapids, Michigan," November 1947, Paul I. Phillips Manuscript Collection, GRPL, 44.

16. *Grand Rapids Herald*, March 5, 1950.

17. Ibid.

18. Citizens League of Greater Grand Rapids, Affordable Housing Task Force, *A Dream Deferred: Affordable Housing in Kent County* (Grand Rapids, MI: Citizens League of Greater Grand Rapids, 1992), 3.

19. *Grand Rapids Herald*, March 5, 1950.

20. For studies of suburbanization, see Kenneth T. Jackson, *Crabgrass Frontier: The Suburbanization of the United States* (New York: Oxford University Press, 1985); Lisa McGirr, *Suburban Warriors: The Origins of the New American Right* (Princeton, NJ: Princeton University Press, 2001); and Becky M. Nicolaides, *My Blue Heaven: Life and Politics in the Working-Class Suburbs of Los Angeles, 1920–1965* (Chicago: University of Chicago Press, 2002).

21. Citizens League of Greater Grand Rapids, Affordable Housing Task Force, *A Dream Deferred*, 2.

22. *Grand Rapids Press*, April 17, 1960.

23. Human Relations Commission, "Housing Questionnaire for State Advisory Committee U.S. Civil Rights Commission," Human Relations Commission–State Advising Committee Records, Helen Claytor Papers, Michigan Historical Collection, Bentley Historical Library, Ann Arbor, Michigan, 5.

24. Mel Ravitz, "Who Wants Racial Integration?" (report), Helen Claytor Papers, Michigan Historical Collection, Bentley Historical Library, Ann Arbor, Michigan, 6.

25. Human Relations Commission, "Housing Questionnaire for State Advisory Committee U.S. Civil Rights Commission," 5.

26. Housing Ordinance No. 1425, passed by City Commission, January 10, 1956.

27. "Negro Housing: A Giant Problem for GR," *Grand Rapids Press,* September 10, 1967.

28. Ibid.

29. Grand Rapids Health Department, "Community Housing Improvement Program," September 4, 1958, Helen Claytor Papers, Michigan Historical Collection, Bentley Historical Library, Ann Arbor, Michigan, 2.

30. Lewis B. Clingman, "The History of the Grand Rapids Human Relations Commission" (Ph.D. diss., Michigan State University, 1976), 13.

31. Nancy King, "Madison Square Blues," *Grand Rapids Magazine,* November 1986.

32. Grand Rapids Human Relations Commission, "Housing and Minorities in Grand Rapids," Helen Claytor Papers, Michigan Historical Collection, Bentley Historical Library, Ann Arbor, Michigan, 1.

33. *Grand Rapids Press,* December 1, 1962. Also for black suburbanization, see Pattillo-McCoy, *Black Picket Fences;* Haynes, *Red Lines, Black Spaces;* and Wiese, *Places of Their Own.*

34. For more on white homeowner associations, see Sugrue, *Origins of the Urban Crisis.*

35. *Grand Rapids Press,* December 14, 1962.

36. Evelyn Brooks Higginbotham, "African-American Women's History and the Metalanguage of Race," *Signs* 17, no. 2 (Winter 1992): 251–274.

37. "Negroes Make Opportunity," *Grand Rapids Press,* December 1, 1962.

38. Harold I. Hatherly, "Negro Housing Effort by Local Group Is Step Backward, He Says" [letter to the editor], *Grand Rapids Press,* December 18, 1962.

39. J. E. Adams Jr., Julius Frank Jr., Joseph W. Lee, and Samuel S. Triplett, "Developers Explain Position in Purchase of 'Fuller Ave.—20 Acres' Area" [letter to the editor], *Grand Rapids Press,* December 28, 1962.

40. Robert Krueger and Ruth Krueger, "Challenges Recent Letter Supporting Integrated Housing Development" [letter to the editor], *Grand Rapids Press,* January 4, 1963.

41. "Negroes Sign Land Pact," *Grand Rapids Press,* December 11, 1962.

42. "Cite Fears of All-Negro Community," *Grand Rapids Press,* December 14, 1962.

43. "City Still Debates Legality of Integrated Housing Deal," *Grand Rapids Press,* January 3, 1963.

44. Ibid.

45. Ibid.

46. "Buyers' Attorney Makes Appeal for 'Fair Play,'" *Grand Rapids Press,* January 16, 1963.

47. "City Hedges Then OK's Land Sale," *Grand Rapids Press,* January 23, 1963.

48. Ibid.

49. "Negro Housing: A Giant Problem for GR."

50. Gordon Olson, *A Grand Rapids Sampler* (Grand Rapids, MI: Grand Rapids Historical Commission, 1992), 17.

51. *Grand Rapids Herald,* March 5, 1950.

52. Olson, *Grand Rapids Sampler,* 18.

53. Ibid.

54. *Grand Rapids Herald,* March 5, 1950.

55. *Grand Rapids Herald,* January 1, 1950.

56. Grand Rapids Urban League, "A Study of Housing in Selected Areas of Grand Rapids" (report), August 1952, African American History Collection, GRPL, i.

57. U.S. Commission on Civil Rights, "Equal Opportunity in Suburbia" (report), July 1974, Special Collections, GRPL, 9. [Also available at http://www.law.umaryland.edu/marshall/usccr/documents/cr12su1.pdf.]

58. Olson, *Grand Rapids Sampler,* 17.

59. Bouma, "Challenges of Our Expanding Community," 2.

60. Charles Vaughn, *The City of Wyoming: A History* (Franklin, MI: Four Corners Press, 1984)121.

61. Bouma, "Challenges of Our Expanding Community," 2.

62. Olson, *Grand Rapids Sampler,* 34.

63. Charles Press, *When One-Third of a City Moves to the Suburbs: A Report on the Grand Rapids Metropolitan Area* (East Lansing: Michigan State University, 1959), 17. [Located in GRPL.]

64. *Grand Rapids Herald,* February 5, 1950.

65. Bouma, "Challenges of Our Expanding Community," 2.

66. John W. McGee, *Bend in the River: The Story of Grandville and Jenison, Michigan 1832–1972* (Grandville, MI: Grandville Historical Commission/Eerdmans, 1973), 324.

67. Ibid., 325.

68. Ibid., 316.

69. *When One-Third of a City Moves to the Suburbs,* 17.

70. McGee, *Bend in the River,* 306, 314.

71. Grand Rapids Public Library, *Final Report of Grand Rapids Metropolitan Area Study,* 1.

72. Sugrue, *Origins of the Urban Crisis,* 60.

73. *Confidential Report of a Survey in Grand Rapids, Michigan and Its Suburban Area for the Home Owner's Loan Corporation* (Washington, DC: National Archives, 1937), 1–2.

74. Federal Housing Administration, *Underwriting Manual* (Washington, DC: National Archives, 1936), sec. 980.

75. Ibid., sec. 935.

76. Ibid., sec. 937.

77. Ibid., sec. 980.

78. A number of racial ordinances were maintained well into the half-century mark despite the 1917 Supreme Court decision of *Buchanan v. Warley,* 245 U.S. 60 (1917), which declared these ordinances unconstitutional. Although considered private agreements, racial covenants received legal merit through the enforcement of the judicial body of the state. The legal use of restrictive covenants functioned freely for three decades before the decision of *Shelley v. Kraemer,* 334 U.S. 1 (1948), declared the use of restrictive covenants a violation of the Fourteenth Amendment. The ruling handed down in 1948 proclaimed restrictive covenants judicially unenforceable, yet the behavior continued well beyond 1948 because of the ensconced racism and interest of white real estate brokers.

79. Federal Housing Administration, *Underwriting Manual,* sec. 982.

80. Ibid., sec. 982.

81. Ibid., sec. 227.

82. Ibid., sec. 229.

83. Poyntz Tyler, *City and Suburban Housing* (New York: H. W. Wilson, 1957), 40.

84. Home Owners' Loan Corporation, *Area Description—Security Map of Grand Rapids* (Washington, DC: National Archives). Security Maps are provided for the entire city and surrounding area.

85. Home Owners' Loan Corporation, *Confidential Report of a Survey in Grand Rapids, Michigan and Its Suburban Area* (Washington, DC: National Archives).

86. David Wier, "Comstock Park: Mill Town to Bedroom Suburb" (master's thesis, Michigan State University, 1981), 108. [Located in GRPL.]

87. Ibid., 108–110.

88. Ibid., 112.

89. Ibid.

90. Ibid., 114, 115.

91. Ibid., 126.

92. Walker Bicentennial Committee, *Echoes of the Past: A Bicentennial History of the City of Walker, Michigan* (Walker, MI: City of Walker, 1976), 28, 31. [Located in GRPL.]

93. U.S. Department of Housing and Urban Development, *Housing in the Seventies: A Report of the National Housing Policy Review* (Washington, DC: U.S. Department of Housing and Urban Development, 1974), 8.

94. On the vital importance of the 1940s for the interlocking of the New Deal order and the future of American social policy, see Steve Fraser and Gary Gerstle, eds., *The Rise and Fall of the New Deal Order, 1930–1980* (Princeton, NJ: Princeton University Press, 1989); and George Lipsitz, *The Possessive Investment in Whiteness.* For a good overview of federal housing policy in the 1930s, see Gail Radford, *Modern Housing for America: Policy Struggles in the New Deal Era* (Chicago: University of Chicago Press, 1996).

95. U.S. Department of Housing and Urban Development, *Housing in the Seventies,* 8.

96. For detailed historiographical contributions on the federal, corporate, and individual development of suburban space see Jackson, *Crabgrass Frontier;* Sugrue, *Origins of the Urban Crisis;* Lipsitz, *The Possessive Investment in Whiteness;* and Elaine Tyler May, *Homeward Bound* (New York: Basic Books, 1988).

97. Kleinberg, *Urban America in Transformation,* 125.

98. Grand Rapids Human Relations Commission, "Addenda to Housing Questionnaire, Michigan Advisory Committee, U.S. Civil Rights Commission," Helen Claytor Papers, Box 4, Michigan Historical Collection, Bentley Historical Library, Ann Arbor, Michigan.

99. U.S. Commission on Civil Rights, *The 50 States Report Submitted to the Commission on Civil Rights by the State Advisory Committees, 1961* (Washington, DC: U.S. Government Printing Office, 1961), 266.

100. Ibid.

101. *Building the American City: Report of the National Commission on Urban Problems* (Washington, DC: National Commission on Urban Problems, 1968), 1.

102. Committee on Research, Grand Rapids Urban League, "Housing of Nonwhites in Grand Rapids, Michigan," 1964, Black History Manuscript Collection, GRPL, 2.

103. National Urban League and Warren M. Banner, *The Negro Population of Grand Rapids, Michigan, 1940: A Study Conducted for the Interracial Committee of the Council of Social Agencies* (New York: National Urban League, 1940), 50.

104. Bouma, "Challenges of Our Expanding Community," 5.

105. Interracial Committee of the Council of Social Agencies, "Negro Population of Grand Rapids," 51.

106. Ibid., 52.

107. Ibid., 49.

108. Samuelson et al., *Heart and Soul,* 146.

109. Grand Rapids Human Relations Commission, "Official Minutes," July 11, 1956, Grand Rapids City Records.

110. Grand Rapids Human Relations Commission, "Addenda to Housing Questionnaire," 5.

111. Grand Rapids Urban League, "A Study of Housing in Selected Areas of Grand Rapids," i.

112. U.S. Commission on Civil Rights, "Equal Opportunity in Suburbia," 9.

113. Ibid.

114. Ibid., 3–9.

115. Message from the President of the United States to the 83d Congress, 2d Session, January 25, 1954 (H. Doc. No. 306), available http://www.presidency.ucsb.edu/ws/index.php?pid=9952

116. Grand Rapids Urban League, "A Study of Housing in Selected Areas of Grand Rapids," 5.

117. Ibid.

118. Ibid., 5–6.

119. Bouma, "Challenges of Our Expanding Community," 5. See also Kenneth B. Clark, *Dark Ghetto: Dilemmas of Social Power* (New York: Harper and Row, 1965).

120. Grand Rapids Urban League, "A Study of Housing in Selected Areas of Grand Rapids," 13, 19.

121. Ibid., 12.

122. Grand Rapids Urban League, "The Negro American and Housing in Grand Rapids" (report), n.d., GRPL, 2.

123. Grand Rapids Urban League, "Model Neighborhoods Proposal," Black History Manuscript Collection, GRPL, 63.

124. Ibid.

125. Ibid.

126. Ibid., 63–65.

127. Ibid., 65.

128. Ibid.

129. Ibid.

130. *Michigan Bell,* September 1961.

131. George B. Kamohuis, "The Racial Riots of 1967: A Comparison of Reactions" (unpublished paper, GRPL, December 4, 1978), 3.

132. Ibid., 4.

133. "Grand Rapids Welcomes You," *Michigan Municipal Review,* 250. [Located in GRPL.]

134. The advent of the 1956 Federal Highway Act, implemented by the Eisenhower administration, provided white suburbanites the freedom to live farther away from the city. Highways had a costly effect, however, as the original $17 million project in Grand Rapids ended up running $10 million over budget.

135. M. Howard Rienstra, "Reflections on Grand Rapids," *Dialogue* (April 1976): 7.

136. Ibid., 22.

137. Samuelson et al., *Heart and Soul,* 141.

138. Rienstra, "Reflections on Grand Rapids," 7.

139. Samuelson et al., *Heart and Soul,* 140.

140. Ibid., 130.

141. Ibid.

142. "Negro Housing: A Giant Problem for GR."

143. Olson, *Grand Rapids Sampler,* 186, 189, 193.

144. Grand Rapids Urban League, "A Study of Housing in Selected Areas of Grand Rapids," 24.

145. George Lipsitz, "The Possessive Investment in Whiteness: Racialized Social Democracy," in *Rethinking the Color Line: Readings in Race and Ethnicity,* 2nd ed., ed. Charles A. Gallagher (New York: McGraw-Hill, 2004), 138.

146. Curt Wozniak, "Twenty Acres Closer to Equality," *Grand Rapids Magazine* (February 2004): 114.

CHAPTER 4

1. According to William Graebner's book *Coming of Age in Buffalo: Youth and Authority in the Postwar Era* (Philadelphia: Temple University Press, 1990), in the 1920s high schools educated less than a third of the nation's population. The numbers increased to 73 percent in 1940, and by 1960 high schools were educating roughly 87 percent of the nation's population ages fourteen to seventeen.

2. Gael Graham, *Young Activists: American High School Students in the Age of Protest* (DeKalb, IL: Northern University Press, 2006), 82.

3. Ibid.

4. Ibid., 86.

5. Ibid., 87.

6. Ibid., 91.

7. Ibid., 97.

8. *Grand Rapids Press,* August 2, 1966. See also David S. Cecelski, *Along Freedom Road: Hyde County, North Carolina, and the Fate of Black Schools in the South* (Chapel Hill: University of North Carolina Press, 1994); and Davison Douglas, *Jim Crow Moves North: The Battle over Northern School Segregation, 1865–1954* (New York: Cambridge University Press, 2005).

9. *Grand Rapids Press,* May 5, 1960.

10. Ibid.

11. *Grand Rapids Press,* October 4, 1960.

12. Kurt Luedtke and Margaret Moore, "Half of GR Negroes Quit School Early: High Dropout Rate Alarms Educators, Sociologist," *Grand Rapids Press,* May 27, 1962.

13. Lewis B. Clingman, "The History of the Grand Rapids Human Relations Commission" (Ph.D. diss., Michigan State University, 1976), 110.

14. Ibid., 112.

15. Luedtke and Moore, "Half of GR Negroes Quit School Early."

16. *Grand Rapids Press,* November 15, 1964. Half of the cities covered in the survey were located in the Midwest, fourteen were in the East, six were in the West, and one was in the South.

17. Ibid.

18. Derrick Bell, *Silent Covenants:* Brown v. Board of Education *and the Unfulfilled Hopes for Racial Reform* (New York: Oxford University Press, 2004).

19. William H. Chafe, *Civilities and Civil Rights: Greensboro, North Carolina, and the Black Struggle for Freedom* (New York: Oxford University Press, 1980); Bell, *Silent Covenants.*

20. Thomas J. Sugrue, "Crabgrass-Roots Politics: Race, Rights, and the Reaction against Liberalism in the Urban North, 1940–1964," *Journal of American History* 82 (September 1995): 551–578.

21. Charles R. Collins to Gerald R. Ford, Congressional Papers, Gerald R. Ford Presidential Library and Museum, Ann Arbor, Michigan.

22. George Spruyt to Gerald R. Ford, Congressional Papers, Gerald R. Ford Presidential Library and Museum, Ann Arbor, Michigan.

23. John Lamse to Gerald R. Ford, Congressional Papers, Gerald R. Ford Presidential Library and Museum, Ann Arbor, Michigan.

24. Luedtke and Moore, "Half of GR Negroes Quit School Early."

25. Ibid.

26. Ibid.

27. Ibid.

28. Charles Sims, "Non-white Student Employment Survey, 1960–61" (unpublished manuscript, Grand Rapids Public Library [GRPL], Grand Rapids, Michigan, May 1962).

29. Charles Sims, "Caucasian Student Employment Survey, Class of 1960 and 1961" (unpublished manuscript, GRPL, September 1962).

30. Luedtke and Moore, "Half of GR Negroes Quit School Early."

31. Grand Rapids Urban League, "A Study of Ten Inter-Cultural Areas in Grand Rapids, Michigan," Paul I. Phillips Manuscript Collection, GRPL, 43.

32. Clingman, "History of the Grand Rapids Human Relations Commission," 139–140.

33. Ibid., 110.

34. Luedtke and Moore, "Half of GR Negroes Quit School Early."

35. Graebner, *Coming of Age in Buffalo,* 13–14.

36. "South Teacher Quits after Attack by Boys," *Grand Rapids Press,* June 6, 1964, 1.

37. Ibid.

38. Clingman, "History of the Grand Rapids Human Relations Commission," 144.

39. "South Teacher Quits after Attack by Boys," 1.

40. Gordon Olson, *A Grand Rapids Sampler* (Grand Rapids, MI: Grand Rapids Historical Commission, 1992), 53. For similar incidents, see Graham's *Young Activists.*

41. *Grand Rapids Press,* August 12, 1966.

42. Francis Ward, "Mustache Ban on Negro Students Stirs Protest," *Jet,* November 24, 1966, 20–22.

43. Ibid.

44. *Detroit Free Press,* October 28, 1966; *Grand Rapids Press,* October 28, 1966.

45. Ward, "Mustache Ban on Negro Students Stirs Protest," 20, 22.

46. *Proceedings of the Board of Education* 66 (November 16, 1966): 166. Grand Rapids Public School Records, GRPL.

47. *Jet Magazine,* November 24, 1966, 20–21.

48. *Grand Rapids Press,* October 26, 1966.

49. *Jet Magazine,* November 24, 1966, 21.

50. *Grand Rapids Press,* October 26, 1966; *Grand Rapids Press,* October 28, 1966.

51. *Jet Magazine,* November 24, 1966, 24.

52. *Grand Rapids Press,* October 26, 1966.

53. Chafe, *Civilities and Civil Rights,* 173.

54. Edgar Z. Friedenberg, "Ceremonies of Humiliation in School," *The Education Digest,* November 1966, 36; emphasis original.

55. *Grand Rapids Press,* October 28, 1966.

56. Eugene Sparrow to Douglas Hilman, November 2, 1966, Grand Rapids Human Relations Commission Records, City Archives and Records Center, Grand Rapids, Michigan.

57. Clingman, "History of the Grand Rapids Human Relations Commission," 201.

58. Ibid., 196.

59. *Grand Rapids Press,* November 19, 1966.

60. *Grand Rapids Press,* November 12, 1966.

61. Chafe, *Civilities and Civil Rights.*

62. *Grand Rapids Press,* November 17, 1966.

63. Ibid.

64. *Grand Rapids Press,* November 16, 1966.

65. *Grand Rapids Press,* November 17, 1966.

66. WOOD-TV Editorial, November 23, 1966, Congressional Papers, Gerald R. Ford Presidential Library and Museum, Ann Arbor, Michigan.

67. Theresa B. Crawford to Gerald R. Ford, November 12, 1966, Congressional Papers, Gerald R. Ford Presidential Library and Museum, Ann Arbor, Michigan.

68. *Grand Rapids Press,* December 17, 1966.

69. Clingman, "History of the Grand Rapids Human Relations Commission," 198.

70. *Grand Rapids Press,* November 19, 1966.

71. *Grand Rapids Press,* December 2, 1966.

72. *Grand Rapids Press,* January 9, 1967.

73. *Grand Rapids Press,* January 26, 1967.

74. "Davidson Tenure Testimony Ends with Counter-Claim," *Grand Rapids Press,* February 14, 1971.

75. "Parents Term Davidson Ineffective, Rigid in Disciplining Creston Students," *Grand Rapids Press,* February 16, 1971.

76. This chapter also extends the scholarship of the "classical" narrative of the civil rights movement. For critiques of this narrative, see Peniel E. Joseph, "Black Liberation without Apology: Reconceptualizing the Black Power Movement," *Black Scholar* 31 (Fall–Winter 2001): 3–19; Jacqueline Dowd Hall, "The Long Civil Rights Movement and the Political Uses of the Past," *Journal of American History* 91 (March 2005): 1233–1263; and Van Gosse and Richard Moser, eds., *The World the 60s Made: Politics and Culture in Recent America* (Philadelphia: Temple University Press, 2003). For "March against Freedom," see Clayborn Carson, *In Struggle: SNCC and the Black Awakening of the 1960s* (Cambridge, MA: Harvard University Press, 1981), 191–211; John Dittmer, *Local People: The Struggle for Civil Rights in Mississippi* (Urbana: University of Illinois Press, 1995), 389–407; Adam Fairclough, *To Redeem the Soul of America: The Southern Christian Leadership Conference and Martin Luther King Jr.* (Athens: University of Georgia Press, 2001), 309–320; and Peniel E. Joseph, *Waiting 'til the Midnight Hour: A Narrative History of Black Power in America* (New York: Henry Holt, 2006).

77. Dionne Danns, *Something Better for Our Children: Black Organizing in Chicago Public Schools, 1963–1971* (New York: Routledge, 2003), 71–72; also, for excellent work on educational opportunities in southern black communities, see Vanessa Siddle Walker, *Their Highest Potential: An African American School Community in the Segregated South* (Chapel Hill: University of North Carolina Press, 1996); Winifred E. Pitt, *A Victory of Sorts: Desegregation in a Southern Community* (Lanham, MD: University Press of America, 2003); and Vivian Gunn Morris and Curtis L. Morris, *The Price They Paid: Desegregation in an African American Community* (New York: Teachers College Press, 2002).

78. Michael Omi and Howard Winant, *Racial Formation in the United States: From the 1960s to the 1990s* (New York: Routledge, 1994).

79. WOOD-TV Editorial, November 16, 1966, Grand Rapids City Archives, Grand Rapids, Michigan.

80. The literature devoted to student participation in the civil rights movement deals mostly with college students, not secondary students. See, for example, August Meier and

Elliott Rudwick, *CORE: A Study in the Civil Rights Movement, 1942–1968* (New York: Oxford University Press, 1973); Carson, *In Struggle*; Chafe, *Civilities and Civil Rights*; and Aldon Morris, *The Origins of the Civil Rights Movement: Black Communities Organizing for Change* (New York: Free Press, 1984). For works devoted to secondary students, see Richard Wormser, *The Rise and Fall of Jim Crow* (New York: St. Martin's Press, 2003); V. P. Franklin, "Black High School Student Activism in the 1960s: An Urban Phenomenon?" *Journal of Research in Education* 10 (Fall 2000): 3–8; Graham, *Young Activists*; Danns, *Something Better for Our Children*; and Matthew J. Countryman, *Up South: Civil Rights and Black Power in Philadelphia* (Philadelphia: University of Pennsylvania Press, 2006), 223–257. For a journalistic account, see Robert C. Smith, *They Closed Their Schools: Prince Edward County, Virginia, 1951–1964* (Chapel Hill: University of North Carolina Press, 1965).

81. For a meaningful contemporary critique of literature on the civil rights movement, see Steven F. Lawson and Charles Payne, *Debating the Civil Rights Movement, 1945–1968*, 2nd ed. (New York: Rowman and Littlefield, 2006). Early literature on civil rights representative of traditional political, institutional, and biographical approaches also includes Donald R. McCoy and Richard T. Ruetten, *Quest and Response: Minority Rights and the Truman Administration* (Lawrence: University Press of Kansas, 1973); Robert Fredrick Burk, *The Eisenhower Administration and Black Civil Rights* (Knoxville: University of Tennessee, 1984); Hugh Davis Graham, *The Civil Rights Era: Origins and Development of National Policy* (New York: Oxford University Press, 1990); David J. Garrow, *Protest at Selma: Martin Luther King, Jr., and the Voting Rights Act of 1965* (New Haven, CT: Yale University Press, 1978); Charles Whalen and Barbara Whalen, *The Longest Debate: A Legislative History of the 1964 Civil Rights Act* (Cabin John, MD: Seven Locks Press, 1985); Steven F. Lawson, *Black Ballots: Voting Rights in the South, 1944–1969* (New York: Columbia University Press, 1976); Steven F. Lawson, *In Pursuit of Power: Southern Blacks and Electoral Politics, 1965–1982* (New York: Columbia University Press, 1985); and Steven F. Lawson, *Running for Freedom: Civil Rights and Black Politics in America since 1941* (Philadelphia: Temple University Press, 1991).

82. Omi and Winant, 99. Also for important insights into agency among oppressed groups and the "hidden transcript," see James C. Scott, *Domination and the Arts of Resistance: Hidden Transcripts* (New Haven, CT: Yale University Press, 1990); James C. Scott, *Weapons of the Weak: Everyday Forms of Peasant Resistance* (New Haven, CT: Yale University Press, 1985); and James C. Scott, *The Moral Economy of the Peasant: Rebellion and Subsistence in Southeast Asia* (New Haven, CT: Yale University Press, 1976). For more on "infrapolitics," specifically dealing with the urban South, see Robin D. G. Kelley, "'We Are Not What We Seem': Rethinking Black Working-Class Opposition in the Jim Crow South," *Journal of American History* 80 (June 1993): 75–112; and Robin D. G. Kelley, *Race Rebels: Culture, Politics, and the Black Working Class* (New York: Free Press, 1994).

83. For information on black power studies, see Peniel E. Joseph, ed., *The Black Power Movement: Rethinking the Civil Rights-Black Power Era* (New York: Routledge, 2006); "Radicalism in Black America," special issue of *Souls* 1, no. 4 (Fall 1999); "Dossier on Black Radicalism," special issue of *Social Text* 19, no. 2 67 (Summer 2001); and "Black Power Studies: A New Scholarship," special issue of *Black Scholar* 31, nos. 3–4 (Fall–Winter 2001). With the exception of Chafe's *Civilities and Civil Rights*, a number of important civil rights movement studies on "local people" stop short of the black power era. For examples of southern civil rights movement studies, see Dittmer, *Local People*; Charles Payne, *I've Got the Light of Freedom: The Organizing Tradition and the Mississippi Struggle* (Berkeley: University of California Press, 1996); and Diane McWhorter, *Carry*

Me Home: Birmingham, Alabama, the Climactic Battle of the Civil Rights Revolution (New York: Touchstone Books, 2002). For examples of northern civil rights struggles, see James R. Ralph Jr., *Northern Protest: Martin Luther King Jr., Chicago, and the Civil Rights Movement* (Cambridge, MA: Harvard University Press, 1993); Martha Biondi, *"To Stand and Fight": The Struggle for Civil Rights in Postwar New York City* (Cambridge, MA: Harvard University Press, 2002); and Randal Maurice Jelks, *African Americans in the Furniture City: The Struggle for Civil Rights in Grand Rapids* (Urbana: University of Illinois Press, 2006). For recent case studies on civil rights and black power, see Robert O. Self, *American Babylon: Race and the Struggle for Postwar Oakland* (Princeton, NJ: Princeton University Press, 2003); and Countryman, *Up South.*

CHAPTER 5

1. McArthour Williams, "Successful Integration?" *Grand Rapids Times,* May 15, 1971.
2. "The Grand Rapids Study Class Presents: Langston Hughes," February 14, 1960, Grand Rapids Study Club Manuscript Collection, Grand Rapids Public Library (GRPL), Grand Rapids, Michigan.
3. "Langston Hughes to Lecture," *Grand Rapids Press,* February 14, 1960, Grand Rapids Study Club Manuscript Collection, GRPL.
4. "61st Anniversary Celebrated by the Grand Rapids Study Club," *Grand Rapids Press,* November 18, 1965, Grand Rapids Study Club Manuscript Collection, GRPL.
5. "Civic Theater's 'Raisin' Has Cast of Extremes," *Grand Rapids Press,* February 1, 1966, Grand Rapids Study Club Manuscript Collection, GRPL.
6. Ibid.
7. "61st Anniversary Celebrated by the Grand Rapids Study Club."
8. Ibid.
9. "Grand Rapids Study Club Gives Scholarship-Aid Award," *Grand Rapids Press,* 1966, in "Grand Rapids Study Club Scrapbook," Grand Rapids Study Class/Grand Rapids Study Club Manuscript Collection, GRPL.
10. "61st Anniversary Celebrated by the Grand Rapids Study Club."
11. Lillian Gill, interview, June 6, 1997, interview #014, Greater Grand Rapids Women's History Council Oral Interviews, Grand Rapids History and Special Collections, GRPL.
12. "Whites Join Protest" *Grand Rapids Press,* September 23, 1963.
13. Ibid.
14. Lillian Gill, interview.
15. Ibid.
16. Ibid.
17. Ibid.
18. *Grand Rapids Press,* April 19, 1967.
19. Lewis B. Clingman, "The History of the Grand Rapids Human Relations Commission" (Ph.D. diss., Michigan State University, 1976), 211.
20. "2,200 March Here in the Cold," *Grand Rapids Press,* March 15, 1965.
21. Clingman, "History of the Grand Rapids Human Relations Commission," 210–211.
22. Ibid., 211–212.
23. Ibid., 212.
24. Ibid., 200.

25. Ibid., 193.

26. "White America 'Uncivilized,' Carmichael Says Here," *Grand Rapids Press,* May 18, 1967.

27. "Carmichael Urges Negroes Organize," *Grand Rapids Press,* May 18, 1967.

28. Clingman, "History of the Grand Rapids Human Relations Commission," 213.

29. Ibid., 214.

30. Ibid., 215.

31. Linda Samuelson, Andrew Schrier, and Grand Rapids Area Council for the Humanities, *Heart and Soul: The Story of Grand Rapids Neighborhoods* (Grand Rapids, MI: Eerdmans, 2003), 151.

32. Maris Brancheau, "Anatomy of a Riot," *Grand Rapids Times,* February 8–14, 2002.

33. Elizabeth Slowik, "Cowboy and the Saint," *Grand Rapids Press,* July 26, 1987.

34. Ibid.

35. Clingman, "History of the Grand Rapids Human Relations Commission," 217.

36. Maris Brancheau, "A Taste of Anarchy" (magazine article, source unknown, Riot Vertical Files, GRPL).

37. Clingman, "History of the Grand Rapids Human Relations Commission," 217–218.

38. Vernis Schad, "Revisiting Racial Segregation in the Mid-1960s: Grand Rapids Public Schools" (unpublished manuscript of presented paper, GRPL, 2003), 28.

39. Mike Lloyd, "Meet Raises Education vs. Integration Issues," *Grand Rapids Press,* May 7, 1968.

40. Grand Rapids Board of Education, "Proposed School Organization and Construction Plan," May 1968, Grand Rapids Public School Records, GRPL, 1.

41. "Schools' Antibias Plan Set," *Grand Rapids Press,* April 22, 1968.

42. Lloyd, "Meet Raises Education vs. Integration Issues."

43. *Proceedings of the Board of Education* 67 (May 6, 1968): 246. Grand Rapids Public School Records, GRPL.

44. Schad, "Revisiting Racial Segregation in the Mid-1960s," 24.

45. *Proceedings of the Board of Education,* May 6, 1968, vol. 67, 246, 247.

46. Ibid., 247.

47. Ibid.

48. Ibid., 248.

49. Ibid.

50. Lloyd, "Meet Raises Education vs. Integration Issues."

51. Pat Shellenbarger, "Not Just Black and White: Key Citizens Remember the Fight to Create a Racial Balance in Grand Rapids Schools," *Grand Rapids Press,* May 2, 2004.

52. Schad, "Revisiting Racial Segregation in the Mid-1960s," 24.

53. *Proceedings of the Board of Education* 67 (May 6, 1968): 249.

54. "School Plan Would Cut Segregation," *Grand Rapids Press,* May 7, 1968.

55. *Proceedings of the Board of Education* 67 (May 6, 1968): 256.

56. *Grand Rapids Press,* May 7, 1968.

57. *Proceedings of the Board of Education* 67 (May 6, 1968): 256.

58. *Grand Rapids Press,* May 7, 1968.

59. *Proceedings of the Board of Education* 67 (May 6, 1968): 256.

60. Ibid., 257.

61. *Grand Rapids Press,* May 7, 1968.

62. *Proceedings of the Board of Education* 67 (May 6, 1968): 257.

63. *Grand Rapids Press,* May 7, 1968.

64. Ibid.

65. *Proceedings of the Board of Education* 67 (May 6, 1968): 258.

66. Ibid.

67. *Proceedings of the Board of Education* 67 (June 3, 1968): 267. Grand Rapids Public School Records, GRPL.

68. Ibid., 271.

69. Ibid.

70. Ibid., 288.

71. Ibid.

72. Mike Lloyd, "Board Approves New Master Plan Calling for Integration of Schools," *Grand Rapids Press,* June 4, 1968.

73. Ibid.

74. *Proceedings of the Board of Education* 67 (May 6, 1968): 288.

75. *Proceedings of the Board of Education* 68 (May 26, 1969): 256. Grand Rapids Public School Records, GRPL.

76. Mike Lloyd, "Temperature Was High," *Grand Rapids Press,* May 14, 1968.

77. Schad, "Revisiting Racial Segregation in the Mid-1960s," 28.

78. Lloyd, "Temperature Was High."

79. Schad, "Revisiting Racial Segregation in the Mid-1960s," 26.

80. Shellenbarger, "Not Just Black and White."

81. Lloyd, "Temperature Was High."

82. Mike Lloyd, "Is Busing the Key to School Crowding, Integration?" *Grand Rapids Press,* April 4, 1968.

83. Ibid.

84. Lloyd, "Temperature Was High."

85. Lloyd, "Is Busing the Key to School Crowding, Integration?"

86. Paul Chaffee, "Busing: A Look at Our Own Bugbear," *Grand Rapids Press,* March 15, 1970.

87. "G.R. Schools and Busing," *Grand Rapids Press,* March 13, 1970.

88. "The Issue of Busing," *Grand Rapids Press,* March 14, 1970.

89. Paul Chaffee, "Schoolmen Clash on Busing, Budget," *Grand Rapids Press,* March 11, 1970.

90. "The Issue of Busing."

91. Chaffee, "Busing: A Look at Our Own Bugbear."

92. "The Issue of Busing."

93. Chaffee, "Busing: A Look at Our Own Bugbear."

94. Robert Gill, "Racial Balance of Students" (internal report of the Grand Rapids Public Schools, GRPL, April 16, 1984), 4.

95. *Proceedings of the Board of Education* 67 (May 6, 1968): 248.

96. Schad, "Revisiting Racial Segregation in the Mid-1960s," 24.

97. Mike Lloyd, "Buses Now Criss-Cross Town under New School Program," *Grand Rapids Press,* September 5, 1968.

98. Ibid.

99. "Union Closes after Fight Sparks Racial Brawl," *Grand Rapids Press,* September 13, 1968.

100. Gill, "Racial Balance of Students," 3.

101. "Union Closes after Fight Sparks Racial Brawl."

102. Ibid.

103. Ibid.

104. Ibid.

105. Schad, "Revisiting Racial Segregation in the Mid-1960s," 24.

106. "Union Closes after Fight Sparks Racial Brawl."

107. Schad, "Revisiting Racial Segregation in the Mid-1960s," 26.

108. Ibid., 3.

109. Ibid., 4.

110. Ibid.

111. Ibid., 33.

112. Gill, "Racial Balance of Students," 4.

113. Schad, "Revisiting Racial Segregation in the Mid-1960s," 39.

114. Ibid.

115. Shellenbarger, "Not Just Black and White."

116. Ibid.

117. Ibid.

118. Curt Wozniak, "Forever South," *Grand Rapids Magazine,* available at http://
www.grmag.com/online-feature-archive.htm (last modified October 2003).

119. Ibid.

120. Ibid.

121. Ibid.

122. *Grand Rapids Press,* February 27, 2000.

123. Wozniak, "Forever South."

124. Schad, "Revisiting Racial Segregation in the Mid-1960s," 43.

125. Ibid.

126. Lloyd, "Is Busing the Key to School Crowding, Integration?"

127. Ibid.

128. *Grand Rapids Press,* June 18, 1969.

129. Shellenbarger, "Not Just Black and White."

130. *Grand Rapids Press,* February 27, 2000.

131. "Where Do We Go from Here? Three Views Are Expressed," *Grand Rapids
Press,* September 22, 1968.

CHAPTER 6

1. Ella Sims, interview, May 2, 1994, interview #029, Greater Grand Rapids Women's
History Council Oral Interviews, Grand Rapids History and Special Collections, Grand
Rapids Public Library (GRPL), Grand Rapids, Michigan, 27.

2. Ibid., 2, 1, 12, 14, 15.

3. Ibid., 11, 16, 17.

4. Ibid., 18, 20, 21.

5. Ibid., 21, 25, 26.

6. Ibid., 26.

7. Michael B. Katz, *The Undeserving Poor: From the War on Poverty to the War on
Welfare* (New York: Pantheon, 1989), 81. See also Allen J. Matusow, *The Unraveling of
America: A History of Liberalism in the 1960s* (New York: Harper and Row, 1984);
Thomas Jackson, "The State, the Movement, and the Urban Poor: The War on Poverty
and Political Mobilization in the 1960s," in *The "Underclass" Debate: Views from History,*
ed. Michael B. Katz, 403–440 (Princeton, NJ: Princeton University Press, 1993); and
Matthew J. Countryman, *Up South: Civil Rights and Black Power in Philadelphia* (Philadelphia: University of Pennsylvania Press, 2006).

8. Mike Niemann, "CAP to Fight Move to Kill On-Job Training," *Grand Rapids Press,* March 17, 1970.

9. Gordon Olson, *A Grand Rapids Sampler* (Grand Rapids, MI: Grand Rapids Historical Commission, 1992), 51.

10. Theresa B. Crawford to Gerald R. Ford, Congressional Papers, Gerald R. Ford Presidential Library and Museum, Ann Arbor, Michigan.

11. Gerald R. Ford to Sargent Shriver, December 14, 1966, Congressional Papers, Gerald R. Ford Presidential Library and Museum, Ann Arbor, Michigan.

12. Sargent Shriver to Gerald R. Ford, January 19, 1967, Congressional Papers, Gerald R. Ford Presidential Library and Museum, Ann Arbor, Michigan.

13. Ella Sims, interview, 28.

14. Ibid., 27.

15. "City Board of Education Candidates Give Views," *Grand Rapids Press,* August 1, 1971.

16. Mike Lloyd, "Paul Phillips Dies; Civil Rights Leader," *Grand Rapids Press,* January 1, 1977.

17. Ibid.

18. Paul I. Phillips, "Brief Account of Our 25 Years of Stewardship," 1947, Paul I. Phillips Manuscript Collection, GRPL, 4.

19. Ibid.

20. "Phillips Challenges Board on Negroes," *Grand Rapids Press,* February 14, 1968.

21. Ibid.

22. Phillips, "Brief Account of Our 25 Years of Stewardship," 5.

23. Ibid.

24. Mike Lloyd, "Paul Phillips Dies."

25. *Grand Rapids Press,* October 24, 1971.

26. Phillips, "Brief Account of Our 25 Years of Stewardship," 3.

27. Vernis Schad, "Revisiting Racial Segregation in the Mid-1960s: Grand Rapids Public Schools" (unpublished manuscript of presented paper, GRPL, 2003), 38.

28. "3 Is the Key" [political advertisement], *Grand Rapids Press,* April 5, 1969.

29. Ibid.

30. "Can't Halt Integration in Schools, Says Post," *Grand Rapids Press,* February 7, 1969.

31. "City School Board, Suburb Race Highlight Monday Vote," *Grand Rapids Press,* April 3, 1969.

32. "Can't Halt Integration in Schools."

33. *Grand Rapids Press,* March 12, 1969.

34. Donald Cooper, "Busing, He Protests, Magnifies Racial Issue," *Grand Rapids Press,* March 9, 1972.

35. Ibid.

36. Mike Lloyd, "3 School-Busing Foes Win Voter Approval," *Grand Rapids Press,* April 8, 1969.

37. Ibid.

38. Ibid.

39. Robert Alt, "Black, White Walk in Hope," *Grand Rapids Press,* April 8, 1968.

40. "New School Board Men Hail 'Mandate,'" *Grand Rapids Press,* April 4, 1969.

41. Ibid.

42. "5 Now in Election Race for City School Board," *Grand Rapids Press,* January 5, 1970.

43. Paul Chaffee, "Mrs. Sleet Quits, Rips Board Policy," *Grand Rapids Press*, February 3, 1970.

44. Ibid.

45. "70 Negro Pupils at Creston 'Walk Out,' but Obey Police," *Grand Rapids Press*, May 27, 1970.

46. Ibid.

47. "Creston to Reopen Monday," *Grand Rapids Press*, May 28, 1970.

48. Phillips, "Brief Account of Our 25 Years of Stewardship," 5.

49. "70 Negro Pupils at Creston 'Walk Out,' but Obey Police."

50. Barbara Savage, "We'll Get Together When We Realize . . . ," *Grand Rapids Press*, November 14, 1971.

51. Ibid.

52. Paul Chaffee, "Anti-Busing Bloc Rules School Board," *Grand Rapids Press*, April 7, 1970.

53. Robert Gill, "Racial Balance of Students" (internal report of the Grand Rapids Public Schools, GRPL, April 16, 1984), 4.

54. Ibid.

55. Hank Bornheimer, "Quiet Returns to Union High," *Grand Rapids Press*, October 7, 1971.

56. Chaffee, "Anti-Busing Bloc Rules School Board."

57. Ibid.

58. Gill, "Racial Balance of Students."

59. *Higgins et al. v. Board of Education of the City of Grand Rapids, Michigan et al.*, 395 U.S., 444 (1973).

60. Mike Lloyd, "NAACP Suit Attacks School Master Plan," *Grand Rapids Press*, August 20, 1970.

61. Mike Lloyd, "Blacks Want City Schools Desegregated," *Grand Rapids Press*, April 22, 1971.

62. *Grand Rapids Press*, March 25, 1969.

63. *Grand Rapids Press*, October 7, 1969.

64. Lloyd, "Blacks Want City Schools Desegregated."

65. Ibid.

66. "Candidates Cite Mrs. Sleet's Frustration," *Grand Rapids Press*, February 4, 1970.

67. Phillips, "Brief Account of Our 25 Years of Stewardship," 4.

68. Pat Shellenbarger, "Not Just Black and White: Key Citizens Remember the Fight to Create a Racial Balance in Grand Rapids Schools," *Grand Rapids Press*, May 2, 2004.

69. *Grand Rapids Press*, April 4, 1972.

70. *Higgins et al. v. Board of Education of the City of Grand Rapids, Michigan et al.*

71. Shellenbarger, "Not Just Black and White."

72. Gerald Elliott, "Bus Ruling Spells More Trouble for Cities," *Grand Rapids Press*, July 31, 1974.

73. Henry Bornheimer, "Grand Rapids Schools May Be Forced to Rejuggle Attendance to Avoid Legal Risk," *Grand Rapids Press*, November 29, 1974.

74. Henry Bornheimer, "School Officials Don't See End to Busing Case Yet," *Grand Rapids Press*, December 7, 1974.

75. Olson, *Grand Rapids Sampler*, 48.

76. Joseph P. Van Blooys, "Grand Rapid's [*sic*] Project 1003," *Michigan Challenge*, February 1968, 20; emphasis original.

77. "Anatomy of a Riot" (report, Grand Rapids Planning Division, Grand Rapids, Michigan, November 1967), 7. [Located in GRPL.]

78. Van Blooys, "Grand Rapid's [*sic*] Project 1003," 20.

79. "Anatomy of a Riot," 21.

80. Fletcher Knebel, "The White Cop and the Black Rebel," *Look Magazine*, February 6, 1968, 18–20.

81. Michigan Civil Rights Commission, "Toward Equality: Two-Year Report of Claims Activity 1968–1969," Chamber of Commerce Manuscript Collection, GRPL, 3.

82. Van Blooys, "Grand Rapid's [*sic*] Project 1003," 21, 27.

83. Ibid., 30.

84. Olson, *Grand Rapids Sampler*, 48.

85. Ibid., 42.

86. Ibid., 40.

87. Ibid., 45.

88. Ibid., 45, 46.

89. Ibid., 46.

90. Ibid.

91. Ibid., 47.

92. Van Blooys, "Grand Rapid's [*sic*] Project 1003," 30.

93. Cathle Bloom, "Lyman Parks: Leader for Grand Rapids," *Grand Rapids Press*, December 26, 1984.

94. Robert Holden, "Lyman Parks the 'Realist': How a Black Man Became Mayor of Grand Rapids without Anyone Noticing," *Grand Rapids Press*, October 10, 1971.

95. Lyman Parks, interview, November 19, 1985, Oral History Collection, GRPL.

96. Olson, *Grand Rapids Sampler*, 200.

97. PBS, "The National Black Political Convention (1972)," available at http://www.pbs.org/wgbh/amex/eyesontheprize/milestones/m13_nbpc.html.

98. Holden, "Lyman Parks the 'Realist.'"

99. David Nicolette, "The Grand Center: A Community Triumph," *Grand Rapids Press*, October 12, 1980.

100. Ibid.

101. Bloom, "Lyman Parks: Leader for Grand Rapids."

102. Nicolette, "The Grand Center."

103. Ibid.

104. Jim Harger, "The Right Man at the Right Time: City's Only Black Mayor, the Rev. Lyman S. Parks, Remembered for Service," *Grand Rapid Press*, November 5, 2009.

105. Jennifer Ackerman-Haywood, "This Year's Giant Was a GR First: Former President Ford Hails Parks," *Grand Rapid Press*, January 26, 2003.

106. Jim Mencarelli, "Riot Legacy. 20 Years Later a Haunting Question: Have We Progressed?" *Grand Rapids Press*, July 26, 1987.

107. Ibid.

108. Ibid.

109. Ibid.

110. Ibid.

111. William H. Chafe, *Civilities and Civil Rights: Greensboro, North Carolina, and the Black Struggle for Freedom* (New York: Oxford University Press, 1980).

112. Thomas J. Sugrue, *The Origins of the Urban Crisis: Race and Inequality in Postwar Detroit* (Princeton, NJ: Princeton University Press, 1996), 267.

113. Ibid.

CONCLUSION

1. Keith Schneider, "Michigan Apartheid: Reforming Land Use Policy Can Help Most Segregated State," Michigan Land Use Institute, April 17, 2003, available at https://mlui.org/pageview.asp?fileid=16480.

2. Ron Stodghill and Amanda Bower, "Welcome to America's Most Diverse City," *Time U.S.,* available at http://www.time.com/time/nation/article/0,8599,340694-1,00.html (last modified August 25, 2002).

3. See Arnold R. Hirsch's impressive book *Making the Second Ghetto: Race and Housing in Chicago, 1940–1960* (Chicago: University of Chicago Press, 1998), xvii.

4. A number of important studies note the construction of the "second ghetto," including Hirsch, *Making the Second Ghetto*; Charles F. Casey-Leinniger, "Making the Second Ghetto in Cincinnati: Avondale, 1925–1970," in *Race and the City: Work, Community, and Protest in Cincinnati, 1820–1970,* ed. Henry Louis Taylor Jr. (Urbana: University of Illinois Press, 1993); and Raymond A. Mohl, "Making the Second Ghetto in Metropolitan Miami, 1940–1960," *The New African American Urban History,* ed. Kenneth W. Goings and Raymond A. Mohl (Thousand Oaks, CA: Sage Publications, 1996). As previously noted, while the "second ghetto" thesis distinguishes the second wave of black migrants from the first, it is primarily helpful in examining larger cities with distinct pre-Depression migrations, such as Chicago, Detroit, Philadelphia, and New York. This does not adequately account for Grand Rapids and numerous other smaller secondary cities in America that had no established first ghetto until the postwar era, when Hirsch introduced the term "second ghetto."

5. The Second Great Migration was larger than the First Great Migration and of different character. The result brought new migrants into numerous secondary cities in America, causing the black population to multiply. My emphasis on a secondary community adds to the few black urban histories, primarily of larger cities, that examine the Second Great Migration, including Hirsch, *Making the Second Ghetto*; Henry Louis Taylor Jr., ed., *Race and the City: Work, Community, and Protest in Cincinnati, 1820–1970* (Urbana: University of Illinois Press, 1993); Carolyn Adams David Bartelt, David Elesh, Ira Goldstein, Nancy Kleniewski, and William Yancey, *Philadelphia: Neighborhoods, Division, and Conflict in a Post-industrial City* (Philadelphia: Temple University Press, 1991); and Nicholas Lemann, *The Promised Land: The Great Black Migration and How It Changed America* (New York: Knopf, 1991). See also Kenneth L. Kusmer and Joe W. Trotter, eds., *African American Urban History since World War II* (Chicago: University of Chicago Press, 2009).

6. David Covin, *Black Politics after the Civil Rights Movement: Activity and Beliefs in Sacramento, 1970–2000* (Jefferson, NC: McFarland, 2009).

7. James Waterman Wise and Alexander Alland, *The Springfield Plan* (New York: Viking Press, 1945), 120.

8. Stodghill and Bower, "Welcome to America's Most Diverse City."

9. Todd E. Robinson, "Up from the Ashes: The Macedonia Church Fire in the Post-racial Era," *Souls: A Critical Journal of Black Politics, Culture, and Society* 12, no. 4 (October 2010), 358–375.

10. David Mayo, "King: Pain of South's Closing Remains," *Grand Rapids Press,* February 22, 1998.

11. Curt Wozniak, "Forever South," *Grand Rapids Magazine,* available at http://www.grmag.com/online-feature-archive.htm (last modified October 2003).

INDEX

Page numbers followed by the letter p refer to photographs.

Adams, J. E., Jr., 57, 83; housing development project of, 57–61
African American Urban History since World War II (Kusmer and Trotter), 180
Alexander School, 47
Alger Heights suburb, 54, 61, 62, 67, 81
All-American City award, 79–80, 83, 171, 183
Alland, Rosemary, 158
Allen, Hezekiah, 118
Allied Construction Council, 55
Alston, Eugene E., 15
Amberg, Callie S., 47, 48
Amberg, David M., 33, 34
Amberg, Julius, 17, 26, 27–28, 33
American Babylon (Self), 52
"American Dream," suburban housing in, 82, 83
American Seating Company, 6, 40
"Anatomy of a Riot" report, 169
Anderson, Melvin D., 47, 48
Antibusing movement, 152–162
Antipoverty programs, 147–149
Assessment of real estate values, discrimination in, 28
Atkins, Georgia, 103
Atkins, Melvin, 103, 141
Auburn Hills, housing subdivision project in, 57–61, 83
Auburn Hills Corporation, 57
Auerbach, Isador, 91–92

Bagnall, Robert W., 15
Baldwin, Louise, 115
Barber, Robert, 56
Barnett, Stanley, 115
Barto, Bernard, 60

Barton, Alex, 120
Baum, Benjamin, 60
Beahan, Michael, 117
Beaman, William H., 47, 48
Benjamin, Thomas E., 15
Biondi, Martha, 181
Birmingham, Alabama: protests on bombing in (1963), 117–118; Sixteenth Street Baptist Church in, 117
Bissell, Hillary, 32–36, 42, 44, 46
Bissell, John, 174
Bissell, Wadsworth, 32
Bissell Carpet Sweeper Company, 32
"Black belt": busing plan for students in, 127–128; health problems in, 76; housing in, 51, 56–57, 61, 73, 76, 78, 79; and Human Relations Commission, 120, 121; lack of insurance coverage in, 79; public schools in, 40, 42, 43, 46, 47
Black power, 105, 110–113, 207n76, 208–209n83
Black Unity Council (BUC), 123, 125, 158
Blandford, Robert, 59
Bliss, Lewis, 30
Blodgett Memorial Hospital, 4, 8
Boelens, Robert, 173
Bolden, Emmett, 2, 23, 86p; as Grand Rapids School Board candidate, 17, 46; in GRNAACP, 2, 15; and Keith Theater seating segregation, 16–18, 21, 28, 93; opposition of, to self-segregation, 20; as South High School student, 93
Bolding v. Grand Rapids Operating Corporation, 26
Boonstra, Jack L., 153, 155, 156, 157
Boozer, Raymond L., 125, 137

Boss Rule, 26
Bouma, Donald H., 42–43, 50, 54, 62, 106
Bowie, Jack M., 60
Bowman, George, 154, 157, 160, 163
Bracey, John, 128
Bracey, Kathy A., 141–142
Bremer Realty Company, 63
Brooklyn Technical High School, 91–92
Brown, Ezell, 56, 167
Brown, Fred, 123
Brown, Milo, 2, 23; as candidate for mayor, 19, 93; Club Indigo founded by, 21–22; in Grand Rapids Urban League, 93; in GRNAACP, 2, 18, 19, 93; mortuary business of, 2, 18–19, 93; in Progressive Voters League, 93; on racism in post–Jim Crow era, 22; as South High School student, 93
Browne, Henri, 4
Brown v. Board of Education, 45, 139, 183
Buchanan School, 44, 47
Buchanan v. Warley, 202n78
Bureau of Public Health Nursing, lack of black workers in, 5
Burgess, Eleanor, 129
Burgess, Ethel, 20, 21
Burkman, Geoff, 92
Burton, Charles Wesley, 16
Burton Heights area, 62, 67
Burton School, 47
Businesses: discriminatory practices of, 3, 4, 5, 16–18, 28–29; political control in postwar era, 176–177
Busing for school integration, 124–144, 152–167; and antibusing movement, 152–162; complaints of black students and organizations on, 137–138, 140, 141; cost of, 137; decision to rescind plan on (1971), 161; Engel ruling on, 164–166; first day of (1968), 136–137; impact of, on black students, 141–142, 143; lawsuit on, 162–166; master plan on, 110, 124–144; Phillips on, 129, 130, 131, 133, 150, 156, 157, 162; school board candidates in opposition to, 153–157, 160; Sims on, 149–150; two-way proposals on, 163; white resistance to, 131–136, 138, 140–141, 143–144, 150, 152–162, 163
Butterworth Hospital, 4, 98–99

Calloway, Cab, 21
Calvin College, 27, 116
Campau Area Schools, 41–48
Campau Park, 147
Campau School Committee (CSC), 43–48
Carlson, R., 103
Carmichael, Stokely, 105, 121
Carter, Sarah, 2. *See also* Glover, Sarah
Caruthers, Marsha, 128, 129
Carver, George Washington, 173

Central High School, 93, 103; in master plan of GRSB, 127, 128, 132, 135, 136
Chafe, William H., 50, 105, 176
Chain migration process, 2
Chamber of Commerce, 120, 144, 168–172; on annexation and merger plan, 81; Cowles speech to (1963), 119; and employment discrimination, 28, 33–35; Grand Rapids Project 1003 of, 169, 172; and Grand Rapids School Board, 47, 49; headquarters of, 86p; and housing discrimination, 55, 71, 74, 75; Kelley as member of, 40; and managerial racism, 75, 96; and Phillips in GRUL, 30, 32; and progressive reform movement, 24, 28; in Republican Home Front, 26; Sonneveldt in, 106; Van Blooys in, 168, 169, 170
Chest Improvement Club, 56
Chicago, Illinois, 2; second ghetto in, 179
Chicago Defender, 18, 111
Christmas Savings Club of GRSC, 12
Ciofu, Monique Marie, 141
Citizens' Action movement, 25, 27–28; Goebel in, 81; Lamberts in, 59; managerial racism in, 25; in opposition to McKay-Welsh political machine, 27–28, 80; and Phillips, 32, 35
The City of Wyoming: A History (Vaughn), 62
Civil Rights Act (1885), 17; amendment of (1919), 17
Clayton, James, 101
Claytor, Helen Jackson, 30, 36–40, 74, 88p; living in suburban area, 52–54
Claytor, Robert, 30, 37, 42, 55, 88p; suburban house purchased by, 52–54, 73–74, 83
Cleaver, Eldridge, 91
Clingman, Lewis B., 100, 105, 120–121, 123
Club Indigo, 21–22
Coe, Ethel B., 46, 115–116
Collins, Charles R., 97
Coming of Age in Buffalo: Youth and Authority in the Postwar Era (Graebner), 205n1
Community Action Program, Sims involvement in, 147
Community Chest Board, 37
Community Relations Service, 40
Comstock Park, 68–69, 164
Comstock Park: Mill Town to Bedroom Suburb (Wier), 68
Concerned Parents of the Inner-City, 138
Congress of Industrial Organizations (CIO), 6
Congress School, 44
Conley, Alda, 167
Cooper, Donald D., 155
C&O Railroad, 146
Corruption, political, 24–25, 26, 27
Countryman, Matthew J., 181
Cowles, Alfred E., 97, 119, 120
Crabgrass Frontier (Jackson), 65
Crawford, Theresa B., 108, 148

Creston High School: busing of South High students to, 136, 158–159; Davidson as assistant principal of, 110; population of black students in, 93, 132; racial tension in (1970), 158–159
Crisis Magazine, 15, 32
Cross, Cleo, 103; and mustache incident, 103–110
Cross, Lettie Ann, 103, 106
"Culture of opposition," 10
Curriculum issues in school integration plan, 130

Danns, Dionne, 110
Darden, Joseph, 175
Davidson, Charles, 102–110; and mustache incident, 103–110, 119, 120
Davis, Stanley, 59, 60
DeBerry, William Nelson, 16
DeBoer, Henry W., 71
DeBoer Brothers Realty Company, 71
Democratic Party, 176
Depression era: Bissell during, 32; black population of Grand Rapids during, 21; Comstock Park area during, 68; school construction during, 44
Detroit, Michigan, 1; public schools in, 46, 47; rebellion in (1967), 122, 168
Detroit Free Press, 103
DeVos, Rich, 174
Dickinson School, 44
Discrimination: "Balance Sheet on Race Relations" report on, 34; in employment opportunities (*see* Employment discrimination); in housing, 51–84; Human Relations Commission on, 38–41; in Keith Theater, 16–18, 21, 26, 28, 93; and northern Jim Crow customs, 3–8; in public schools, 41–51, 129, 130; in real estate assessment, 28; in recreational facilities, 19, 20–21; in restaurants, 3, 4, 28, 29
Donley, Richard, 123
Downtown Development Authority, 174
Drake, Beverly, 175–176
Dress code and grooming policies in high schools, 92, 100–113; and mustache incident, 103–110 (*see also* Mustache issue at South High School); student-led demonstrations on, 107–109
Dropout rates from high schools, 94–100; and employment opportunities, 95–99
DuBois, W. E. B., 7, 14, 20, 173
Dunham, M. L., 16
Dutch residents, 5–6, 96

Eardley, J. Warren, 154
East Grand Rapids, 61, 81, 142, 143, 164; black residents of, 61; crisis prevention tactics in, 122

Edmond, Mary, 140
Education: and employment opportunities, 95–99; in Grand Rapids Study Club, 8–14; in public schools, 41–51 (*see also* Schools); in southern black communities, 207n77
The Education Digest, 105
Eisenhower, Dwight, 76
Elections: Citizens' Action in, 28; Parks as candidate in, 173; Progressive Voters League in, 14, 19, 172; Republican Home Front in, 26–27; voter registration for, 14, 19
Emery, John G., 71
Employment discrimination, 4–7, 25; "Balance Sheet on Race Relations" report on, 34; Cowles on, 120; and Fair Employment Practices Commission, 25, 33–35, 41; and lack of opportunities for black youth, 95–99; Michigan Civil Rights Commission investigation of, 169–170; and Phillips in GRUL, 29–30, 33–34, 97; in public schools, 5, 49, 95, 165
Engel, Albert, 164–166
English, Cortez, 15
Equal Educational Opportunity Department (Michigan Department of Education), 142
Esbaugh, Kent, 101
Eschels, Carl, 174, 175
Executive Order 8809 of Roosevelt, 25
Expressway construction, 80–81, 204n134

Facial hair and mustache issue at South High School, 103–110. *See also* Mustache issue at South High School
Fair Employment Practices Commission and legislation, 25, 33–35, 41
Fair Housing Ordinance (1963), 61
Federal Housing Administration (FHA), 51, 182; discriminatory practices of, 51, 52, 54, 55, 65–67, 70, 71, 72, 182; Residential Security Maps used by, 65, 67–68, 71, 182; underwriting manual and policies of, 65–67, 70
Federal Housing Administration Underwriting Manual, 65–67
Federal housing policies, 70–71, 203n94. *See also* Federal Housing Administration
Federal National Mortgage Association (FNMA), 70
Fenstermaker, Marsh', 92
Ferrey, Glenn A., 75
First Great Migration, 1
Fisk Jubilee Singers, 11, 115
Fletcher, Harold T., 71
Fletcher Realty Company, 63, 71
Ford, Benson, 34
Ford, Gerald R., 3, 27, 92, 97, 108, 148–149, 175
Ford Motor Company, 34
Forest Hills neighborhood, 142, 164
Fountain School, 44

Fountain Street Baptist Church, 27, 28, 50, 54, 114

Franklin School and School District, 42, 43, 44, 75–76

Franks, Julius, Jr., 83; housing development project of, 57–61, 83

Freeman, Emery T., 138

Freeway construction, 80–81, 204n134

Frey, Edward J., 75, 81, 174

Furniture industry, 5–6

Gaines, Louisa, 9, 23

Gaines, William, 4

Gardella, Charles B., 71

Garner, Alexander C., 16

Gary, Indiana, 1, 3, 7

General Motors Corporation, 6, 63

German population in Grand Rapids, 5

Ghetto areas, 79; in postwar period, 199nn2–3; pre–World War II, 192n37, 199n2; second ghetto, 51, 179–180, 188–189n24, 199n2, 216nn4–5

Gilbert, Walter A., 137

Gill, Bill, 109

Gill, Frances, 118

Gill, Kenneth, 118

Gill, Lillian, 29, 116–118

Gill, Robert, 118, 136, 139, 140

Gill, Robert Earl, 116

Gillett, Richard, 174

Gillis, Victor, 122

Glenn, William, 17

Glenn v. Grand Rapids Operating Corporation, 17

Glover, Henry, 2

Glover, Sarah (neé Carter), 2, 4, 7, 23, 85p; at Blodgett Memorial Hospital, 4, 8; in Grand Rapids Study Club, 8–9, 13–14; in Progressive Voters League, 14

Godfrey Lee school district, 164

Godwin Heights, 164

Goebel, Frank, 28

Goebel, Paul, 28, 38, 80, 81

Gold Coast Negro community, 33

Gould, Vivian, 20

Graebner, William, 205n1

Graham, Gael, 91

Grand Center project, 174

Grand Rapids Bar Association, 2

Grand Rapids Brough Community Association, 30

Grand Rapids Civic Club, 14

Grand Rapids Health Department, on housing conditions, 56

Grand Rapids Herald, 62

Grand Rapids Ladies Literary Club, 9

Grand Rapids Magazine, 10, 11

Grand Rapids Metropolitan Area Study (GRMAS), 81

Grand Rapids National Association for the Advancement of Colored People (GRNAACP), 2, 7–8, 15–19, 25; activist members of, 22; Bissell in, 32–36, 42; Brown in, 2, 18, 19, 93; Claytor in, 38; compared to Grand Rapids Urban League, 25, 31, 32, 33, 35–36; confrontational approach to, 35–36; on educational inequalities, 42, 44–45, 46, 50, 94, 138; on employment discrimination, 25; formation of, 15; Gill in, 116, 117; on housing discrimination, 55; on Human Relations Commission, 40; and lawsuit against Grand Rapids school system, 152, 162–166; on master plan of GRSB, 130, 138, 140, 162; and National Urban League, 20, 21; occupations of members, 15; Skinner in, 2, 19, 32, 33; white members of, 32–33; women in, 14

Grand Rapids Negro Welfare League, 21

Grand Rapids Operating Corporation, 17, 18, 26

Grand Rapids Planning Division, "Anatomy of a Riot" report, 169

Grand Rapids Police Department: Gillis as captain of, 122; Green beaten by police officer, 17–18

Grand Rapids Press: on "Balance Sheet on Race Relations" report, 34; on Creston High School racial tensions, 159; on decline in property values, 82; on DuBois speech, 14; on education inequalities and segregation, 165; on employment discrimination, 29, 100; on first day of busing plan, 136–137; on interracial protest against Birmingham bombing, 118; on Keith Theater seating segregation, 16; on legal fight of Coe for civil rights, 115; on master plan of GRSB, 124, 127, 132, 134, 135, 142, 155–156, 161, 163, 165; opening new building (1966), 172; on opposition to busing, 154; on Parks as mayor, 174; on *A Raisin in the Sun* play, 115; on real estate assessment system, 28; on school discipline and grooming policies, 102; on school dropout rates, 94, 95, 100; on school integration lawsuit, 164; on school mustache policy, 106, 108; on student reactions to busing, 138; survey by, on racial attitudes (1971), 159–160; on twenty-acre housing subdivision proposal, 57, 58; on urban renewal projects, 172

Grand Rapids Project 1003 of Chamber of Commerce, 169, 172

Grand Rapids Real Estate Board (GRREB), 73, 74, 182

Grand Rapids School Board (GRSB), 42–49; and academic standards at South High School, 93–94; Bolden as candidate for, 17, 46; and busing for school integration, 124–144, 150, 152–165; candidates for, opposing busing, 153–157, 160; discipline as focus of, 93, 94, 102; and GRNAACP lawsuit on school segregation, 162–166; master plan of, 110, 124–144, 152–162; members of, 47; on mustache issue, 103, 104, 107, 109, 110, 113; open enrollment plan of, 166; Phillips as member of, 48–50, 107–108, 129, 130, 131, 133, 142, 150–151, 164; police state policy of, 161; postwar building patterns of, 44, 46, 62, 134, 136; Racial Imbalance Committee of, 124, 125, 127, 132, 143; Sims as candidate for, 160, 161, 163; Sleet as member of, 157–158; and student dropout rates, 95

Grand Rapids Study Club (GRSC), 2, 7–8, 8–14, 25; Coe in, 115–116; guest speakers of, 11, 115; headquarters of, 12; Idlewild investment of, 12; members of, 85p; scholarship awards of, 115–116; Skinner in, 11, 12–13, 14, 22

Grand Rapids Times, on mustache issue, 104, 106

Grand Rapids Urban League (GRUL), 2, 7–8, 11, 19, 20; accommodationist approach of, 31, 33, 35–36; "Balance Sheet on Race Relations" report by, 34; Brown in, 93; Claytor in, 38; compared to GRNAACP, 25, 31, 32, 33, 35–36; creation of, 20, 30; on education inequalities, 42, 138; on employment discrimination, 25; Gill in, 117; on housing discrimination, 55, 73, 74, 75, 76, 77–78; on master plan of GRSB, 138, 162, 164; at meeting on busing plan, 125; Phillips in, 28–31, 33–34, 35, 95, 129; Pilot Placement program, 33; recreation programs of, 31; on Sheldon School District, 77; on student dropout rates, 95; women in, 14

Grand Rapids Urban League and Brough Community Association, 30

Grand Rapids Welfare Union, 20

Grandville area, 61, 63, 64, 164

Grant, Roger, 17, 93

Green, Oliver M., 2, 23; in Keith Theater court case, 15, 17, 18; police beating, 17–18

Greensboro, North Carolina, 120, 176, 183

Griffin, Robert P., 165

Groce, Nolan, 98–99

Grooming policies and dress codes in high schools, 92, 100–113; and mustache incident, 103–110 (*see also* Mustache issue at South High School); student-led demonstrations on, 107–109

Hain, Elwood, 164

Hall, Doris G., 108

Hall, Jacquelyn Dowd, 22

Hall Elementary School, 47

Hannah, John, 92

Hansberry, Lorraine, 115

"Harlem" poem (Hughes), 115

Harlem Renaissance, 15

Harris, James F., 71

Harrison Park Junior High School, 135

Hatcher, Richard, 173

Hatherly, Harold, 58

Hawkins, Wilbur, 129

Hayes Manufacturing Company, 116

Henry School and School District, 42, 43, 44, 77

"Hidden transcript," 112, 208n82

High schools. *See* Schools

Highway construction in suburban expansion, 80–81, 204n134

Hillcrest Elementary School, 44

Hine, Darlene Clark, 10

Hirsch, Arnold R., 179, 182

Hirsh High School (Illinois), "Operation Snatch" in, 110–111

Hoek, Peter, 71

Homeowner associations, 201n34

Home Owners' Loan Corporation, Residential Security Maps of, 65, 67–68

Hoogterp, Dorothy, 109

Hospitals: employment in, 4, 8, 98–99; segregated wards in, 4

House of Styles Barber Shop, 123

Housing, 50; absentee owners of, 56; in "American Dream," 82, 83; barriers restricting access to, 67; in "black belt," 51, 56–57, 61, 73, 76, 78, 79; de facto segregation in, 167–168; and FHA discriminatory practices, 51, 52, 54, 55, 65–67, 182; "gentlemen's agreements" on, 74; historical trends in new housing starts, 71; mortgage lending practices for, 74–75; New Deal era programs on, 65–67, 70–71, 203n94; overcrowding problems in, 76, 77–78; and racial imbalance in schools, 66, 152, 162, 163, 165, 166; rent discrimination in, 73, 79; Residential Security Maps on, 65, 67–68, 71, 182; restrictive covenants on, 65–66, 78, 202n78; and school district boundaries, 32, 44–48, 72; segregation patterns of, in Michigan, 178; substandard conditions of, 55–56, 73, 75–78; in suburban development, 44, 51–84; twenty-acre subdivision proposal on, 57–61

Housing Ordinance (1956), 55–56

Hughes, Langston, 11, 116–117

Human Relations Commission (HRC), 38–41, 119–122; on Clayton assault, 101; Cowles as director of, 119, 120; gap between "black belt" residents and, 120, 121; on housing discrimination, 54–55, 58, 62, 72, 74, 75; limited effectiveness of, 120, 121; reduction in size of, 105; on school dropout rate, 97–98, 99–100; on South High School mustache incident, 105, 120–121; Study Committee on, 38–39

Hurd, Robert, 176

Idlewild investment of GRSC, 12

Immigration Commission, 6

Inner-City Organizing Committee, 130

Interracial Committee of the Council of Social Agencies, 73
Interracial Council, 20, 21
It Happened in Springfield (movie), 180

Jackson, Al, 110
Jackson, Kenneth T., 65, 182
Jamo, Robert, 59–60, 61
Jefferson, Thomas E., 20
Jefferson School, 42, 48
Jelks, Randal M., 16, 17–18, 32, 83
Jenison area, 63
Jensen, Norma, 180
Jet Magazine, 104, 109
Jim Crow era, 2–8; Grand Rapids NAACP in, 15–19; Grand Rapids Study Club in, 10, 11
John Birch Society, 121
Johnson, Carl H., 157, 160
Johnson, Charles, 20
Johnson, Fred, 108
Johnson, John Allen, 175
Johnson, Lyndon B., 147
Jones, Deborah, 184
Jones, Eugene Kinckle, 20
Jones, J. Ed, 15
Jones, John Paul, 81, 171
Jones, LeRoi, 92
Jones, Robert E., 16
Judd, Dorothy, 81

Kall, Richard, 58
Katzman, David M., 179
Kaufman, Irving R., 45, 48
Keeler, Mary Ann, 157, 174
Keith Theater, seating segregation in, 16–18, 21, 26, 28, 93
Kelleher, William J., 110
Kelley, Harry, 40, 75
Kelley, Robin D. G., 11, 12, 112
Kennedy, John F., 97
Kenowa Hills, 164
Kensington School, 44
Kent County Board of Education, 47
Kent County Board of Social Welfare, 5
Kent County Emergency Relief, 32
Kent Industrial Park, 171
Kent Intermediate School, 164
Kentwood Township, 122, 143, 164
Kerner Report, 124, 142
Kilgore, William, 141
King, Martin Luther, Jr., 104, 117, 156, 173, 175
King, Paul, 141, 184
"The King" poem (Purnell), 156
Kleinberg, Benjamin, 71
Krueger, Robert, 58
Krueger, Ruth, 58
Ku Klux Klan: club at South High School, 93; public rally and parade in Grand Rapids,

2–3, 15; and racial tensions in Creston High School, 159
Kusmer, Kenneth L., 179–180

LaBelle, Tom, 29, 30
Labor unions, in maintenance of racial barriers, 5, 6
Lafayette School, 42
Lamberts, Evangeline, 59–60, 61
Lampkins, Daniel B., 20
Lamse, John, 97
Lansing, Michigan, 1, 2
LaPenna, Tony, 95
Lawrence, Howard C., 75
Lee, Joseph W., 57, 83; housing development project of, 57–61
Levittown, New York, 62
Lewis, Earl, 10
Lewis, John L., 117
Lincoln School (New Rochelle, New York), 45
Lipsitz, George, 10
Littlefair, Duncan E., 27, 28
Livingston Hotel, refusal to serve black pastors in, 16
Lomax, Louis, 11, 115
Look magazine, 80, 169
Los Angeles, California, 120
"Lost classes" of South High School, 141, 184
Lowe, George, 98–99
Lubbers, Arend, 174

Madison Park School, 42, 48
Making the Second Ghetto: Race and Housing in Chicago, 1940–1960 (Hirsch), 179
Malcolm X, 173
Managerial racism: Chamber of Commerce in, 75, 96; and Citizen's Action movement, 25; de facto segregation in, 168; direct-action protest against, 116; in education policies, 150, 165; and Human Relations Commission, 121; and interracial protest on Birmingham bombing, 117–118; limiting progress of blacks, 22; prestige and economic prosperity of Grand Rapids in, 22; and progressive movement, 25, 26, 29, 40, 75, 120, 183; promise of racial progress and reform in, 176; and racial geography of Grand Rapids, 168; regulatory function of, 84; and South High School mustache incident, 105, 106–107, 111; suppression of black equality in, 183; youth protest as challenge to, 119, 177
Manufacturing employment, discrimination in, 5, 6, 34
Maplewood School, 42, 47
Mariemont High School (Ohio), 92
Marris, Webb, 137
Marshall, Thurgood, 32
Martens, Mrs. Raymond, 54

Master plan of Grand Rapids School Board, 110, 124–144, 152–162; decision to rescind (1971), 161; school board candidates in opposition to, 153–157, 160; white resistance to, 131–136, 143–144, 152–162

Masters, Edgar Lee, 68

Matthews, Buck, 174

McAllister, Dorothy, 40

McCullough, Evan, 128

McGee, John W., 63

McKay, Frank D., 24, 26–27, 80, 87p

McKee, F. William, 60

McMillan, Joseph H., 102, 118, 143, 163

McNamara, David J., 40

McNamara, Patrick, 171

Meijer, Frederik, 174

Metcalfe, Ralph, 29

Michigan Bell Telephone Company, 31

Michigan Civil Rights Commission, 142, 169–170

Michigan Civil Rights Committee, 32

Michigan Committee on Civil Rights, 76

Michigan Consolidated Gas Company, 171, 172

Michigan Social Security Area Office, 5

Michigan State Association of Colored Women (MSACW), 9

Michigan State Employment Service (Grand Rapids Office), 5

Michigan State News, 16, 19

Michigan Tannery, 68

Michigan Trust Company, 75

Migration, 1–2, 192n37; chain migration process in, 2; clubs and networks in, 2; and enroll-ment of black students in public schools, 42; First Great Migration, 1; Grand Rapids Study Club assisting in adaptation to, 9–10; and housing segregation, 67; Second Great Migra-tion, 31, 41, 51, 62, 179, 216n5; and unem-ployment, 95–96, 97, 120

Milanowski, John P., 133

Mileski, Terri T., 142

Miller, James, 60

Mirel, Jeffrey, 47

The Mis-education of the Negro (Woodson), 41

Model Neighborhood, 78, 79

Mohl, Raymond A., 179

Morris, Harold, 123

Moss, R. Maurice, 20–21

Moten, Etta, 115

Mustache issue at South High School, 103–110, 111, 113, 114; Davidson in, 103–110, 119, 120; Human Relations Commission in, 105, 120–121; Phillips on, 107–108; Sims in, 148–149

Muth, C. Robert, 125, 128, 135, 137

Nabers, Henry B., 82, 122

Nash-Kelvinator Corporation, 6

National Association for the Advancement of Colored People, 32–36; Grand Rapids chapter of (*see* Grand Rapids National Association for the Advancement of Colored People [GRNAACP]); history of, 193n67; lawsuits of, on school segregation, 162; and National Urban League, 20, 21

National Association of Real Estate Boards (NAREB) Code of Ethics, 74

National Black Political Agenda, 173

National Black Political Convention (1972), 173

National Commission on Urban Problems, 72

National Congregational Council of America conference (1919), 16

National Municipal League, 80, 170

National Urban League, 30; on discriminatory practices in employment, 5, 6, 7; Grand Rap-ids chapter (*see* Grand Rapids Urban League [GRUL]); migrant family study by, 2; and NAACP, 20, 21; recreational facility study by, 20–21

Neighborhood Block Clubs, 56

New City Plan, 81–82, 171, 176

New Deal era, 203n94; Comstock Park area during, 68; federal housing programs during, 65–67, 70–71, 203n94

New Hope Baptist Church, 106

"New Negro Movement," 10, 15

New Rochelle School Board (New York), 45–46, 48

"Nigger Heaven," 16, 22

Nixon, Richard, 173

Noel, Janice, 141

Northeast Junior High School, 124, 125

Northview school district, 164

Nursing profession, discriminatory practices in, 4, 7

Oakdale School, 44

Obama, Barack, 180, 181

Office of Equal Opportunity (OEO), Sims involvement with, 147–149

Old Kent Bank and Trust Company, 75, 171, 172, 174

Old Mill Creek Tannery, 68

Olson, Gordon, 17, 61, 63, 171, 175

Open enrollment plan, 166

"Operation Snatch" in Hirsh High School, 110–111

The Origins of the Urban Crisis (Sugrue), 179

Osofsky, Gilbert, 179

Oswego Community High School (Illinois), 92

Ottawa Hills School, 44, 47, 93, 103; busing of black students to, 161

Ottawa Hills suburb, 67

Ottawa Junior High School, 135

Owens, Jesse, 29

Palmer, Walter S., 71

Pantlind Hotel, 17, 30, 146, 174

Park Congregational Church, 14
Parks, Gordon, 104
Parks, Lyman Sterling, 90p, 172–175; as mayor, 173–175, 177
Patterson, W. L., 117
Pearson, Donald, 104
Persons against Racism, 154
Pew, Robert, 174
Phillips, Paul, 89p, 144, 150–152; "Balance Sheet on Race Relations" report coauthored by, 34; on busing for school integration, 129, 130, 131, 133, 150, 156, 157, 162; elected to City Charter Commission, 35; on employment discrimination, 97, 170; employment program of, 95–96; as Grand Rapids School Board candidate, 46, 48; as Grand Rapids School Board member, 48–50, 107–108, 129, 130, 131, 133, 142, 150–151, 164; in Grand Rapids Urban League, 28–31, 33–34, 35, 95, 129; on housing discrimination, 55; on mounting racial tensions, 168; on mustache issue in South High School, 107–108; non-confrontational approach of, 31, 32, 35, 40–41, 95–96, 108; on racial prejudice in Grand Rapids, 159; and retirement from GRSB, 151, 157, 158, 163; on student drop-out rates, 95; on student motivation problems, 95, 99
Pickens, William, 11
Pinkney, Hattie, 12, 23
Pittsburgh Courier, 32
Plainfield Township, 61, 143; crisis prevention tactics in, 122
Plummer, William Wilberforce, 35, 95
Pojeski, Lawrence F., 132, 153, 155, 156, 157, 158, 160
Polish residents, 5, 6, 96; in Westside community, 152–153
Porter, Charles F., 133–134, 142
Post, David, 144, 154
Pritchett, William, 123, 167
"Program of Education for Democracy," 180
Progressive movement, 24, 25–27; Citizens' Action in, 25, 27–28; managerial racism in, 25, 26, 29, 40, 75, 120, 183; and racial politics, 28–41
Progressive Voters League (PVL), 14, 19, 93, 172
Prothro, W. B., 56
Public accommodations, discrimination in: in Keith Theater, 16–18, 21, 26, 28, 93; in recreational facilities, 19, 20–21
Public schools, 41–51. *See also* Schools
Purnell, Marshall, 156
Pylman, Jay, 139; on Clayton assault, 101; discipline and grooming policies of, 101–102; on master plan of GRSB, 128, 129, 134; on mustache issue, 103, 104, 106, 107

Racial Balance Building Utilization Committee, 167
"Racial baptisms," 199n4
Racial covenants on real estate, 65, 202n78
Racial Imbalance Committee, 124, 125, 127, 132, 143
Racial uplift: assimilationist approach to, 108; Grand Rapids Study Club in, 8–14
Racial uprisings, 122; in Detroit (1967), 122, 168; in "Red Summer" (1919), 29; youth participation in, 91–113, 119, 124, 183–184, 207–208n80
A Raisin in the Sun play, 115, 116
Ramona Gardens dance hall, 21
Raniville Company, 47
Ray, Basil, 15
Reactionary populism, 189n27
Reagan administration, 175
Real estate: assessment discrimination in, 28; Residential Security Maps on, 65, 67–68, 71, 182; restrictive covenants on, 65–66, 78, 202n78. *See also* Housing
Reavis Survey (1949), 42, 44
Recreational programs: of Grand Rapids Urban League, 31; segregation in, 19, 20–21
"Red Summer" (1919), 29
Reform movement, progressive. *See* Progressive movement
Reid, Ira, 104
Report to the Commission on Civil Rights (1961), 53
Republican Home Front, 26–27, 28
Republican Party, 176; on Fair Employment Practices legislation, 34; Parks in, 173, 174; reform movement of, 24, 25, 27–28
Residential Security Maps, 65, 67–68, 71, 182
Restaurants, discriminatory practices of, 3, 4, 28, 29
Rienstra, M. Howard, 31
The Rise and Fall of an Urban School (Mirel), 47
Roberts, Jack, 174
Rockford school district, 164
Romani, Romulus, 103
Romney, George, 122
Roosevelt, Franklin D., 25, 70
"Row, not drift" mentality, 22, 177
Rust Belt, 2, 179, 185
Ryman, Wilbur, 3

Sacramento, California, 178, 180, 181
Schad, Vernis, 139–140, 153, 154; on busing for school integration, 127, 132, 143, 154; as Grand Rapids School Board member, 49, 50; on Racial Imbalance Committee, 124, 132, 143
Schermer, George, 39
Schneider, Nanette, 59
Schneider, Stanley, 59

Schools, 41–51; in "black belt," 40, 42, 43, 46, 47; black teachers in, 164, 165; busing for integration of, 124–144 (*see also* Busing for school integration); class size in, 42; discipline focus in, 93, 94, 100, 101–102, 104, 106; district boundaries for, 32, 44–48, 72, 124, 125, 127; dress codes and grooming policies in, 92, 100–113; dropout rates in, 94–100; employment discrimination in, 5, 49, 95, 165; expectations of white teachers in, 118; and FHA underwriting guidelines, 66; importance of student contributions to black freedom movement, 183–184; open enrollment plan, 166; "Operation Snatch" in, 110–111; "platoon system" in, 46; police state policy on, 161; racially homogeneous, 66; rise of black youth protest in, 91–113, 114, 183–184; socioeconomic class–based analysis of, 189n27; student-led demonstrations in, 107–109, 111, 112, 119, 183–184, 207–208n80; trends in student populations, 72, 93; vocational training in, 48

Schroeder, Willard, 174

Scott, James C., 112

Scott, Rebecca, 108

Secchia, Peter, 175

Secondary cities, urban experience of blacks in, 178–185

Second ghetto, 51, 179, 188–189n24, 199n2, 216n4; in Chicago, Hirsch on, 179; studies on construction of, 179–180, 216nn4–5

Second Great Migration, 31, 41, 179, 216n5; housing discrimination in, 51, 62

Security Maps, Residential, 65, 67–68, 71, 182

Self, Robert, 52, 181, 182

Self-help and self-improvement in Grand Rapids Study Club, 8–14, 22

Selma, Alabama, 119, 120

Seymour Christian Church, 62

Shagaloff, June, 42

Sheldon Complex social welfare agency, 103–104, 106, 108–109, 125; in mustache incident, 148–149; programs of, 148, 149; Sims involvement with, 148–149; Task Force of, 122–123

Sheldon School and School District, 42, 43, 44, 77, 147

Shelley v. Kraemer, 202n78

Shopping malls in suburban areas, 81

Shriver, Sargent, 148–149

Sigsbee School and School District, 47, 77

Simerink and Duthler real estate firm, 62, 63

Sims, Charles, 97

Sims, Ella, 90p, 145–150, 160, 161, 163

Sinking Fund, twenty-acre housing subdivision request to, 57–61

Sixteenth Street Baptist Church (Birmingham, Alabama), 117

Skill Bank program, 96

Skinner, Floyd, 2, 15, 17, 23; Club Indigo founded by, 21–22; death of, 61; in GRNAACP, 2, 19, 32, 33; on housing segregation, 57, 61, 79; opinion of, on National Urban League, 21; opposition of, to self-segregation, 20, 21, 22; in Progressive Voters League, 19; as suburban resident, 57

Skinner, Lucille, 2, 4, 23; in Grand Rapids Study Club, 11, 12–13, 14, 22

The Slave play, 92

Sleet, Nina, 157–158

Smith, Carl, 130, 131, 132, 137–138, 140, 169

Smith, George M., 23; as candidate for City Commission, 19; in GRNAACP, 15, 16; opinion of, on National Urban League, 21; opposition of, to self-segregation, 20

Social workers, black professional, 20

Something Better for Our Children (Danns), 110

Sonneveldt, Christian, 105, 106, 121, 122, 124, 171, 172

Soodsma, Herbert, 172

Sorrells, Jerome, 130, 162, 163

South Congregational Church, 62

South High School, 92–94; academic standards in, 93–94; busing of students from, 124–144, 150, 164; Clayton assault in, 101; Coe as graduate of, 115; conference on dropout problem in, 100; dress code and grooming policies in, 100–113; expectations of white teachers in, 118; Gill family attending, 118; history of, 92–93; impact of closure of, 184; "lost classes" of, 141, 184; mustache issue in, 103–110 (*see also* Mustache issue at South High School); Sims involvement with, 147, 148–149; student-led demonstrations in, 107–109, 114, 119; Vocational Information Institute, 89p

South Middle School, 140, 167

Sparrow, Eugene, 105

Spatial mismatch theory, 185

Spear, Allan H., 179

Springfield, Massachusetts, 180–181

Springfield Plan, 180, 181

Spruyt, George, 97

Stark, Robert, 137

Stauffer, Norma, 37

Steenland, William, 157, 159

Steketee, Robert, 174

Stiles, Jack, 27

Stillman, C. C., 20

St. Mary's Hospital, 4

Store owners, discriminatory policies of, 3, 4

The Story of Grandville and Jenison, Michigan (McGee), 63

Student Nonviolent Coordinating Committee (SNCC), 105, 121

Suburban areas: annexation and merger proposal, 81–82; black teachers in, 164;

Suburban areas (*continued*)
busing black inner-city students to, 124–144,
152–167 (*see also* Busing for school integration); commuting to work from, 63, 69; and
expressway construction, 80–81, 204n134;
housing discrimination and racial segregation in, 51–84, 182, 199–200n5; population
of black students in, 164; rapid growth of,
62–64; shopping malls in, 81; studies of, 199–
200n5, 200n20, 203n96
Sugrue, Thomas J., 40, 179, 181, 182
Sunday Evening Club, 14
*Sweet Land of Liberty: The Forgotten Struggle for
Civil Rights in the North* (Sugrue), 181
Sys-Con Company, 171

Tableman, Marvin, 142
Taggart, Ganson, 3
Tardy, Betty, 163
Tardy, Melvin, 104, 147, 148
Tardy, Ray, 103–104, 109, 147, 148
Taylor, Lucille, 175
Taylor v. New Rochelle, 45, 48
Theaters, seating segregation in, 16–18, 21, 26,
28
Till, Emmett, 145
Time Magazine, 178, 180
Todd, Stanton W., 26, 27
Tolliver, Elizabeth, 11, 23
Tregre, Q. S., 54
Triplett, Samuel, 57, 83; housing development
project of, 57–61
Trotter, Joe W., 179–180
True Light Baptist Church, 11
Truman, Harry S., 117
Tubbs, Robert S., 47

Uhl, John, 174
Unemployment rate, 96; of black high school
graduates, 100; Chamber of Commerce concerns about, 168–170; migration trends
affecting, 95–96, 97, 120; and unfair employment practices, 120
Union Bank and Trust Company, 75, 171, 172
Union High Parents Association (UHPA), 153
Union High School, 93; boycott by white students, 161; busing of inner-city students to,
132–133, 135–140, 152–156, 161, 184; faculty
at, 139; racial unrest in (1968), 138, 139, 140
Unions, in maintenance of racial barriers, 5, 6
United Automobile Workers, 6
Urban experiences of blacks in secondary cities,
178–185
Urban renewal projects, 171–172

Van Blooys, Joseph, 157, 168, 169, 170
Vandenberg, Arthur H., 172
Vandenberg Center, 172

Vandenberg School, 42, 43, 44, 48
Vanderkooi, Ronald, 80–81
VanOveveren, Robert K., 101
Van Slyke, Everett, 153, 154, 155, 156, 157
Verdier, Leonard, 18
VerMeulen, W. B., 26
Veterans Administration: discriminatory prac-
tices of, 55; housing programs of, 70, 72
Voluntary Home Mortgage Credit Program,
74–75
Voter registration, 14, 19
Vruggink, Elmer H., 102, 125

Waer, Oscar E., 27
Walker Township, 61, 69, 81, 143
Wallace, George, 117
Ward, Cedric, 175
War on Poverty programs, 147–148, 149, 175
Washington, Booker T., 7, 173
Waters, Russell, 158–159
Weinheimer, Norman P., 159, 162
Wellesley High School (Massachusetts), 92
Welsh, George W., 24, 27–28, 80, 87p
Western Michigan Catholic, 28, 29
Westgate neighborhood, 69
Westinghouse Electric Corporation, 47
West Middle School, 135
Westside community, opposition to busing plan
in, 132–133, 152–153
Wheeler, Albert, 109
White, Harry C., 19
White Citizens Committee, 58, 61
Whittington, Jerry, 115, 116
Wier, David, 68, 69
Wilkins, Roger, 52, 53, 83
Wilkins, Roy, 33, 35, 37, 104
Williams, John V., 95
Wilson, Ida W., 20
Wilson, William Julius, 83
Women, black: employment discrimination
against, 4, 7; in Grand Rapids Study Club,
8–14, 115–116
Women's City Club, 9
Woodson, Carter G., 41
WOOD-TV, 120, 174
Works Progress Administration (WPA), 5
"The World's War and the Darker Races"
speech (DuBois), 14
Wyoming Township, 61, 64, 67, 81, 143, 164;
black residents of, 61; crisis prevention tactics
in, 122; rapid growth of, 62–63

YMCA and YWCA: Claytor in, 36–38; segrega-
tion in facilities of, 20–21, 36, 38
Young, Whitney, 173
Young Activists (Graham), 91

Zoning regulations, 66–67, 72